MAKING IT

The Encyclopedia Of How

To Do It For Less

MAKING IT
The Encyclopedia Of How
To Do It For Less

by Arnold and Connie Krochmal

DRAKE PUBLISHERS INC.

NEW YORK - LONDON

Published in 1975 by
Drake Publishers Inc.
381 Park Ave. South
New York, N.Y. 10016

Library of Congress Cataloging in Publication Data

Krochmal, Arnold, 1919-
    Making it: the encyclopedia of how to do it for less.

    1. Home economics. 2. Cost and standard of
living.   3. Consumer education.   I. Krochmal, Connie,
joint author.   II. Title.
TX147.K66   640.73   74-22582
ISBN O-87749-775-3

Printed in The United States of America

Contents

Contents

Acknowledgements

We acknowledge a debt of gratitude to a number of people who provided illustrations, information, and assistance that made this book possible, as well as several contributors who wrote sections.

Karen Snipes, a graduate student in the School of Design at North Carolina State University, took the time to write the section on Finishing and Refinishing Furniture.

Beverly Lenk, a school teacher and mother of an active and time-consuming 18-month old son, found time to write the section on Breast Feeding based on her own experience.

Dr. Ron Sakolsky, of Sangamon State University, Office of Academic Affairs, Springfield, Illinois, didn't hesitate when asked to write the section on Consumers' Guide to Doctors.

Bob Biesterfeldt, woodchopper and editor, did the home haircut section.

Information on consumption of energy was provided by Carolina Power and Light, and Public Service Company of North Carolina, Inc. Tom Thielke of Asheville, N.C., helped provide information on comparison shopping of different brands of food. Dave Chesson, of Sears Roebuck, Asheville, let us test one of their microwave ovens.

Special thanks for providing photos go to Mary Cowell, Photo Librarian, U.S.D. Agriculture, Washington, D.C.; Charlotte Olsson, Assistant Chief, Marketing Service Branch, of U.S.D.A., Washington, D.C.; to Leviton, Inc. of Little Neck, N.Y. for the photo of their lamp kit; and to our son Maurice who was our photographic assistant.

For the generous use of their illustrations we turned to the Cooperative Extension Services of the Louisiana State University, University of Illinois at Urbana-Champaign, University of Kentucky, University of Arizona, University of Arkansas, Michigan State University, University of Wisconsin, University of Vermont, Auburn University, University of Tennessee, Oregon State University, and Pennsylvania State University.

MAKING IT
The Encyclopedia Of How
To Do It For Less

Chapter 1
Leisure and Vacations

NATIONAL FORESTS

Our national forests, administered by the Forest Service of the United States Department of Agriculture, offer a tremendous variety of outdoor pastimes. If you are a hunter or a fisherman, there are forests which provide opportunities for either or both of these activities. If you are a back-packer there are wilderness areas available to you. If you like to take the family camping there are forests which provide tentgrounds as well as trailer facilities, and toilet and washrooms. National forest facilities are one of the greatest bargains around, charging only a nominal fee per night for pitching a tent or setting a trailer into position.

Many of the national forests now have interpretive centers that help tell the visitor what is happening in the nature around him. Most of the forests offer unmatched experiences of wild beauty and conservation concern.

Many of these forests are open to the public all year. The Forest Service does a great deal more than manage the forests for timber. Visit one near you and see. We have made a list alphabetically by states, of places you can write to get information about the facilities and location of national forests in your state. In some states there are none, including Maryland, New York, New Jersey, and Delaware.

NATIONAL PARKS

People very often confuse forest rangers and park rangers. They are quite different. Park rangers are employees of the National Park Service of the U. S. Department of the Interior. They manage national parks, national parkways, national monuments, recreation areas, national historic sites, and they have a special group in Washington, D.C., called the National Capital Park Police.

The National Park Service is solely concerned with preservation of national monuments, historical and natural sites. The number of parks, sites, and monuments is huge, and extends from Alaska to the Virgin Islands. In the Virgin Islands we have often visited the Buck Island National Monument with its underwater trails, and the Virgin Islands National Park on St. John Island. An example of the work of the National Park Service is the old and historic town of Christiansted, St. Croix in the Virgin Islands. The downtown area of town is a national historical area and no architectural changes can be made that alter the appearance of the area. Such regulations are made with the support of local communities and are important for encouraging tourism.

National parks and forests have camping, picnicing, nature trails and back packing, and some national recreation areas allow fishing and hunting as well. One summer, when we worked in the Great Smoky Mountains National Park with the rangers, we became so indoctrinated with the preservationist philosophy of the parks that we would not so much as pick up a pebble or a fallen leaf!

We have included a list by state and region, of the National Park Regional Office from whom you can get detailed information on parks and monuments near you. Costs are low too, matching those for the national forests. Drop a postcard to the nearest regional office for information on facilities, as well as maps and leaflets.

FEDERAL GOVERNMENT AREA ENTRANCE FEES

Certain national park areas charge an entrance fee. We have provided a list of those that do as of December 1974. In addition to entrance fees special recreation use fees will be charged at certain designated areas. No national forest area charges an entrance fee, but some have fees for special use areas.

If you are an infrequent visitor to the designated areas that charge, then the single entrance fee is probably the cheapest way to get in. However, if you are a frequent visitor to these areas, The Golden Eagle Passport may save you money.

This admission ticket costs $10, from January 1 to December 31, and is non-transferrable. It covers the entrance fee for the owner and all the people with him in a non-commercial vehicle, which means the family car, truck, camper, motorcycle, etc.

In addition to the entrance fee, there are special recreation use fees for specialized sites, facilities, or equipment such as camping or boat launching facilities which the federal government provides. The special use fees may be charged by several different government agencies.

The Golden Age Passport is a very marvelous thing issued free to anyone over 62 years old with the same privileges as the Golden Eagle Passport, PLUS a 50% reduction on special recreation use fees. This very thoughtful deed on the part of our federal government is heart warming. The pass is good for the lifetime of the bearer.

Golden Eagle and Golden Age Passports can be obtained from either National Parks Regional Offices or National Forest Regional Offices, or by writing Forest Service, U.S. Department of Agriculture, Washington, D.C., 20250 or National Park Service, U.S. Department of the Interior, Room 1013, 18th and C Streets, N.W., Washington, D.C., 20240

FEDERAL ENTRANCE FEE AREAS

Arizona

Casa Grande Ruins National Monument
Chiricahua National Monument
Grand Canyon National Park
Montezuma Castle National Monument
Petrified Forest National Park
Pipe Springs National Monument
Saguaro National Monument
Tonto National Monument
Tumacacori National Monument
Tuzigoot National Monument
Walnut Canyon National Monuments

Arkansas

Pea Ridge National Military Park

California

Kings Canyon National Park (Joint fee with Sequoia National Park)
Lassen Volcanic National Park
Pinnacles National Monument

Sequoia National Park (Joint fee with Kings Canyon National Park)
Whiskey Town National Recreation Area
Yosemite National Park

Colorado

Black Canyon of the Gunnison National Monument
Colorado National Monument
Great Sand Dunes National Monument
Mesa Verde National Park
Rocky Mountain National Park

Florida

Everglades National Park

Georgia

Fort Pulaski National Monument

Idaho

Craters of the Moon National Monument

Maryland

Assateague Island National Seashore (See Virginia)

Massachusetts

Cape Cod National Monument

Montana

Glacier National Park

Nebraska

Scotts Bluff National Monument

New Mexico

Aztec Ruins National Monument
Bandelier National Monument
Capulin Mountain National Monument

Carlsbad Caverns National Park
El Moro National Monument
Fort Union National Monument
White Sands National Monument

North Dakota

Theodore Roosevelt National Memorial Park

Oregon

Crater Lake National Park

Texas

Fort Davis National Historic Park

Utah

Arches National Park
Bryce Canyon National Park
Golden Spike National Historic Site
Zion Canyon National Park

Virginia

Appomattox Court House National Historical Park
Assateague Island National Seashore (See Maryland)
Colonial National Historical Park (Jamestown Island)
George Washington Birthplace National Monument
Shenandoah National Park

Washington

Mount Rainier National Park

Wyoming

Devil's Tower National Monument
Grand Teton National Park (Joint fee with Yellowstone)
Yellowstone National Park

To obtain information about national forests and facilities of the National Parks, contact the offices listed here alphabetically by state. The abbreviations listed under the National Park Service refer to the abbreviations for the National Park Service Regional Offices which are listed on page 7.

State	Forest Service, U.S.D.A.	National Park Service, U.S.D.I.
Alaska	Box 1628 Federal Office Building Juneau, Alaska 99801	P.N.W.
Alabama	Box 40 Montgomery, Alabama 36101	S.E.
Arizona	517 Gold Avenue, SW Albuquerque, New Mexico 87101	W.
Arkansas	1720 Peachtree Road NW Atlanta, Georgia 30309	S.W.
California	630 Sansome Street San Francisco, California 80225	W.
Delaware	none	N.A.
Florida	214 S. Bronough Street Box 1050 Tallahassee, Florida 32302	S.E.
Georgia	322 Oak Street NW Gainesville, Georgia 30501	S.E.
Hawaii	none	W.
Idaho (northern region) (southern region)	Federal Building Missoula, Montana 59801 324 25th Street Ogden, Utah 84401	P.N.W.
Illinois	633 West Wisconsin Avenue Milwaukee, Wisconsin 53203	N.W.
Indiana	633 West Wisconsin Avenue Milwaukee, Wisconsin 53203	M.W.
Kentucky	1720 Peachtree Road NW Atlanta, Georgia 30309	S.E.
Louisiana	1720 Peachtree Road NW Atlanta, Georgia 30309	S.W.
Maine	633 West Wisconsin Avenue Milwaukee, Wisconsin 53203	N.A.
Maryland	none	M.A.
Michigan	633 West Wisconsin Avenue Milwaukee, Wisconsin 53203	M.W.
Minnesota	633 West Wisconsin Avenue Milwaukee, Wisconsin 53203	M.W.
Mississippi	350 Milner Building Box 1291 Jackson, Mississippi 39205	S.E.
Missouri	633 West Wisconsin Avenue Milwaukee, Wisconsin 53203	M.W.
Montana	Federal Building Missoula, Montana 59801	R.M.

Nebraska	Denver Federal Center Building 85 Denver, Colorado 80225	M.W.
Nevada	324 25th Street Ogden, Utah 84401	W.
New Hampshire	633 West Wisconsin Avenue Milwaukee, Wisconsin 53203	N.A.
New Jersey	none	N.A.
New Mexico	517 Gold Avenue, SW Albuquerque, New Mexico 87101	S.W.
New York	none	N.A.
North Carolina	Box 2570 Asheville, North Carolina 28802	S.E.
Ohio	633 West Wisconsin Avenue Milwaukee, Wisconsin 53203	M.W.
Oregon	Box 3623 Portland, Oregon 97208	P.N.W.
Pennsylvania	633 West Wisconsin Avenue Milwaukee, Wisconsin 53203	M.A.
Puerto Rico	none	S.E.
South Carolina	1801 Main Street Columbia, South Carolina 29201	S.E.
South Dakota	Denver Federal Center Building 85 Denver, Colorado 80225	R.M.
Tennessee	1720 Peachtree Road NW Atlanta, Georgia 30309	S.E.
Texas	Box 969 Lufkin, Texas 75901	S.W.
Utah	324 25th Street Ogden, Utah 84401	R.M.
Vermont	633 West Wisconsin Avenue Milwaukee, Wisconsin 53203	N.A.
Virginia	1720 Peachtree Road, NW Atlanta, Georgia 30309	M.A.
Virgin Islands	none	S.E.
Washington	Box 3623 Portland, Oregon 97208	P.N.W.
West Virginia	633 West Wisconsin Avenue Milwaukee, Wisonsin 53203	M.A.
Wisconsin	633 West Wisconsin Avenue Milwaukee, Wisconsin 53203	M.W.
Wyoming	324 25th Street Ogden, Utah 84401	R.M.

National Park Service Regional Offices

M.A. Mid-Atlantic
143 South Third Street
Philadelphia, Pennsylvania 19106

M.W. Midwest
1709 Jackson Street
Omaha, Nebraska 68102

N.A. North Atlantic
150 Causeway Street
Boston, Massachusetts 02114

P.N.W. Pacific Northwest
523 Fourth & Pike Building
Seattle, Washington 98101

R.M. Rocky Mountain
P. O. Box 25287
Denver, Colorado 80225

S.W. Southwest
Old Santa Fe Trail
P. O. Box 728
Santa Fe, New Mexico 87501

W. Western
450 Golden Gate Avenue
Box 36036
San Francisco, California 94102

S.E. Southeast
3401 Whipple Avenue
Atlanta, Georgia 30344

STATE PARKS

Every state has some parks with a range of facilities. Even a cookout at a roadside park can be relaxing. Camping sites are also available. Some state parks have cabins available to groups, such as Girl Scouts, Boy Scouts, and outing clubs. For information write the State Department of Parks, at your state capital.

FOOD FOR THE FIELD

We find that the cheapest way to get our food supply if we are going camping or backpacking is to buy standard dehydrated foods at the supermarket, either in small packages or in large containers, and repackage them ourselves.

The fancier and more appealing dehydrated foods are simply sky-high in price for most budgets. No doubt they may be tastier than single dried foods, but for a few days in the field, they are not worth the difference.

Pre-cooked rice and a packet of whatever seasoning mixture you like, (a taco seasoning mix for example) is fine. We use a small amount of the seasoning for a unit of instant rice to minimize the thirst problem on the trail. A teaspoon of dried seasoning in a half cup of rice works well.

Instant potatoes come in a variety of flavorful mixes, and a small packet will do for two or three people easily enough.

Dried beef jerky in a jar is easily found on the grocery shelf. Re-pack the meat in aluminum foil and add it to your rice mixes.

Dried fruits are not too cheap, but pitted prunes, raisins, apples, make a nutritious dessert or breakfast at low cost. They can be eaten as they are or cooked for a little more substance.

Instant eggs are sold commonly in small foil packets, enough for two or three people. Small cup size packets of soups can be tasty, particularly the vegetable kinds which are full of goodies. A little rice mixed with one of these packets makes a fine stew, and dehydrated onions are lightweight and savory.

Chocolate is always a good energy source, but it can make you thirsty on a long hike. Also, unless you get Army D rations, which are guaranteed not to melt at body temperature, you run the risk of a sticky mess on a hot day.

If you are going camping with a trailer or tent, the only limitations are budgetary. Many of the dehydrated foods we suggest for hiking trips work just as well, and are just as cheap for a trailer or camper or tent.

ZOOS

Hardly a county in the United States fails to have either a small public zoo or someone who keeps animals to lure customers in. Commercial zoos are often quite distressing, but some city zoos can be a joy. Here in Asheville with about 70,000 people there is a small city zoo that is a good example. Admission is 25ᶜ for anyone, and the city provides an operating budget. Gifts from individuals and corporations help greatly. With 1 elephant, 30 members of the monkey family, some birds of prey, several of the local birds, 2 African lions, 2 mountain lions, and 2 black bears, young and old can spend some very relaxing hours watching the animals. We are zoo lovers and never fail to rush madly to the zoo wherever we are. We have seen Sam and Samantha, the hugable diapered baby gorillas in Cincinnati; the free roaming llamas in the San Diego Zoo; the baby animal nursery in the Dallas Zoo. The Bronx Zoo is our favorite and a child can spend hours there riding

the camel and the elephant, peering at snakes and monkeys.

Zoos generally charge for admission, but it is a lot less than paying for a movie, and a lot more fun as well.

BOTANICAL GARDENS

If you like plants, a visit to a botanical garden can be relaxing fun as well as a learning experience. Whether it is the giant and beautiful New York Botanical Garden, or the far smaller North Carolina Botanical Garden at Chapel Hill, this is an inexpensive way of taking a break. Many universities have small botanical and indoor tropical gardens with no admission charge. Take a package lunch along and a thermos of coffee and you will come home refreshed and ready to go back to the salt mines. A good wild plant guide can help you recognize some of the plants on display. Gardens have a range of activities, from spring flower walks to short courses in natural dyes.

MUSIC

The opportunities for live concerts of all kinds of music from rock to local symphonies are tremendous in any part of the United States. The amount of live music available is infinitely greater here than in any other part of the world. In small towns and cities, concerts are rather inexpensive. In New York, Washington, and larger urban areas, they are higher. However many, many concerts have special prices for students, some have areas for standing room which can lead to a seat at intermission, and all have cheap balcony seats. In some larger cities, tickets that have not been sold until the day of the concert go on sale then very cheaply.

Many universities have concert series which permit students free admission because their activity fee helps pay for the costs of concerts and plays. In different parts of the country there are often competitions of all sorts of small music groups that cost very little to go to.

If you are lucky enough to live in or visit some of the western states, many of the Indian ceremonies have hauntingly beautiful old songs, unchanged for centuries. The soft beating of a hide drum and the chanting are deeply touching. One memory Arnold will always carry is of a visit to Zia Pueblo, in New Mexico, to see a student of his. Juan was a drummer in the buffalo dance, a proud and happy member of the pueblo family, who made the transition from the white man's university in Las Cruzes to his heritage without a tremor.

MUSEUMS

There are few towns too small to have some local museum or historical spot open to the public. Of course seeing the Smithsonian or the Museum of the American Indian is more time consuming, but local museums have much to offer, especially now as they become more oriented to the needs of the community they serve.

Entry to museums is no longer free as it was in years past, but the cost is still relatively small. A little reading before you go, on some aspect of the museum's specialty, will add greatly to the pleasure of what is to be seen.

When we visit Washington, D.C. or New York, a good part of every trip is devoted to the tremendous exhibits at the Smithsonian as well as the American Museum of Natural History. The Metropolitan Museum of Art in New York has a continuous series of programs all during the week that provide lovely three dimensional stories of days gone by. But if you are lucky enough to visit a large museum don't try to do it all in one day. It is simply overwhelming.

At some museums there are planetariums that put on dazzling displays of the earth and stars and planets. In Chapel Hill the University of North Carolina has a small but much used planetarium. Every day it welcomes flocks of school buses from neighboring areas.

The National Park Service usually has a museum at each area. These are free, and are unequaled in showing the man-made history and natural history of the places visited. One of the best to be seen is at the Visitor's Center on the Gatlinburg side of the Great Smoky Mountains National Park, covering the original settlers, the birds, plants, animals, and natural history. You can even see a sound movie.

On a smaller scale, the National Forests provide similar visitor's centers. These too are free.

In Washington there are some out of the way museums worth visiting. The Space Museum, the Museum of the Medical Corps of the Armed Forces, the F.B.I., Treasury and a lot of others are tremendously enlightening.

COUNTRY FAIRS

Country fairs, county or state, are not free, but if you can get to one, they are lots of fun. If you live in an urban area, drop a postcard to your state extension service, whose mailing address we have given on pages 203–5. Ask them the date of the state fair, which usually is in the fall, and is sometimes but not always in the state capital. The extension people should also be able to provide you with a list of county fairs and their dates, usually held in late summer. If the county information is not available, drop a postcard to your state Department of Agriculture, in the capital city.

Fairs are divided into three major areas. Entertainment sometimes seems to be the biggest part, with ferris wheels, games of chance and much more. Another part is the food stands which frequently sell their goods at low prices. Many of the food concessions are run by local churches and similar groups, and sometimes they serve surprisingly good food. Of course cotton candy and candied apples are abundant too. And you can carry a lunch easily enough if you care to.

The best part of the show are the exhilarating exhibits of livestock, home baking, produce, and sewing crafts. Handsome, well trimmed sheep stand around hopefully; large boars and sows, cleaned and husky, wait to be judged; cattle low in their stalls; horses prance in the arenas. The variety of chickens to be seen is unbelievable. Tiny bantams, guinea hens, pheasants, and a rainbow-hued variety of egg layers and meat producers cluck and crow. The smells are clean and rich, the sense of excitement of the exhibitors and judges is spine tingling. In the midst of crows, moos, bleats and neighs a local high school band may tune up with a stirring Sousa march.

If you are lucky you may see a weight pulling contest with teams of husky well cared for horses pulling concrete blocks. Once, at the Tennessee State Fair, Arnold was one of the judges for the honey exhibit but he almost made himself ill tasting all the honey!

Bread and cake baking contests still attract large numbers of competitors, and nearby, bunches of green onions and carefully arranged displays of shiny apples all crowd into view.

There are also business exhibits of machinery, books, life insurance, special foods and odds and ends. These too can be a lot of fun.

If you go, wear your most comfortable walking shoes, a hat of some sort, and sun-glasses if you have them. If you take lunch bring something that won't be hurt by high temperatures. We carry some bread, tomatoes, salt and cheese. Not gourmet but filling and cheap. If you have a camera, picture-taking can be fun too.

RIDING THE FERRY

Not everybody can do this, but if you are near the coast check around for public ferries going out to islands, parks, or other parts of the city.

The best 10¢ leisure buy in all the world is the city ferry boat ride from South Ferry in Manhattan to Staten Island, and back. You are "at sea" for 20 minutes each way, there are closed cabins, a quick food counter which sells such exotica as excellent hot knishes. On one of our recent visits to New York we had the sheer pleasure of hearing a concert given on the boat by a stocky Japanese man, dressed in a long kimono and a quilted outer kimono, who strummed a guitar and sang all across the bay. Friendly pigeons tagged along on deck, getting handouts from people like us. Circling the boat were a number of graceful sea gulls.

In North Carolina there are state operated ferries all along the coast to the outer banks areas. In Charleston, South Carolina there are no ferries but two excellent tour boats there are quite inexpensive. One goes to Ft. Sumter, a national monument with museum and guides, and the other tours the harbor area. Miami has this sort of excursion boat as well. And the old Hudson River Day Line Excursions were a source of joy for families in New York City in the 30's and 40's. Scraping a few cents together, packing a lunch of chopped meat with lettuce, the whole family would go up the Hudson for the day. It costs a little more, but you can still do that today.

Check around for ferries and boat rides. They are inexpensive, lots of fun and you get a view of the area that is to say the least, rather unusual.

BUS TRAVEL

We have travelled extensively by bus and there is a lot to be said for that mode of travel. Firstly it is very cheap. The distance you can travel for $25 is hard to believe. The buses stop frequently for snacks, and have toilets aboard.

Travelling by bus provides an opportunity to get to know people a little better than you would on a plane, or even on a train.

People who use the long distance bus systems have in common with their fellow travellers a sense of belonging to a group-the thrifty ones.

TRAINS

AMTRAK and other railroads are cheaper than flying, but from what we hear, they are just as chancy about keeping to schedules. The one time we wanted to try AMTRAK we were unable to get return reservations from New York. Living as we do in the mountains of North Carolina it is an academic question for us because few passenger trains even go near us.

We feel that train travel could be a tremendous thing, if we could model it on the Japanese and European systems which are fast, cheap, frequent and above all meant to serve the traveller. With the airlines pricing themselves out of the market and reducing the services they offer the traveller, rail transport is desperately needed now.

There is every reason for the Federal government to establish the railroads as a federal agency to meet the needs of the people of this country. Railroads complain that their passenger trains lose business. We would rather our tax money went into a government operated railroad system than for excess profits for railroad owners and stockholders.

AIRLINES

We find airlines expensive, indifferent, and careless with their customers' rights, and we try to avoid them unless we have no other choice. The scroungy sandwiches served in the states in economy seats should be a source of embarrassment to the airlines. They aren't. Flying overseas we have used a lot of airlines and found a few that please us most - the Dutch KLM, British West Indies Airlines. In the Virgin Islands, island hopping by seaplanes is a joy.

Means of travel	Round-trip fare	Changes	Hours of travel time	Meals bought	Limousine
Bus	$71.20	one	20	two	not needed
Train	$89.00	two	18	two	not needed
Plane	$120.74	none	2¼	none	twice

We've put together a table to show some of the factors to consider in deciding whether to travel by train, plane or bus. The trip we have theorized is from Asheville, North Carolina to New York, as of January 1975.

Meals during a bus trip are somewhat cheaper than on a train. Plane travel requires a limousine from the airport to the city which runs from $3.50 to $5.00 per person in our area, and more elsewhere. The greatest advantage to the plane is the time. Two hours by air would be a lot easier than 18 to 20 hours by train or bus. However, if money is tight, the bus will get you there almost $50.00 cheaper. There is no reason that sandwiches or a sack lunch cannot go on the train or bus to save the cost of at least one meal. And sometimes there is good reason to carry a snack on the airplane!

RESTAURANTS

Getting out of the house once in a while is an important emotional outlet, and a good meal served by someone else is a pleasant change for the cook in your house.

When we travel we are often in a hurry, and rather than prepare a meal in the hotel, will have something to eat along the way. Finding a good restaurant on the road isn't an easy task, and we have found the most unsatisfactory restaurants on the Pennsylvania and New Jersey Turnpikes. These we avoid like the plague because the food is expensive, the servings are small and the service indifferent.

We have found that by going off the turnpikes and driving a few miles we can often find some decent place to eat. However, the curse of eating on the road in the United States is the all pervading presence of french fries. Their smell is everywhere.

When we look for a restaurant at home or while travelling, we have certain rules of thumb we follow. We avoid places that provide entertainment, and if possible those with bars. In both cases we feel the emphasis is on something other than preparing meals. We don't look for a fancy place, but one that seems to be clean. We peer at the rugs. You would be surprised at the numbers of restaurants we find with crumbs and food on the floor.

We try to see a menu on the window. If there isn't one in view we have no hesitation about asking to see one. We often save ourselves some searching by phoning beforehand and asking what is served, and the prices as well.

We never expect "gourmet" food, whatever that may mean. We want hot food, adequate portions, prompt service and water refills; if we have a pleasant waiter or waitress we are completely happy. . . . *helpful takelist of food and utensils*

2 forks, knives, teaspoons
jam or jelly, small jar
peanut butter, small jar
2 small cans boned turkey
   or chicken
2 small packets dehydrated potatoes
2 boxes dehydrated soups,
   cup size portions
1 small jar ground coffee
   or instant coffee
tea bags

small jar sugar
small salt shaker
fresh or canned fruit
1 jar cheese spread
1 box of cookies

FORMING GOURMET CLUBS

A gourmet club offers you two advantages: you get to eat out without paying the high prices of restaurants and still have variety and a decently prepared meal, and you can also meet and make new friends.

There are several ways of sharing the cost of meals in the club. One way is for the club to agree on a menu for each meal and decide who will cook what. This is a creative outlet for many of us who love to cook because you can cook and serve things that you never get a chance to make at home. The club usually rotates the meetings at different members' houses, with the cleaning detail also being rotated so the burden doesn't fall on the same people time after time. With this approach, the cost of each meal can be divided equally between all the members. Another method is to divide the club into several groups of people, rotating so that each group takes turns buying and preparing the food. Then the cost of the meal is divided equally between the members of the group that prepare the food. Still another method is to publish a roster of dates, with each family listed. Then the family whose turn it is prepares a meal of their selection for the other members and pays for the complete meal.

In any of these methods once or twice a month is a good schedule for the dinners, or slightly less often if desired. Meetings are necessary to make up the menus. Wine and cheese tasting sessions can also be arranged. The group should not exceed eight to twelve people, or four to six couples.

If you live in a college town, a variation of the gourmet club is to invite students from various countries to participate, making some native dish of their own choosing. It is a never ending source of wonder to us to find foreign men go ape when the opportunity to cook presents itself here in the United States. They can do a tremendous job indeed, and these are men who would sooner be caught dead than cooking in their own countries!

HOTELS AND MOTELS

The hotel or motel you choose can determine whether your trip will be pleasant or disappointing. Since the prices are so expensive now it is more important than ever that you feel you are getting your money's worth.

Many chains, including Howard Johnson's, Holiday Inn, and unfortunately the Sheraton, all vary in the condition of the rooms and the quality of the service. The good ones are far outnumbered by the bad ones. When we are in doubt of the condition of the rooms, we ask first to have a key so we can look at the room before we take it. Most of these are owned by corporations which aren't concerned with your complaints. The Sheraton, owned by I.T.T. took a year to answer a complaint we voiced about one of their hotels.

If you have a complaint it is best to talk to the assistant manager, who usually will try to straighten things out for you. Unfortunately, assistant managers are frequently "out" when you want to talk to them.

If you are taken to a room in a hotel that you don't like, talk to the bellhop about it before he unloads your luggage. It is amazing the amount of pull that the bellhop can have, and he can usually get you a better room if he is encouraged.

Be as generous with praise as you are with your complaints. The staff of hotels and motels appreciate knowing that they are doing a good job. The manager of a hotel in Washington, D.C., sent a bottle of champagne to our room after we told him how pleased we were with his hotel.

RAISING MONEY AT BOOK AND BAKE SALES

These two devices for raising modest amount of money for community projects require the usual cooperation of people. Books for the book sales can be gathered in several designated areas. A supermarket or covered area in a shopping mall are fine. You need a large box clearly marked to show what you are doing, and advance publicity over radio, television, and newspapers to let people know you will be collecting books on a given date at certain hours, for resale at a given time and place to raise funds for a project.

When the collection time ends, someone will have to collect the books and haul them to a garage or other place where the prices can be entered.

If you want to sell the books, they will have to be marked very very low, or no one will want them. Anything above 25ᶜ for paperbacks will make sales almost impossible. The ordinary fiction hardcover will not sell for much over 50ᶜ or 75ᶜ. When you begin your book sale, select a covered area for protection against rain and sun, and have a table or two in place with some of the books on display.

A bake sale is another pleasant way to raise funds. Here you need some cooperative people who will provide the material to be sold

—cakes, pies, cup-cakes, cookies and bread. The same preliminary publicity is needed as for a book sale. You need a table to place the items on display, and some waxed paper or such to cover the baked goods to protect them from invading flies. If you plan on a sale in hot weather, you might consider asking the people who are providing the goods to freeze them and deliver them to the sale right in that shape. This will keep them fresh at the end of the sale.

READING

Buying Books

We buy used paperbacks because they are cheap, and we can trade them in for another batch. Some stores give you one replacement for two you bring in. Other stores give a small cash allowance. We delight in used paperback stores and will buy up to one hundred or more at a time.

There are several mail order booksellers, but the one we have dealt with satisfactorily has been New World Books, 2 Cains Road, Box 89, Suffern, New York, 10901. They sell at 30% off for books listing at $10 or more, 25% for books selling at less than $10, 15% off on University Press trade books, and 10G off on texts and references, with some exceptions. No paperbacks are discounted. Parcel post and handling is 35ᶜ per book, and if you live out of New York, there is no applicable sales tax for many states. We have found New World prompt in delivering and have never had a problem.

Similar concerns are Bookquick, Inc., 160 Eagle Rock, New Jersey 07068, and The Bookpost, Inc., 141 44th Street, New York, New York 10017.

In our house we have a set of the Book of Knowledge dating from 1922. Would you believe that you can find a lot of useful information in the set? Early polar exploration, Indian legends, plant uses, World War I, the Civil War and a legion of other useful bits are there. So if you want an encyclopedia or set of reference books for your own use, or for your kids of school age, buy what you want second-hand. We have had eminent success with Literary Mart, 1261 Broadway at 131st Street, Room 701, New York, New York 10001. A used encyclopedia five or six years old may not have the latest element discovered at the University of California or in the Soviet Union, and may not cover Watergate, but it has almost all you need for ordinary purposes of reference. And at a fraction of the cost of a new set.

If you form a book co-op you can trade off your books; if not they will always be welcome at your nearest public or school library, or for sale at some community fund-raising.

Local bookstores sometimes run special sales, and they are worth watching for. Marboro Books of New York have some tremendous buys; you can get your name on their mailing list by writing a postcard to Marboro Bookshop, Inc., 205 Moonachie Road, Moonachie, New Jersey 07074.

We have tried several book clubs but with two exceptions dislike them. We prefer to buy exactly the books we want, at a discount. We dislike having to buy any set number of books over a period of time, and find that a good many book clubs offer selections we wouldn't want to read. The exceptions are (1) The Detective Book Club, and (2) The Natural History Book Club. The Detective Book Club is pure escapism, and of the three stories in each voluem, at least two are usually excellent. Their address is Roslyn, New York. The Natural History Book Club has se-

lections to suit most everyone's interest, whether you are a bird watcher, ecologist, biologist, or botanist, or if you are just interested in natural history. Their address is Riverside, New Jersey 08075.

EXERCISE

Golf is considered a good moderate exercise. Tennis is more strenuous. Jogging seems to be a big thing and wherever you go these days, from Central Park to the campus of a university, the familiar joggers with their sweat bands can be seen hard at it. This is great, but you have to be in shape for it. If you have not been exercising for awhile and have gotten a "spare tire," go very very slowly in getting into the heavy exercise routine.

We've tried cutting firewood with a power saw and that is exercise too. A garden also demands a good bit of bending and stooping which is good exercise but somewhat limited to the warmer months of the year.

We've looked at rowing machines and cycling machines, but they are not an easy way to exercise. It takes as much effort to climb into one of those things as it does to do anything else.

Horse back riding if you can afford that or live in a rural area is pleasant exercise, but few of us have the necessary resources. Remember though that horses should not be ridden on highways and other blacktop areas. This is very bad for the horse's feet, and only a very insensitive person would insist on using the highways as a bridle path.

One of the better ways of exercising, particularly if you are middle aged, is bicycling. More and more towns and cities are setting aside bike paths free of auto traffic. Eventually bikes will probably be licensed to help pay for the costs of these programs, just as part of the gasoline tax which motorists pay is used to improve highways.

A simple bike with three speeds is adequate for most people. The ten speed bikes are a lot more expensive, and are not really worth the cost to the ordinary person just wanting to ride around for exercise. If you get more serious and join a bike club that goes on long excursions, then a ten speed may well be worthwhile. A ten speed also makes it easier to go up hill, so if you live in a mountainous or hilly area a ten speed may be called for. Biking is great fun, but remember that five miles of bike riding is only equal to the exercise you would get in walking one mile.

Outing clubs often reduce the expense of the equipment needed for outdoor activities by sharing the cost and the use of the equipment cooperatively. If you only bike or backpack infrequently this makes more sense than tying your money up in equipment that you will only use perhaps 12 times a year.

ORGANIZING A COMMUNITY THEATRE

The need for each of us to provide entertainment and services for pleasure and fulfillment is great, and the outlets for such endeavors are expanding. Community theatre is a nice and inexpensive way to encourage those in the community who need outlets for creativity, as well as provide relaxation for the rest of the community.

The principal ingredients for a community theatre are a script, actors, director and technical support, and a theatre site. The script and the actors are by far the major ingredients. Almost any place can be used for a theatre, indoors or outdoors.

Many community theatre programs are based on some aspect of local history; some incident in the past that has become a part of community tradition. This serves the purpose of having material readily available and provides a continuity of tradition. From the largest cities to the smallest there is no lack of fascinating legends or historical happenings that can be written up into a one or two act play.

How do you get a script? We think the smartest way is to ask for volunteers and have a group work together. Undoubtedly this will take a lot longer than having a contest or delegating one person to do the job, but it widens the feeling of participation. Also, if you have someone in the community with writing experience, whom you can get as an advisor, that can help matters.

The group will need two or three meetings to discover what incident they want to dramatize. Sources of information for larger communities are libraries. For smaller ones, court records and city records, old newspaper files, and the memories of older residents all can be a rich source for a start.

Having decided on the incident, the group should then decide on the essential cast of characters, preferably keeping it to a small group initially. From then on, the actual writing must be determined by the group's ability to delegate responsibility and authority, and the enthusiasm of the members.

Chapter 2
Food

BUYING FOOD FOR LESS

Grades and Standards

Grades and standards do not measure nutritional value or economic value. Most grades are for aesthetic appeal. But here are a few facts to remember.

Fancy grades of canned fruits mean nothing in the way of nutrition, and heavy syrup in a canned fruit is a waste of money. Fruits in light syrup are tasty, lower in calories, less sweet, and should be cheaper, particularly with sugar prices skyrocketing.

Most canned vegetables are not graded. A possible exception are peas and carrots. Peas come in four sizes, with the smallest size the most expensive. Baby carrots in cans or jars are also higher than carrot slices. Needless to say the larger sizes are just as nourishing and cheaper by far.

A few canned fruits and vegetables are graded B and C, which means the can's contents may be slightly malformed, or in chunks rather than some attractive shape. These are usually a good buy because they are cheaper. Don't forget that any canned item sold MUST meet government standards of cleanliness and can be eaten safely.

Fresh produce that is graded Fancy or Extra Fancy is more attractive to the eye, and more expensive. The other fruits are just as tasty and nourishing and a lot cheaper.

Grade B eggs do not appear very often, but when they do we have no hesitation in buying them. These are eggs with a less than firm white and a slightly flattened or runny yolk. They should be cheaper. But we have seen them sold at the same price as the Grade A. There is no difference nutritionally between white eggs and brown eggs, and we are unaware of any nutritional difference between fertile and nonfertile eggs.

Read The Label

The label on a can of a one-item pack, such as peaches, string beans, or beets, for example, will give you an idea of what you are buying and can serve as a rough basis of comparison between two brands. The label will tell you what is in the can (sliced beets, pickled beets, or tiny whole beets, for example), the contents' weight, the manufacturer's name, and any additives, whether salt or preservative.

No one brand of a single item can claim to be better or cheaper than any other brand. A label on a can saying "Inspected by United States Department of Agriculture" is a guarantee of cleanliness only, not quality.

To help you with this tricky aspect of shopping, we have included a table of can sizes and can contents.

Drained vs. Net Weight

Any weight you see marked on a can of fruits or vegetables is the net weight of the product PLUS the water or liquid in the can. The drained or edible weight of the product you are buying varies greatly. Vacuum packed corn has less liquid than ordinary canned corn, for just one example.

Frozen vegetables are labeled to tell you the weight of the vegetable; no water is used. In many instances frozen vegetables are a better buy than canned vegetables. Frozen fruits often have sugar syrup added before freezing.

We prefer frozen vegetables because we know how rapidly the freezing process takes place after harvest, to provide a fresh product with all its nutrition locked in. However, like most people, we have to compromise because we do not have a freezer, and our refrigerator-freezer holds only a limited supply.

Efforts by consumer groups to require the drained or edible weight of the contents to be listed on the can, have been successfully fought by commercial canners, who argue that the liquid may contain additives that are nutritious and may make the product more tasty. But how many of us just pour that canned juice right down the drain?

Unit Pricing

This consumer aid is not in use in all food stores. But unfortunately the number of shoppers who use unit pricing is far smaller than it should be.

Unit pricing makes it possible to contrast prices of comparable items such as canned vegetables, canned fruits, rice, beans, flour, and similar one-of-a-kind items. It is pretty useless with items like corned beef hash, stews, and mixed foods, because here the contents vary.

In stores using unit pricing, the labels on the shelves can help you save money. Unfortunately many stores use such small print as to be almost unreadable, and some include so much information that the consumer is baffled. The simplest method is shown below.

Eggs-By The Dozen or Pound?

A similar approach to egg buying can result in cash savings. Pricing eggs by the dozen is a convenience in packing them, but makes no sense to the consumer who should know how much a dozen eggs weigh. It is fairly easy to convert the cost of eggs by the dozen, to the cost per pound, using Table 1. If you can, copy the table on an index card and carry it with you when you shop. Or if you forget, just remember that if two sizes of eggs differ by more than 7ᶜ a dozen, the smaller size is the better buy.

Practice using the conversion table a little and you will see that it is simple and very practical. Suppose your grocery store is selling large eggs at 84ᶜ a dozen, and medium eggs at 69ᶜ a dozen. Run your finger down the large column to 84ᶜ, then to the right of the chart to the cost per lb. column. The price is 56ᶜ a lb. Now do the same with the medium column to 69ᶜ, then across to the price per lb. of egg which is 52ᶜ. The medium eggs are the better buy because you are getting a pound of medium eggs for 4ᶜ a pound less than a pound of large eggs.

If prices go above the highest price listed on the chart, divide the *price per dozen* you are paying by two, and then multiply the *price per pound* by two, which will give you the price per pound for one dozen eggs.

UNIT PRICE
60ᶜ
dried split peas   75ᶜ per lb.
12 ozs.

UNIT PRICE
70ᶜ
dried split peas   70ᶜ per lb.
16 ozs.

Although this item comes packed in two different sizes, 12 ozs. and 16 ozs., it is easy to see by reading the shelf sign that one is 5ᶜ per lb. less than the other.

Converting egg prices by the dozen
to prices by the pound

PRICE BY SIZE			CONVERTED PRICE PER POUND
Large	Medium	Small	
44	38	33	29
46	41	35	31
48	42	36	32
49-50	43	37	33
52	46	39	35
54	47	41	36
56	49	42	37
58-59	51-52	44	39
60	53	45	40
62	54	46	41
63	55	47	42
64	56	48	43
65	57	49	44
66	58	50	44
68	59	51	45
69	60	52	46
70	61	53	47
72	63	54	48
74	64	56	49
76	66	59	51
80	69	60	52
84	74	63	56
89	79	67	69

CONVENIENCE FOODS

These are foods which have been partially prepared for eating. Although canned and other packaged items could be included in this category, we usually think of things like dehydrated soups, cut up chicken, fillet of fish, vegetables in plastic bags with sauce and butter, baked goods, frozen fruits and juices, and such.

How much your shopping list revolves around convenience foods is influenced by several factors and only you can decide how important they are.

The general advantages of convenience foods are: quick and ready dishes, the distribution of seasonal crops over a long period of time, and the pleasure of having foods from all parts of the United States as well as imported from other countries. There is a savings in time of preparation, and a reduction in cleaning up.

In times such as these, costs loom high. Are convenience foods actually more expensive than the home preparation of the same foods?

Cost

In 1973, the U.S. Department of Agriculture came up with some surprising figures. Like most people we had always considered convenience foods a luxury. However, the U.S.D.A. statistics indicated this is not necessarily true.

Starting from scratch was found cheaper for some items but convenience foods were found to be cheaper in other cases. The study pointed out that 59% of the selected convenience foods studied had a serving cost equal to, or less than, comparable food started in raw form and prepared at home.

A good example was frozen concentrate orange juice which was cheaper than orange juice squeezed at home. Here are the figures.

Produce	Unit	Cost	Servings	Cost per ½ cup serving
fresh orange juice	1 dozen	59ᶜ	8	7.3ᶜ
frozen orange concentrate	1 can	35ᶜ	6	5.9ᶜ

For vegetables, seven out of ten ready-to-cook items had a lower cost per serving than the same items bought fresh. This is because there is no waste when preparing frozen vegetables as there is for fresh.

Baked goods, however, are a different story. Here, 75% of the convenience products had higher costs than the same product prepared at home. We find that we can make biscuits at home for about 40% less than ready-to-bake refrigerated biscuits. But most

people we know do not bake their own bread. For real economy you need a freezer, and an oven large enough to handle several loaves of bread at once to keep energy costs down.

Slightly over half the pork, beef, and poultry convenience foods were less expensive per serving because commercial processors are more efficient in the use of the animal carcass.

In some cases convenience foods may be cheaper in price but not really comparable in quality. We once tried a dehydrated chili mix, adding the necessary ground beef but the beans were tough, the flavoring and seasoning were skimpy, and the tomato was almost invisible. It was not any cheaper to buy this mix than to buy a can of beans, a can of tomatoes, and chili powder.

So much for cost.

Time

Time is always a factor in deciding to use convenience foods. Will the built-in service provide some extra time to do something personal? Do you have unexpected guests drop in and too little time to start a meal from scratch?

Does the built-in service relieve you of a chore you would rather avoid? Some people dislike the task of cutting up a chicken for cooking. We always buy poultry whole and cut it up ourselves because it is cheaper by several cents a pound, and we can segment the bird to suit our needs, but if this is distasteful to you then the added work is not worth it.

OUTDATED, DAMAGED, AND RIPE ITEMS

Bakery outlets can be an excellent source of cheaper baked goods. Here in Asheville we patronize one that sells "crippled" baked goods, items that are a little crumbled at one corner, or the ends of fruit cakes, or day-old breads. We save 30 to 50% on each thing we buy and find them all fine.

Supermarkets will sometimes reduce bread that is a day or two old. But check carefully to be sure the loaves are not moldy.

Some supermarkets offer reduced prices on Saturday evenings. When we lived in Kentucky we had the good fortune to live near one such store, and we bought excellent barbecued items at half price, including chickens, pork chops, pork ribs, and more. The foods were reduced to avoid keeping them in the store over the week-end. A find like this can cut your meat costs way down, and allow you to eat a lot better than your income would ordinarily permit.

Other markets may mark down a package of meat when it gets a little off-color. We grab these and find no lesser quality.

On the subject of aging food items, we think the best bananas for eating are those with black spots. Most people like them a bright clear yellow. When they are spotted most markets will mark them down, at which point we buy them. You can also buy green peppers, cantaloupes, cauliflower, green beans, citrus, and potatoes at these reduced counters. Check to make sure the fruits and vegetables are not overly spoiled or bruised, because then there will be more waste than usual and your savings will be reduced.

Never hesitate to ask salespeople if overripe fruits or vegetables are to be reduced. Half the time you may get a huffy answer. The other half you will save money.

Quite a few towns have a "salvage" food store that specializes in selling damaged canned goods. Many of these items are 25 to 40% cheaper than the same brand undamaged. Sometimes government food surplus items appear in damaged cans, and you can save 50% or more on such things as butter, peanut butter in quart and gallon size cans, canned boned turkey and chicken and luncheon meat. These are of excellent quality. If you have such a store around check carefully to be sure that the cans are not leaking, and know what comparable prices are, to be sure you are saving.

Some grocery stores will have a wagon of damaged goods around, but this is getting common as food prices spiral upward. Before buying a damaged can be sure that it is not on special at a lower price elsewhere and in perfect condition. We have seen a damaged can of fruit marked at 39ᶜ in a store, and the same can of fruit--undamaged--on sale in the store at three for $1.00!

One sure way to save money on your food bill is not to throw any food away. Make it a habit to serve all leftovers as soon as possible to avoid spoilage and waste. Keep all leftovers at the front of the refrigerator in clear view where you can't miss them. Leftover vegetables and meats can be added to soups and salads. After making a pot roast, take the drippings and the bone, and cook it up to make a broth for soup. The same thing can be done with all chicken bones and turkey bones. The liquid from cooked or canned beans shouldn't be thrown out but can be added to other foods. Odd scraps of cheese can be grated and added to spaghetti sauce or salad dressings.

Contents of the most frequently seen canned foods

Can Size	Contents	Used for
4 oz.	¼ cup	mushrooms, oysters
6 oz.	¾ cup 6 fluid oz.	frozen concentrates, fruit juices
8 oz.	1 cup 8 oz. 7¾ oz.	fruits, vegetables, mixed foods
# ½	6½ oz.	tuna, salmon

# 1	1¼ cups 10½ oz. 9½ fluid oz.	condensed soups, fruits, vegetables, mixed foods
# 300	1¾ cups 15½ oz. 13½ fluid oz.	pork and beans, spaghetti, chili, hash, fruits
# 303	2 cups 1 lb. 15 fluid oz.	vegetables, fruits, apple sauce
# 2	2½ cups 1 lb. 4 oz. 1 pint, 2 fluid oz.	vegetables, fruits, fruit juices
# 2½	3½ cups 1 lb. 11 oz. 1 pint, 10 fluid oz.	vegetables, fruits
46 oz.	5¾ cups 1 qt. 14 fluid oz.	juices
# 10	12 cups 6 - 7 lbs.	tuna, salmon, fruits, vegetables

National Brands vs. Store Brands

We made some comparisons between national brand prices and store brand prices here in Asheville, using Winn-Dixie, a national chain, and Ingles, a local chain.

In many, many cases the store brand is packed by a national company, with the label changed. Few chains care to have the responsibility of managing canneries and food processing plants. A&P does produce its own dairy products and push them in their stores. We find A&P has a relatively poor selection of dairy products outside of their own brands.

We noted that the Winn Dixie house brand fruits were mostly in light syrup, and were cheaper than the national brands which were almost always in heavy syrup. Here at least the difference is clearly due to the sugar. By all means buy those in light syrup. It is better for you by far and cheaper.

We have not attempted to compare foods like pork and beans, hash or stews because although federal law sets a minimum of meat content, it does not set a ceiling for the meat in these foods and it is almost impossible to compare them.

There is not much difference between national and store brands, but in general the store brands seem to have gone up faster in price than the national brands. When the store brand is only one or two cents cheaper than the national brand, then the supermarket is trying to make a high profit since they don't spend money on advertising as the national brands do. When we see a store brand the same price as the national brand, we buy the national brand.

A&P recently announced a freeze on the prices of some of their own brand of items. This noble gesture on their part was hailed as a step forward against increased prices, but it is interesting that the signs announcing the price freeze do not list any specific items covered by the freeze. One wonders how many items are not covered by the freeze. In the fall of 1974 when it was announced that the corn crop was a disaster, anticipating higher prices of corn and corn products, A&P was one of the first to raise the price of the 1973 corn oil still on their shelves.

Comparing store brands and national brands of a number of foods at two supermarkets in Asheville, North Carolina. All have to meet federal standards of cleanliness and safeness for human use.

ITEM	NATIONAL BRAND	STORE BRAND
Whole tomatoes	39¢	35¢
Spinach, 15 ozs.	3/$1.00	4/$1.00
Corn, whole kernel	39¢	33¢
Green limas	47¢	3/$1.00
Sweet peas, large	39¢	3¢$1.00
Ketchup 1 lb. 4 ozs.	59	55¢
Apple sauce	37¢ (16½ ozs.)	22¢ (16 ozs.)
Vegetable oil	$1.25	$1.19
Evaporated milk	30¢	27¢
Shortening, 3 lbs.	$1.66	$1.59
Sliced beets	25¢	29¢
Peaches, cling halves	47¢ (heavy syrup)	3/$1.00 (light syrup)
Pears, Bartlett halves	69¢ (heavy syrup)	55¢ (light syrup)
Instant tea, 3 ozs.	$1.59 & $1.79	$1.38

BUYING VEGETABLES

Whether you buy fresh, frozen, or canned vegetables is a personal preference. We prefer frozen to the canned because the canned are usually overcooked and lack proper texture. Some vegetables aren't overcooked during canning, such as corn, lima beans, and dried beans. Even in the summer at the peak of the harvest we often prefer frozen vegetables unless there is a tremendous savings on the fresh, or unless we are buying locally grown produce at the farmers' market or fresh local produce from the supermarkets. Often there is such a delay from the time the produce is picked to the time that you buy it, that the produce loses its freshness.

Frozen vegetables are subject to slight thawing and refreezing during movement to the store, because of overloading and faulty refrigerator cases, and further thawing from the time you buy it until you put it in the freezer. But weigh the problems of fresh vs. frozen produce, and choose for yourself.

Of course, fancy mixed vegetables, such as Japanese style vegetables, or vegetables in butter or sauce are going to cost more than if you make the dish yourself.

Fresh, canned, and frozen vegetables all give different number of servings because of waste or cooking liquid. The price per pound or unit is an indication of which vegetable is cheaper, but the number of servings is also important. The tables here list the number of servings you can expect from a 1 lb. can of vegetables, 1 lb. of fresh vegetables, and a 10 oz. package of frozen vegetables. Divide the cost of the unit by the number of servings to get the cost per serving. Then compare the price of a serving of the fresh, frozen, and canned. Some things are naturally going to cost more frozen than fresh, such as potatoes. Here the freezing is a convenience because the potato is peeled and sliced or chopped, so you are paying for the convenience as well as for the potato. During the winter when the price of green peppers goes so high, the frozen chopped green pepper can be cheaper than the fresh. Buy only the amount of fresh vegetables that you can use before they spoil. Even if a vegetable is on sale or cheaper per pound in large amounts, don't buy any more than you can use before it loses quality or spoils.

The number of servings per lb. or unit of vegetable.

Vegetable	Fresh 1 lb.	Frozen 9 or 10 oz. pkg.	Canned 16 oz. can
asparagus	3-4	2-3	3-4
beans, lima	2 (bought in pod)	3-4	3-4
beans, snap	5-6	3-4	3-4
beets, diced	3-4 (bought without tops)	-	3-4
broccoli	3-4	3	-
brussel sprouts	4-5	3	-
cabbage	raw-shredded 9-10	-	-
	cooked 4-5	-	
carrots	(bought without tops) raw-diced or shredded 5-6	-	-
	cooked 4	-	3-4
cauliflower	3	3	-
celery	raw-diced or chopped 5-6	-	
	cooked 4	-	-
corn, whole kernel	-	3	3-4
kale	5-6	2-3	2-3
okra	4-5	4	-
onions, cooked	3-4	-	-
parsnips	4	4	-
peas	2 (bought in pod)	3	3-4
potatoes	4	-	-
spinach	4	2-3	2-3
squash, summer	3-4	-	-
squash, winter	2-3	-	-
sweet potatoes	3-4	2-3	-
tomatoes	raw-diced or sliced 4	-	3

Dry beans give 10 servings per lb.
Dry split peas and lentils give 10-11 servings per lb.

Number of servings per pound or unit of fruit

Fruit	Fresh	Frozen	Dried	Canned
	1 lb. or unit	10 or 12 oz. pkg.	8 oz. pkg.	16 oz. can
apples	3-4	-	8	All canned fruits
apricots	5-6	-	6	give 2-3 servings
bananas	3-4	-	-	per can when drained.
blueberries	4-5 per pint	3-4	-	If served with the
cherries, sweet	5-6	-	-	liquid they give
grapes, seedless	5-6	-	-	4 servings per can.
aches	3-4	2-3	7	
pears	3-4	-	7	
plums	3-4	-	-	
prunes	-	-	4-5	
mixed fruit	-	-	6	
raspberries	4-5 per pint	2-3	-	
strawberries	8-9 per quart	2-3	-	

BUYING FRUITS

Fruits come in fresh, frozen, canned, and dried forms, but it isn't easy to judge the amount of waste on fresh fruit or the sugar syrup in canned fruit. The following table helps give you the number of servings per unit, whether the unit is a lb. of fresh fruit, a 1 lb. can of canned fruit, or a 10 oz. package of frozen fruit. Divide the price by the number of servings to get the price per serving.

Some canned fruits are available in light syrup, and cost less than the ones in heavy syrup. Frozen fruits with sugar usually have a better texture, while the ones frozen without sugar are more likely to be mushy and lose their flavor.

MILK

You can save the most money by drinking instant nonfat dry milk. The taste is identical to any of the skimmed milks sold in the dairy case. But if you cannot get used to the taste, try mixing equal amounts of whole milk and reconstituted nonfat dry milk. You can also make your own buttermilk from the nonfat dry milk. Despite all our progress in agriculture here in the United States, dairy herds are still an expensive and inefficient method of producing milk. We hear how much grain it takes to produce meat, but it also takes grain to produce milk and dairy products, and even eggs. The imitation milks that are now being sold are expensive and cannot realistically ever replace milk. There is usually less than 20^c difference in the price of a gallon of whole milk and the imitation milk. The consumption of milk has gone down in the United States in recent years, and so most of the surplus of milk has been made into cheese, causing a cheese surplus, but without the lowering of cheese prices!

RICE

Converted rice used to be much more expensive than ordinary enriched rice, but with recent price increases there isn't that much difference between the two. Quick cooking rice is an expensive luxury. By planning meals ahead of time you can cook regular rice and have a better quality product, for less than the quick cook. The quick cook is convenient to have for meals in a hurry. If you plan on making a rice casserole, or a dish where the rice is cooked first (such as fried rice, curried rice, or rice and beans), the rice can be cooked the day or night before at your convenience. You can cook enough for several meals and store it in the refrigerator for as long as several days until needed.

Frozen rice casseroles, such as rice pilaf, rice and green peas, rice with mushrooms, are very expensive per serving. These dishes are sold in plastic cooking bags and aren't really any more convenient than what you make yourself except for the cleanup. You can mix your own ingredients much more cheaply than you can buy these dishes.

A 1 lb. package of rice equals 2½ cups uncooked rice, or 7½ cups cooked rice.

BREADS

Regular loaves of bread are the cheapest you can buy. Rolls and fancy breads, whether fresh or frozen, are more expensive than regular bread. English muffins, hard rolls, onion rolls, waffles, and toastees are all included as fancy breads. The fancy breads are usually twice the price of the regular bread. An 8 oz. package of fancy bread costs the same as a 1 lb. loaf of bread.

BABY FOODS

With the use of a blender you can make your own baby food. Most fruits, vegetables, and meats that are cooked for the rest of the family only need to be blended to be suitable for baby food.

You can make a large amount of baby food and freeze it in convenient size containers for use later. Baby food can also be canned and the process is the same as canning any other food. (see directions for canning on pages 53–58). Baby food cannot be kept in large amounts in the refrigerator for longer than several days because it will spoil.

DRY BEANS AND PEAS

Dry beans and peas are usually more expensive when bought already cooked in the can. You can save money by cooking your own. They can be cooked very quickly in a pressure cooker if you have one. It usually saves energy if you soak them for 24 hours before cooking. You can also save energy by cooking in an electric hot pot or electric casserole rather than on top of the stove. Cook about twice or three times the amount of beans or peas you need, and freeze the extra ones in the freezer until needed. This will save you energy as well as being more convenient for you. Allow time for the frozen cooked beans to thaw before attempting to use them. Try to buy dry beans of a uniform size because the smaller ones cook quicker than the larger ones. If the pot is covered during cooking, beans will cook faster.

Dry beans will give you about 11 servings per lb. Dry split peas and lentils will give you 10-11 servings. 1 lb. dry beans equals 2 cups of uncooked or 6 cups cooked.

CEREALS

The cheapest and the most nourishing cereals are the hot cereals that have to be cooked, whether regular or instant. Granola cereals are good too, but most of the natural granola cereals contain too much sugar even if it is natural brown sugar or honey, as well as other sweet tasting ingredients including coconut and raisins. The packaged ready-to-eat cereals are more expensive, and are not as nutritious as the cooked ones. The quick cooking cereals only require 2½-5 minutes to cook.

1 lb. of quick cook rolled oats equals 4⅔ cups of uncooked oats.

POTATOES

Potatoes that exhibit damage, growth cracks, sprouts, or that are shriveled, spongy, flabby, or bruised should not be bought. Some defects such as hollow spots and internal discoloration cannot be seen just by looking at the potato. Potatoes should not smell musty or moldy.

If you store potatoes in plastic bags, tear a few holes in the plastic to allow moisture to evaporate rather than condense on the potatoes which will cause them to spoil quickly. Potatoes do better in a slightly cooler storage place. During very warm weather they may spoil if closed up in a warm closet or storage place. When buying a large amount of potatoes, such as a 5 or 10 lb. bag or larger, check for spoiled ones or signs of decay before storing since the decay will spread to the other potatoes.

Ready to cook frozen potatoes such as tater-gems, hash browns, shoestring, and home fries, are more expensive per pound than frozen french fries. Compare the price to see which is the best buy. If the price of fresh potatoes rises too high, the frozen product will sometimes be cheaper than the fresh. Most frozen potato dishes (scalloped, stuffed, and so on), are convenient but very expensive. Since french fries are usually the cheapest frozen potato, keep them in the freezer for their convenience and use them in various ways. Add sauteed onion and green pepper to french fries and you have potatoes O'Brien, or add beaten eggs to the potatoes just before placing in the serving dish.

NOODLES

One way to save money is to make your own noodles. You don't need any special ingredients or special kitchen tools. You can't achieve all the fancy shapes that store-bought noodles come in, but the home made noodles are much tastier and have more of an eggy flavor. All you need is flour and egg which you combine into a dough. The dough is rolled out and allowed to dry. Some people prefer to place the dough over a chair back to dry. After the dough dries, which takes several hours, it is sliced into the size you want. It can be cooked or stored in jars in the refrigerator until needed. The only difficult part about making noodles is rolling out the dough, which takes a little effort and practice, but even at the first try your noodles will be perfectly delicious and edible.

If flour is 89ᶜ for 5 lbs., and large eggs are 75ᶜ for a dozen, you can make 2½ cups cooked noodles (5 oz. uncooked weight) for the low price of 11ᶜ. Compare this with the price of store-bought noodles.

It takes one cup of uncooked noodles to make 1¼ cups cooked. A 1 lb. package of macaroni equals 3 cups uncooked or 6 cups of cooked.

COFFEE

Coffee filters on coffee pots like Mr. Coffee or Norelco can be used twice by putting fresh coffee on top of the old grounds. Since coffee grounds will sour and spoil like any other food, begin with a new filter the following day. Coffee will also go farther if it is ground very very fine, as in an electric grinder. Even an electric blender can be used to grind coffee. Already ground bought in cans and bags can be ground finer in the grinder or blender.

CHEESE AND CHEESE PRODUCTS

There's alot of confusion about cheese and cheese products and alot of people are uncertain whether to buy a process cheese food. Natural cheeses do contain all milk but are very expensive. The other three types of cheese contain as much protein as the natural cheeses, and some of them are even higher in protein than certain types of natural cheeses.

Pasteurized process cheese is a blend of natural cheeses which have been shredded, mixed, and heated with other ingredients. It comes in several flavors, and contains 23.2 grams of protein for every 4½ oz. of cheese. It is usually about 70ᶜ to a $1.00 per lb. less than natural cheeses.

Pasteurized process cheese spread has higher moisture content and lower milkfat than cheese food and process cheese. It contains 16.0 grams of protein for every 4½ oz. of spread.

Pasteurized process cheese food contains some natural cheese but also has such ingredients as nonfat dry milk added. It contains 19.8 grams of protein for every 4½ oz. of cheese food. Today process cheese no longer costs more for slices than for blocks.

EXTENDERS AND ADDITIVES

The manufacturers of soybean extenders have priced themselves out of the market and most nutritionists agree that adding bread, egg, and oatmeal is just as satisfactory as adding soybean extenders, and for less cost. Even meat products containing soy-

bean extenders are usually not bargains when you consider the amount of meat in proportion to the amount of soybean they contain. For example, chicken bologna with soybean was introduced at 49-59ᶜ per lb., which was then $1.00 cheaper per lb. than regular bologna. It slowly inched up in price despite the fact that none of the contents had gone up in price.

Several other meat extenders and protein supplements are available at the wholesale level. Peanut grits is one of them. Cottonseed flour is another, but it is quite bitter and does have a noticeable odor, despite the advertising claim.

Nitrates And Nitrites

This is an area of confusion and all the facts are not in yet.

In "organic" health food stores we have seen products being sold free of nitrates and nitrites. They are of course more expensive than the foods without nitrates and nitrites. Is the extra cost justifiable? Let's take a look.

Nitrates and nitrites are naturally occurring substances found in foods, water, and even human saliva. The maximum amount permitted in drinking water is 45 parts per million. There are federally imposed ceilings for nitrates and nitrites in our food.

These two compounds are much used in curing and processing meat and fish, which helps meat keep its red color, as well as keeping ham, bacon and sausage red. Bacon without nitrite is salt pork, and ham is salty roast pork.

The value of these two is that they prevent botulism, an often fatal food poisoning. The F.D.A. believes that the use of nitrates and nitrites are essential to prevent the growth of poisonous substances in certain meats, poultry and fish.

The drawback is that laboratory animals have developed cancer when nitrites and nitrates break down and form new products. At this time there seems to be no information on the effect of nitrates and nitrites in the human diet. The trouble causing product, nitrosamines have turned up very rarely in the meat examined by the U.S. Department of Agriculture. Three out of 48 processed meats showed nitrosamines to be present; three out of 50 samples of cooked sausage showed nitrosamines present. The levels found in these meats were much lower than required to cause cancer in laboratory studies with animals.

Meat Tenderizers and MSG

A few years ago the newspapers were full of the "Chinese restaurant syndrome," which turned out to be that some people experienced headache after eating Chinese restaurant food. Research turned up the culprit of MSG (monosodium glutamate), a natural compound made from wheat, corn, soybeans, yeast and other vegetable sources. It is used to enhance flavors and is reported as safe to use unless you are allergic to it and develop headaches.

Meat tenderizers are a plant product, papain, and are totally safe when used on foods that are cooked, although they can sometimes spoil the texture of the meat.

FOODS FAD COSTS PLENTY SOMETIMES

Vitamins

Vitamin C is best had from citrus fruits, and tomatoes, green peppers, and other fruits and vegetables. Large doses of Vitamin C do not and will not prevent catching the common cold. But for some small part of the population, massive doses of Vitamin C may

alleviate the symptoms of a cold. If your diet includes the four basic groups of food each day no additional Vitamin C is needed. Remember too that the body does not store that vitamin.

Vitamin E has traditionally been held as the bearer of the "fertility factor." In lab experiments, male rats without Vitamin E became sterile. However, dosing faltering human males with Vitamin E to treat either sterility or impotence has failed. Vitamin E is needed to continue pregnancy in humans, but no proof exists that it is a factor in fertility.

For awhile some commercial cosmetics included Vitamin E, but a popular deodorant containing Vitamin E was recalled by· the F.D.A. because there were widespread reports of rashes after its use.

Brewer's yeast, a source of Vitamin B as well as protein, has had its day. We tried it at home but we found the smell discouraging to say the least. Some faddist writers have suggested that panthothenic acid, a Vitamin B complex, will restore gray hair to its original color. It won't.

Vitamin A is now under special regulatory control by the F.D.A. There is sound evidence that excess Vitamin A can lead to weak bones, as well as some symptoms like those related to brain tumors. This vitamin can accumulate and be stored in the body, particularly in the liver.

Vitamin D excess can cause calcium deposits in tissues and result in changes in bone structure. However, milk fortification with Vitamins A and D at modest levels provides the two vitamins in amounts needed for normal growth and development.

In general, an adequate and average diet, even with reduction in luxury foods, but in keeping with the suggestions we have given for the basic food groups, will provide all of the vitamins and minerals the average healthy person needs. Taking modest amounts of supplemental vitamins will not hurt one's health, but taking massive doses can be expensive and may lead to poor health.

Organic Food Fads

Organic Vitamins

The back-to-nature movement has always been with us. Carried too far it can be a budget wrecker and can ruin the results of a good diet.

Some people claim that "natural" vitamins are infinitely better than "man-made" vitamins, but this is a superficial and untrue statement. A vitamin has a very specific molecular structure made up of unvarying building blocks. Whether it comes from plants, a test-tube, or an animal, its structure is absolutely the same. The human organism cannot differentiate one from the other. Part of the fallacy of "natural" vitamins is that they do not contain any man-made substances. In making tablets and capsules the manufacturer must use binders and excipients such as ethyl cellulose and other synthetic emulsifiers.

Often the "natural" vitamins contain unnecessary materials, such as honey, pushing the price way above that for the same vitamin man-made.

Organic Foods

We buy "organic" bread not for any miraculous qualities it may have, but because we like its flavor. However, to the organic food enthusiast, what he buys is supposed to be produced without man-made chemicals, such as fertilizers, pesticides, herbicides and he is supposed to prepare the food without any additives.

Some believers think that the term "organic" should be applied to foods produced free of traces of chemicals. This definition is not used because it has almost no validity. In 1972 the State of New York held hearings on organic foods which suggested that even if foods were produced without any chemicals, many of the resulting products contained chemicals anyway. This could be a carry-over from previous land use, or caused by wind drift from nearby farm areas.

As far as we know from the limited number of studies to date, there is no nutritional difference between organic foods and the usual farm products. Processed foods may sometimes be lower in certain nutritional factors, destroyed or reduced by the processing, but the loss is no greater for processed standard foods as compared to processed organic foods.

The source of fertilizer, whether natural like manure, green manure, limestone or others, as compared to those whose origin is more chemical or a little more complex, has no known effect on the nutritional value of crops. Plants absorb what is in the soil in an available form. They cannot distinguish between natural and synthetic fertilizers in what they absorb or what they use. How nourishing the plant will be to man depends on the minerals available, rainfall, sunlight, disease, and so forth. There is no reason to believe that we are better off for eating plants that have been fertilized one way over another.

Furthermore, there is ample opportunity for clever businessmen to dupe the unsuspecting consumer who wants to believe that organic foods are safer, more nourishing, and better in general than other foods. The F.D.A. has pointed out some weird examples. Cashews, mostly imported from India and Africa, are grown under conditions beyond any American market control. Yet some are sold as organic at almost twice the price of others not labeled organic. Dried apricots sold as organic were priced at $1.24 a pound and those not labeled as organic sold for $.74 a pound. Undoubtedly the organic growers may have added expenses such as a large crop loss because of failure to use insecticides, but as the F.D.A. puts it "...the opportunity for economic fraud is considerable."

One problem with organic foods is that they are not treated with preservatives. Some foods that contain oils, such as wheat germ and sunflower seeds, turn rancid very quickly if they do not have a preservative. Studies have shown that foods preserved with additives retain their nutrients longer than those without additives. One study included such things as grains, nuts, seeds, and flours. So if you store the organic food in your pantry too long you may be getting less nutrition than you would from the ordinary enriched product.

Another problem with some of the organic foods is that the fruit trees and nut trees are not sprayed to kill insects. When they are not sprayed this means that the food may be contaminated with insects that will not reveal themselves for quite some time after the harvest, usually waiting until after you have bought it and had it in your pantry for some time. A package of organic filberts became a swarmy mess of larvae, and organic dried Italian chestnuts produced bunches of moths which we at first assumed to be clothes moths until we examined the chestnuts. These moths can spread to grain, such as bags of flour, and even bags of noodles.

Special Foods

Most of us have seen the bumper sticker which says "Eat fish—live longer, eat oysters—love longer." These are amusing, but not particularly truthful. Food fads have run through blackstrip molasses, honey, wheat germ and a host of others. Each was part of a cult. Certainly these kinds of foods do not harm you if taken within reason. However, whatever qualities they have can be found in other products as well. We like honey at home and use it on pancakes because it is sweet. But it is no more a natural sweetener than beet sugar or cane sugar, both of which are plant products. In your house, you may find white bread too light and airy, and you may prefer pumpernickel, rye, or whole wheat. This does not necessarily mean that they are better for you, though they are certainly not harmful.

Fast Foods

Like a voice in the wilderness a professor is heard claiming that a teenager eating a quick lunch of a cheeseburger, french fries and a vanilla milk-shake will get about one third of the daily recommended diet allowance for most nutrients, except iron. Using foods from McDonalds, Burger Chef, and Burger King, Dr. Howard Appledorf analyzed these foods and found they provided a teenager with 39% of daily calories needed, 46% of calcium, 63% of phosphorus, 49% of zinc and 42% of copper. To make up the iron shortage Appledorf urges the government to require additional iron supplements in bread. However, some people would take exception to this suggestion since some types of supplemental iron are not easily digestible, especially for those with ulcers and other common digestive problems, and can be potentially harmful.

Diets

The number of diets that become fads and crazes varies little from year to year or decade to decade. There is no secret or trick way to lose weight, no special food or special formula. The best way to lose weight is to reduce the number of calories you eat. Weight losing pills can be dangerous.

According to U.S.D.A. most of the

special diet foods that are sold (other than those with artificial sweeteners) have as many calories as the ordinary non-diet food item. So it doesn't make sense to pay a lot of extra money for special diet dinners. Some yogurts and cottage cheeses advertise that they have less fat than the others, but they are all equally lowfat.

If these frequently appearing short-cuts sold on the market really worked well, would so many new ones keep popping up

FOOD STAMPS

15,000,000 Americans are thought to be using food stamps, with at least another 15,000,000 eligible who are not getting them. The stamps are bought for less than their face

value and are then used in the grocery store for food. Tobacco, liquor, beer, soap, and pet foods cannot be bought with the stamps.

Very simply, you are eligible for food stamps if you meet the following criteria:

Unemployed
Part-time worker
Low earnings
On public welfare
On Social Security or with small pensions

Eligibility is determined from the following table. The amount of net monthly income is for a family not on welfare or public assistance.

Persons in household [1]	Net monthly income [2]	Other resource limit [3]
1	$183.00	$1500.00
2	$260.00	
3	$373.00	
4	$473.00	
5	$560.00	
6	$646.00	
7	$726.00	
8	$806.00	
9	$873.00	
10	$940.00	$3000.00

1 Household is an individual or certain group of people who live in the same house, share food costs and eat together.

2 Money received on a regular basis including wages, pensions, unemployment compensation, Social Security, net earnings from farm operations, disability payments or public assistance.

3 Cash on hand, stocks, bonds, U.S. Savings Bonds, bank accounts, certain real or personal property.

The Food Stamp program is administered at the county level in each state.

In order to qualify, in addition to the economic guideline above, each and every member of the family from 18-65 years old who is able-bodied, must register to work. If one person in the household refuses to register, and remains a member of the household, everyone becomes ineligible to receive the stamps.

In considering qualifications, the following items are not counted as assets: one car; non-licensed vehicles; home; life insurance policies; real estate that produces income; vehicle needed for work; tools of a tradesman; and farm machinery.

If you meet these requirements the next step is to visit the local office of your welfare department with the following papers to expedite your application:

Social security card
pay stubs from employer or pay records
rent receipt or record of mortgage payments
income tax records for previous year or two
records of any other income
bank book
name, age, and income of everyone living in the household

After the necessary paperwork and usual return trips for things you might have forgotten, you will get a stamp allowance depending on the number of people in your household. Cost of the stamps will be based on the number of people and net family income. In no case will the cost of the stamps exceed 30% of the household's net income or take home pay. The allotment of stamps can be bought twice a month, or once a month. Older people have difficulty getting to the office to buy the stamps once a month, as well as difficulty getting enough money to buy the entire allotment once a month. Twice a month is easier financially, but pretty impossible for older people or people living in isolated communities and without transportation.

Having registered for work, all able-bodied members of the household in the 18-65 age bracket must report for job interviews at the Employment Service upon request; provide the Employment Service with information when needed; report to an employer if referred by the Employment Service, and accept an offer of suitable employment when made.

If you do get food stamps and move, simply ask the local office for a transfer certification. This form is good for 60 days, at which time it must be re-issued in the new locality.

Unfortunately, inflation has reduced the buying power of the stamps for people with minimal incomes, and the program is in trouble. But it is a worthy program that should definitely continue with government support. Feeding our own poor and needy, our old and disabled is a non-negotiable requirement of the government of the United States.

In some instances communes have qualified for food stamps, apparently meeting the household description by pooling food and income. Numbers of college students over 18 have been using the stamp program on the grounds that they were over 18 years old, were self-supporting, and their income was below poverty level. In January 1975, however, the United States Department of Agriculture was ordered by the Congress to stop selling food stamps to middle class students. Any student over 18 years old whose parents are not eligible for food stamps, and who receives over half his income from his parents, is now considered an income tax dependent and is ineligible for food stamps. When you consider that most college scholarships are closed to middle class students, and that many, many colleges will not permit on-campus jobs, this is indeed a questionable policy.

GROWING YOUR OWN

Vegetable Growing

You can grow vegetables in your house, in your backyard, or many places in between! You can grow modest amounts of a pretty wide selection of vegetables in an apartment if you have a location which gets some sunlight. A windowsill, a balcony, or a door stoop protected from dogs, are good locations. By law, fire escapes are out of bounds.

All you need to be in the indoor vegetable business is a suitable container, seeds, and synthetic soil mixture. You can't feed a family, but you can have some fun and a modest amount of home grown produce.

Containers

Just about anything that allows for drainage will serve the purpose. You can use flower pots, an old pail, a simple plastic freezer bag, an old plastic dish, a wooden bushel basket lined with plastic, or an old work bucket.

Be sure that you punch holes for drainage, usually four to six holes, ¼ inch in diameter, along the bottom side.

The size container you select as well as how many, will depend on how much space you have available. Six inch pots are fine for chives. Radishes, onions, and miniature tomatoes grow well in ten to twelve inch pots.

Large five gallon plastic containers are fine if you have a large enough space to hold them.

Growth Medium

One of the best soil substitutes can be made by mixing this formula. It can be cut in half if need be, or increased;

¾ cubic feet package of shredded peat moss

equal quantity of vermiculite
½ cup ground limestone
¼ cup 20% superphosphate
½ cup 5-10-5

Add a little water and mix well. We use a garbage can with a tight fitting cover for this, to minimize inhaling the dust.

Seeds

Small packets are readily available in almost any grocery, garden store and discount stores. I have never found an out-dated packet of seeds and doubt that you will. This refers to the year stamped on the packet which tells you in which year the seeds were meant to be grown.

Light Requirements

Some vegetables need more sun than others. This will influence the kind of vegetables you plant. If you have limited space with sunlight you will need to specialize in those vegetables that grow with less sunlight.

Some vegetables can be grown entirely in the house, using supplementary light sources. In this group fall radishes, leaf lettuce and the dwarf "Tiny Tim" tomato.

Light adaptability of some vegetables

Partial Shade	Full Sunlight
beets	eggplant
cabbage	peppers
carrots	tomatoes
chives	
leaf lettuce (tolerates low temperatures)	
leek	
onions, green	
parsley	
radishes	

Backyard Gardens

If you have a small space which receives at least half a day of sunlight and is not under a tree or shrub, you can produce an amazing quantity of vegetables from your small backyard garden. During World War II backyard gardens became a community venture. These Victory Gardens were in the backyards of apartment buildings and churchyards.

The trick we adapted when we had a space three feet wide by six feet long was to go for vertical planting. We simply used the principal that governs architecture in big cities: build up because the air space is a lot cheaper than the ground space.

We grew tomatoes and bell peppers and trained them on stakes. The amount we produced from three plants each, was amazing. We bought some tomato plants and some pepper plants from a garden shop and set them out about a foot apart. When the plants had reached a foot in height, we tied them carefully to stakes.

The first thing we planted in the spring were some radishes and lettuce, both of which do well in cool weather. But go easy on the radishes. How many radish salads can you eat in a day?

If you have a space, try to dig it up either early in the spring or late in the fall. If the space is big enough it may be worth your trouble to get a hand cultivator from Sears. We have one which cost us about $30 delivered with several small attachments. After the ground has been dug up with a shovel, or a rented rototiller if you have a larger plot, and just before you plant, run the wheeled cultivator over it to break up the clods. For a small backyard garden it is usually not practical to invest money in a roto-tiller because this expense adds enormously to the cost of the food you produce.

Some extension leaflets advise the selection of a garden spot that is well drained. Beautiful. But how do you know? Dig a hole about a foot deep, and in the afternoon fill it with water. If the water has disappeared in the morning, drainage is fine. If not, look for another spot.

Last October we decided to have a garden on our front lawn. We marked out an area about 50 feet x 75 feet, rather larger than needed. Our neighbor had a roto-tiller and we roto-tilled the area. Just before we did this we put 500 lbs. of decayed animal manure we had bought on sale at the local K-Mart, and 50 lbs. of 5-10-5. Then we sowed a crop of barley to give us a little winter protection as well as to produce some green manure.

In the latter part of October we bought onion bulbs or sets and planted four rows, and two rows of asparagus roots. In January we roto-tilled the barley crop under. We then went over the area with the wheeled cultivator. At the end of February we began planting cool weather crops.

The most important tool needed is a hoe. To lay out the rows fairly straight, drive a piece of wood at each end and tie a cord between them. Then use the top of the hoe handle and make a little furrow under the string to plant the seed in.

Most people plant much too much. One friend planted so many tomatoes that he had tomatoes in the drawers, tomatoes on the bed, and about 70 pint jars of home-made tomato juice. His last wish each night before going to sleep was that the neighbors would help themselves to the tomatoes.

Write your extension service at your state agricultural college or university for gardening leaflets, or call your county extension service. Some will be helpful in selecting varieties of vegetables and quantities to plant. Some will assume you know more than is reasonable to expect a non-farmer to know.

A small garden can be a real way of saving money, if you have access to inexpensive tools, equipment, and the place for one. You can grow a variety of plants for eating, but it's a good idea to plant a lot of onions because you can dry them easily in a shaded well-ventilated place, and they will store for a period of time. That saves you money. An ample tomato crop will yield enough to can as pastes and sauces. Again, you can save a tidy sum if you grow and process your own. We prefer jars because they can be used year after year, and their cost can be distributed over a number of crops.

If you are planning a vegetable garden, you will need to know the date of the last frost in the spring. This is only an average date, which can fall earlier or later in a given year. We add seven days to the date to allow margin of safety. The local office of the National Climatic Center of the U.S. Department of Commerce, or the county agricultural extension agent, can tell you this date for your locality. The average date of the first fall frost helps decide the varieties to select, since some take longer to yield a crop than others.

If you start your own plants indoors four to eight weeks before the last frost, they will be ready to move to the garden area you have in mind. You can start the plants in small pots. About two or three weeks after seeding, the plants to go outside should be hardened; that is done by reducing water and putting the plants in a cooler spot.

Gardening is work, but the exercise is healthful, and the harvest money saving and tasty.

Raising Chickens For Meat And Eggs

During World War II many people raised a few chickens in a backyard pen for meat and eggs. The interest in this home food production plan is again growing rapidly and is worth consideration.

If you decide you want to be a backyard poultryman be sure you know the local ordinances relating to the growing of domestic livestock in your community. These ordinances will tell you whether or not it can be done, and if so, how far from houses and the property line the chickens must be.

There are two kinds of pens suited for small scale poultry raising. One is built directly on the ground, with chicken wire six feet tall. The dimensions will be related to available space and the number of chickens planned for.

A rule of thumb is to have three laying birds for each family member, which theoretically provides an egg a day per person and some chicken to eat later on. Each laying hen is allowed three to four square feet of floor space, and each broiler about 1¼ square feet of floor space.

If you use baby chicks they will need a source of warmth for about a month or more. Very early spring is a good time to begin. Warmth can be furnished by a small home-made brooder with an electric bulb in it. A local garden store will have one that you can look at and copy. Each week the brooder is raised a little higher above the ground level so that there is a gradual lowering in the temperature to ready them for the time when there is no heat needed.

The best egg laying breed is the White Leghorn. Dual purpose birds include New Hampshire, Barred Rocks, and Plymouth Rocks, all of which lay well and make good eating.

An average layer will eat about 100 lbs. of feed over 11 months. In 1974, 100 lbs. of feed cost about $10. An average hen can be expected to produce between 15 to 16 dozen eggs in a year. Litter is needed on the ground, four inches deep, to absorb moisture. Straw, hay, sawdust, and woodshavings can be used. The last two can be picked up for very little if not free, at your nearest lumberyard.

To maintain egg production during the shorter days of winter, a 40-watt bulb in the hen house will do. Such supplemental light can be turned on and off with an inexpensive timing device. The light may have to be on for eight to ten hours, which is an energy use, and you may decide it is not worth the trouble for a small, ten bird flock.

A family of five would want 12 to 20 laying hens. This number of birds would require 36 to 80 square feet of floor space. The length and width would depend on the space available. 50 broilers would require 60 or so square feet of floor space.

Each cage needs a covered area, or coop, with a roof and three sides to protect the birds from rain. In the coop are roosts, and laying boxes for the egg factories if necessary.

Hens and broilers can be kept in raised cages, about 30 inches off the ground. We don't like this system for layers because getting the eggs out intact is a bit of a problem. For broilers it works well and means the droppings fall out of the cage, and can be shoveled out.

Feeders are needed and can be a part of the cage, as hoppers to be a part of the cage, or hoppers to be filled from the outside, or small portable feeders placed on the inside of the cages.

Watering is also needed, and a simple watering device can be bought at a farm and garden store, or Sears. These are large jars that let the water come out as the level in the drinking fountain goes down.

Feeders will be needed in the ground cages and they can be bought just as the waterers are. The feeders have a wire cover to keep the birds from sitting on the feed and dirtying it.

You cannot leave your flock to go off on a week-end. Someone must be around to feed and water them.

Vaccines for certain diseases are needed. A small flock cannot afford much veterinary care in case of disease.

Finally, write your extension service for leaflets on home poultry growing.

USING WILD PLANTS AS FOOD

Wild plants are an abundant source of food free for the taking. You can save a lot of money if you only gather wild greens and dry your own teas. But you must have security that you are not mistaking a poisonous plant for a similar or look-alike edible plant. Our book, *A Naturalist's Guide to Cooking with Wild Plants,* (published by Quadrangle/The New York Times) has illustrations and descriptions of the most common and plentiful wild plants that are used for food, as well as recipes for using the plants. Directions for gathering, cleaning and storing the plants are given as well. Some plants, such as jack-in-the-pulpit, require special handling before they can be eaten since they contain ingredients that could be harmful if not removed by drying or boiling as directed.

Greens should be washed, leaf by leaf, under cold running water to remove any soil and insects. Some leaves of trees can also be eaten when young and luscious, as well as seeds including the redbud pods when green.

Wild nuts are also edible, but if you hold them for long periods they need baking to prevent insect damage. Do not store wild nuts in your pantry until they are well dried and baked, otherwise the insects may also spread to your flour, cornmeal, or other foods.

Most species of acorns can be gathered, dried, and used to make acorn meal through a special process. Used in baking this meal is an excellent source of protein, even higher in protein content than soy flour or cottonseed meal. Acorns must be treated to remove all the tannic acid because people may become ill from eating too many raw untreated acorns. Acorns must also be baked either before or after shelling to prevent further spoilage from mold, mildew, and insects.

Some nuts such as chestnuts will dry and harden badly if stored at room temperature and humidity. Shelled chestnuts can be kept better in the refrigerator or freezer; in the refrigerator they will keep for six months, or as long as nine months in the freezer.

Teas from wild plants are popular because they contain no caffeine. You can easily gather enough tea to last you until the next growing season.

NUTRITION AND MEAL PLANNING

Nutritional Claims

In November 1974, the F.D.A. moved to adopt regulations requiring foods sold with a claim for nutritional value to provide information supporting that claim.

The requirements are limited to foods making some specific claim for nutritional benefit, and require that specific information on vitamins, calories, and protein be released to the public. We feel that this rule should be expanded to cover all food labels.

As of now, the F.D.A. requires that food package labels give the daily percentage of vitamins A, B 12, C, D and E, plus niacin, iron and riboflavin. The drawback here is that if a consumer reads the unit pricing carefully, figures out the best buy, and then tries to figure out the percentage of required nutrients provided by each serving, he will have scarcely any time left for cooking, or eating.

However, this new labeling is an improvement. These requirements are valuable but we feel that the economic protection we have talked about earlier-drained weight, meaningful grades and standards-are of far greater importance to the consumer than % nutriet figures. If income, dietary preferences, and education combine to help the food buyer know what is required in daily consumption, no vitamin deficiency should occur.

Nutritional claims can also be misleading if you don't read the list of contents. When the label lists the number of calories a serving contains, it doesn't tell you where the calories come from. The nutritional content doesn't tell you the source of the nutrients, so cardboard could conceivably have vitamins and minerals added, and coated with sugar, and still be labeled as being nutritious.

These four food groups list only the minimum levels needed, and the minimum number of servings.

Group 1-Vegetables and Fruits

Four or more servings are needed daily.

One serving needs to be high in Vitamin C, another high in Vitamin A; the other servings can be any common vegetables or fruits desired. The two vitamin sources A and C can be combined to save money, and the other three can be any of the cheaper vegetables and fruits

Fruits and vegetables high in Vitamin C: citrus fruit and juices, tomatoes, strawberries, cantaloupe, dark green vegetables, raw greens, broccoli, green cabbage (do not overcook), green and red peppers, pimentos, potatoes, turnips and rutabagas have small amounts of Vitamin C.

Fruits and vegetables high in Vitamin A: yellow, orange, and dark green vegetables including carrots, sweet potatoes, pumpkin, broccoli, spinach, chard, winter squash, beet greens, collards, kale, mustard greens, asparagus, okra, green peas, apricots, cantaloupe, peaches (yellow varieties only), persimmons, pawpaws, prunes and tomatoes.

A serving is ½ cup sliced fruit or vegetable, 1 medium size fruit or vegetable, or ½ grapefruit or cantaloupe.

Group II Milk

The milk requirement is not the same for everyone.

For children up to 9 years	2-3 cups
children 9-12 years	3 cups
teenagers	4 cups

adults	2 cups
pregnant women	3 cups
nursing women	4 cups

Milk is considered to be the most complete food. Unfortunately fresh milk is very expensive and many people cannot afford it. Milk is important because it contains large amounts of calcium, riboflavin, and Vitamin D if it is fortified. Some home economists feel that about ¼ or 1/5 of the food budget should be spent on milk and milk products. But if other foods are eaten that make up these nutrients then such amounts of milk are not necessary. If you are not a milk drinker and don't usually eat the dairy food equivalents of the milk servings, then you should turn to other sources of food to provide you with the nutrients.

Other sources of calcium other than milk products include turnip greens, mustard greens, kale, collards, broccoli, canned fish containing bones, such as sardines, salmon, mackeral, clams and oysters.

Other sources of Vitamin D include eggs, herring, tuna, sardines, salmon, and fish liver oils.

Other sources of riboflavin include green leafy vegetables, dried peas and beans, whole grains (wheat flour, cornmeal, dark rye flour, rolled oats or oatmeal, kasha, bulgar), eggs, lean meats, and organ meats including kidney and heart.

Equivalents of 1 cup of milk are 1½ oz. (6 tbs.) grated cheddar or swiss cheese; or 11 ozs. (1½ cups) cottage cheese. Cream cheese, ice cream, ice milk, and custard are expensive ways to get your milk equivalent. It takes 15 ozs. or 1⅛ cup of cream cheese to equal 1 cup of milk, and 1⅔ cup of ice cream to equal 1 cup of milk. ⅓ cup of nonfat dry milk powder in cooking is equal to 1 cup of milk.

Group III Bread

Four or more servings are needed daily.

This group includes all baked goods as well as spaghetti, and noodle products, dumplings, barley, cereals-both cooked and ready-to-eat.

Very few of us have any problem getting our required servings of bread and cereal. Because it is one of the cheaper foods, most people rely on it to make up a large part of their diet. But breads and cereals contain a lot more than empty fattening calories. They provide protein, vitamins, and minerals as well.

Group IV Meat-Protein

Two or more servings of the meat-protein group are needed every day. Depending on age, weight, and sex, the average person needs 40 to 50 grams of protein every day. The recommended two servings will provide only about half of the protein needed. The rest of the protein must come from other foods eaten from the other food groups, including milk and milk products, breads and baked goods, cereals, corn and corn products including hominy and grits, green peas, noodles, nuts, and seeds.

A serving is:

2-3 ounces boneless lean meat, fish or poultry

2 eggs

1 cup cooked dry peas, beans, lentils

4 tbs. peanut butter

2-3 ozs. of cheese

DAILY PROTEIN NEEDS OF DIFFERENT AGE GROUPS

	Age-Years	Weight-Lbs.	Heights-inches	Protein Grams Needed
children	1-3	26-31	32-36	25
	3-6	35-42	39-43	30
	6-8	51	48	35
	8-10	62	52	40
males	10-12	88	55	45
	12-14	95	59	50
	14-18	130	67	60
	18-22	147	69	60
	22-35	154	69	65
	35-55	154	67	65
females	10-12	77	56	50
	12-14	97	61	50
	14-16	114	62	55
	16-18	119	63	55
	18-22	128	64	55
	22-35	128	64	55
	35-55	128	63	55
	55-75	128	62	55

PROTEIN CONTENT OF SELECTED FOODS

Food-100 grams or 4½ ozs.	Grams of Protein

MEAT DISHES

beans and franks, canned	7.6
beef potpie, home made	10.1
commercial	7.3
chicken a la king, home made	11.2
chicken and noodles, home made	9.3
chicken chow mein, without noodles-home made	12.4
canned	2.6
chicken fricassee, home made	15.3
chicken or turkey potpie, home made	10.1
commercial, frozen	6.7
chili con carne, canned-with beans	7.5
without beans	10.3
chop suey with meat, home made	10.4
canned	4.4
oyster stew, home made	4.9
commercial, frozen	4.2
peppers, stuffed with beef and crumbs	13.0
pizza, home made with cheese	12.0
with sausage	7.8
spaghetti	
home made with cheese (meatless)	3.5
canned (meatless)	2.2
with meat balls, home made	7.5
with meat balls, canned	4.9

VEGETABLE DISHES

bean sprouts, mung, cooked and drained	3.2
beans, common dry	
cooked	7.8
with sauce	6.1
red, cooked	7.8
canned, eaten with liquid	5.7

FOOD - 100 grams or 4½ ozs.	GRAMS OF PROTEIN
lima, mature seeds, cooked, drained	6.0
frozen, thick seeded type	
cooked and drained	6.0
thin shell or baby limas	
cooked and drained	7.4
broccoli	3.1
brussel sprouts	3.2
collards	3.6
corn, sweet whole kernel, drained	3.2
cream style	2.1
cowpeas and blackeye peas	
immature, drained	8.1
young pods with seeds	2.6
dry mature seeds, cooked	5.1
lentils	7.8
mustard greens	2.2
okra	2.0
peas, green, frozen or fresh	5.4
edible pod	3.9
and carrots	3.2
peas, split, cooked, dry	8.0
potato, baked	2.6
boiled	1.9
french fries	2.6
mashed with milk added	2.1
scalloped or au gratin	
with cheese	5.3
without cheese	3.0
salad	2.7
Spanish rice, home made	1.8
spinach, drained	3.0
succotash	4.2
sweet potato	2.1

BREADS AND BAKED FOODS

biscuits	7.4
bread, Boston brown	5.5
cracked wheat	8.7
French, Vienna, American rye, and pumpernickel	9.1
raisin	6.6
salt rising	7.9
white (depends on how much milk is used)	8.7
whole wheat	9.1
bread crumbs, grated	12.6
cheese straws	11.2
cornbread, home made or from mix	7.1
crackers, peanut-cheese sandwich type	15.2
saltine and soda	9.2
muffins	7.1
pancakes	7.2
pretzels	9.8
rolls and buns, home made, including sweet rolls	8.2
rye wafers	13.0
rusk	13.8
salt sticks	12.0
waffles, home made	9.3
frozen, commercial	7.1
made from mix	4.8
zwieback	10.7

DESSERTS

cakes (this is an average figure, a few such as sponge, chiffon will be higher)	4.0
chocolate fudge with nuts	4.9

FOOD - 100 grams or 4½ ozs.	GRAMS OF PROTEIN
cream puff with custard filling	6.5
custard, baked	5.4
eclair with custard filling	6.2
pies, fruit	2.6
chiffon, meringue, and custard	4.4
popovers, home made	8.8
pudding, home made or mix	3.6
rice with raisins	3.6
tapioca cream	5.0

CEREALS AND GRAINS

barley	8.2
bran flakes 40%	10.2
with raisins	8.3
oats, instant or cooked	2.0
buckwheat, whole grain	11.7
millet	9.9
rice, white	2.2
brown	2.5

DAIRY PRODUCTS

cheese	
Blue or Roquefort	21.5
brick	22.2
camembert (domestic)	17.5
cheddar	25.0
cottage cheese, creamed	13.6
limburger	21.2
Parmesan	36.0
Swiss	27.5
pasteurized process cheese, American	23.2
Swiss	26.4
pasteurized process cheese food,	
American	19.8
pasteurized process cheese spread,	
American	16.0
ice cream cone	10.0
ice milk	4.8
milk, skim or whole or buttermilk	3.5
canned evaporated, undiluted	7.0
yogurt	3.4

COOKED DISHES

bread stuffing made from mix	6.5
cheese fondue, home made	14.8
cheese souffle, home made	9.9
corn grits	1.2
corn fritters	7.8
macaroni	5.0
with cheese, homemade	8.4
canned	3.9
noodles, egg	4.1
Welsh rarebit	8.1
white sauce	4.0

NUTS

almonds	18.6
almond meal, partially defatted	39.5
filberts	12.6
macadamia	7.8
peanuts	26.0
peanut butter (depends on amount of	
fat added)	25.2-27.8

FOOD - 100 grams or 4½ ozs.	GRAMS OF PROTEIN
pine nuts	
pignolia	31.0
pinon	13.0
pecans	9.2
sunflower seed kernels	24.0
walnuts, black	20.5
English	14.0
pumpkin and squash seed kernels, dry	29.0

MISCELLANEOUS DISHES

eggs	11.0
papaw	5.2
popcorn, oil and salt added	9.8
potato chips	5.3
soybean curd	7.8
soybean milk	3.4
raisins, uncooked	2.5
soy sauce	5.6

MEAT

Although there are increasing numbers of people who avoid eating meat, most of us like it in one form or another, and many of our meals are built around it.

We use the word meat to describe the flesh of beef, pork, lamb, fish, poultry, and any game we might have. Meats are a source of protein, although as prices go up substitutes are becoming more and more popular. In our house we have reduced the amount of meat we use, and replaced one meal a day with beans, bread, cheese, eggs, peas, and lentils.

Unfortunately the price of cheese and beans has risen greatly too. The cheapest way to get a serving of protein is still 4 tablespoons of peanut butter.

We have never bought the fancier grades of meat because we try to keep our animal fat intake to a minimum because of cholesterol problems. The lower grades have more lean and less waste fat, and can be prepared to be tender, tasty and nutritious.

Beef

The grades of U.S.D.A. are based on the theory that marbled beef (with streaks of fat) is tastier, juicier and more tender. Try telling that to a cowhand in New Mexico or Arizona, a man accustomed to eating lean range beef. He will tell you in no uncertain terms that grass-fed beef has a flavor beyond description and that is what he likes. Recently a scientist at the New Mexico Agricultural Experiment Station put it into clear terms: "...large amounts of fat make no contribution to tender beef." Recently the Canadian government revamped their beef standards to reduce requirements for marbling, and the U.S.D.A. is doing something along those lines now.

Just as in canned foods, the government grades that you may see on the fatty side of a roast or a steak are indications that the meat is fit for human consumption. It guarantees nothing in the way of taste or tenderness.

In buying meat it is good to have an idea of how many servings per pound you can plan on. Of course the way the meat is served has a lot to do with that. We recently had sukiyaki with breakfast steak. By slivering the steak and using generous amounts of vegetables, we served five people with ½ lb. of beef to everyone's satisfaction.

To help you plan meat buying we have included a table giving the approximate number of servings to expect from different cuts of meat.

Variety Meats

These are usually cheaper than other meat cuts, and have little waste. Liver, tongue, heart, kidney, sweetbreads, brains, and tripe are in this category. Try them for a high protein, low cost meat treat.

Such meats, sometimes labeled by unimaginative food stores as offal, are particularly good sources of Vitamins A and B,

iron and protein. Pork liver is very high in iron.

We have prepared a table of servings per pound and cooking directions. If you are not familiar with them, try them for an inexpensive and high protein treat.

MEAT	SERVINGS PER LB.	COOKING IDEAS
kidneys		
beef	1 lb. serves 4-6	Remove membrane; split through the center, remove fat, tubes and tough parts. Wash, soak in salt water 1 hour. Marinate in red wine, soy sauce, or other liquid. Boil in several changes of water. All are tasty when grilled.
calf	1 kidney, ¾ lb. serves 3	
pork	1 kidney, ¼ lb. serves 1	1 inch cubes can be used in stews. Cooked kidneys can be ground with herbs and mixed with mashed potato for patties.
lamb	2 kidneys serves 1	
tongues	1 lb. serves 3	Smoked or pickled tongue should be soaked to remove excess salt. Cook beef tongue in water to cover and add a celery stalk, an onion and a bay leaf, and let simmer until tender. Then remove the skin and slice. Other tongues can be cooked in the same way. Served cold as a sandwich meat it is delectable. It is served hot with various sauces.
	weight	
beef	3 to 5 lbs.	
calf	1 to 2 lbs.	
lamb	3 ozs.	
liver	1 lb. serves 4	Can be broiled, baked, fried, chopped. Pork liver is sometimes stronger tasting than beef liver. Pour boiling water over the pork liver and drain before cooking.
heart	1 lb. serves 3 to 4	Wash well in cold water. Cut in the center, remove tough parts and vessels. Marinate overnight. It can be stuffed, then sewn up, and either braised or baked. It can be added to soups and stews.
	weight	
beef	3-4 lbs.	
pork	½ lb.	
lamb	¼ lb.	

Tripe or "Mundungo"

This is the lining of a beef animal's stomach, usually with a honey combed appearance. A second, less common kind is smooth looking, but not as tender as the honeycomb type.

It is prepared by simmering for one to four hours, adding herbs to taste, such as bay leaf, onion, and garlic.

When tender, slices can be dipped in butter and fried, or cut in chunks and used in spicy stews, broiled or boiled.

Sweetbreads

This is the pancreas and is sold from beef and lamb. These are not cheap and are often hard to find, but they are a delicious treat. Simmer the meat for about two hours until tender in salt water, then remove the outer membranes, slice the sweet bread and charcoal broil it.

Hot Dogs

Not all hot dogs are the same. Some are beef, some are pork and beef, some have cereal added, some have non-fat dry milk or soybean added. Hot dogs with dried milk and cereal usually are cheaper, but they all have the same food values and there is no difference in taste.

Hot dogs come in 12 oz. and 16 oz. packages, and in 2 lb. packages. Be sure you know the size you are buying because the 12 and 16 oz. sizes are hard to distinguish just by looking at them casually.

A lb. of hot dogs can serve 4 to 5 people or more if they are used in a casserole, soup, or stew.

The new U.S.D.A. labeling system for hot dogs distinguishes between hot dogs made with meaty cuts from those made with variety meats, and those that have milk, cereal, or soybean added.

Which is the better buy - chicken parts or whole fryers?

If the price per lb. of whole fryers, ready to cook is	Then chicken parts are as good a buy if the price per lb. is			
	Breast half	Drumstick and thigh	drumstick	thigh
39	55	50	48	52
41	57	52	53	55
43	60	55	53	57
45	66	58	55	60
47	66	60	58	63
49	69	63	60	65
51	71	65	63	68
53	74	68	65	71
55	77	70	68	73
57	80	73	70	76
59	82	76	73	78
61	85	78	75	81
63	88	81	78	84
65	91	83	80	86
67	94	86	82	89
69	97	88	85	92

Buying Meat

A meat with a lot of bone, fat, and waste gives you fewer servings per pound, and may be more expensive per serving than the meats which cost more per pound but have less waste. So you can't go by the price per pound, you need to figure out the price per serving by using the following tables. The thing to remember is that a serving is 3-3½ oz. of cooked lean meat with a little fat. Most of us are accustomed to at least a 5 or 6 oz. serving of meat. So the price per serving is determined by the size of the serving as well. In calculating the cost of a serving of meat you also need to keep in mind the number of grams of protein that each person needs each day. Some meat products are low in cost per serving but provide very little of the protein needed. Bologna, hot dogs, sausage and bacon may be cheap per serving but they are low in protein content, therefore it would take a much larger serving to make up the protein needed. Those meats low in protein should be alternated with those that are higher.

How Far Will Your Meat Go?

To get a general idea of the servings per pound for different meats, use this table. For specific cuts of meat refer to the next table.

Number Of Servings	Cut Of Meat
8 servings per lb.	chipped or dried beef, bologna, or other cold cuts for sandwiches
4-5 servings per lb.	frankfurters, sausage, liver, ground beef and hamburger, canned luncheon meat, canned corned beef, beef kidney, boneless beef stew, cube steaks, flank steaks, ham slices, pork chops (rib and center), fish fillets, Canadian style bacon, eye and heel of round,
4-5 servings per lb.	pork tenderloin
3-4 servings per lb.	round steak, veal steak, well trimmed boned shoulder cuts, boned chunk ham.
3 servings per lb.	pork shoulder chops, beef tongue, boneless beef chuck or rump roast, fryer legs (with drumstick and thigh), chicken fryer breasts, boneless turkey roasts, fish steaks, roast sirloin of beef, pork steak (blade).
2 servings per lb.	rib and chuck steak, beef rib roast, sirloin steak, beef chuck roast, picnic shoulder, whole turkey, whole turkey leg.
1-2 servings per lb.	short ribs, spare ribs, chicken broilers and fryers, chicken wings, chicken roaster or stewing hen, drawn fish.

Number of servings per lb. of meat

This assumes that most of the fat has been trimmed from the meat before it is eaten. These figures allow no more than 10% fat on a cooked, bone-in cut and no more than 15% fat on a cooked boneless cut. If your meat is fatter than these figures allow, then the price per serving is increased.

Cut Of Meat	Number Of Servings Per Lb.
Fish	
fresh or frozen whole	1-2
fresh or frozen fillets or steaks	2-3
frozen breaded portions, canned tuna, salmon, sardines, mackerel, frozen breaded shrimp	4
frozen fish steaks, and cooked peeled cleaned shrimp	5-6
Variety Meats and Cold Cuts	
canned corned beef	4
frankfurters	4-5
liver	4
sausage	4-5

Cut Of Meat	Number Of Servings Per Lb.
sliced luncheon meats	4-5

Poultry

duckling	2
goose	2
turkey under 12 lbs. whole	1½-2
12 lbs. and over	2-2¼
boneless turkey raost	3¼
turkey roll	5
pieces, breast	2½
leg	2½

The larger the turkey the less bone in proportion to the size. A 15 lb. turkey will make twice as many servings as a 10 lb. turkey because the larger one has less bone per pound.

Chicken

whole, broiler-fryer	1½-2
whole, stewing	2½
pieces, breast	3¼-4
drumsticks	2¾
thighs	2½-3
whole leg	2½-3
wings	1½
canned chicken and turkey, boneless	4

Beef

brisket, bone in	2
boneless	3
chuck roast	
arm bone-in	2½
boneless	3¼
blade bone-in	2½
boneless	3-3½
chuck steak	2
Club or t-bone steak, bone in	2
flank steak, boneless	3½
ground beef	4
heart, lover, kidney	5
porterhouse steak, bone in	2¼
rib roast, bone in	2½
boneless	3
rib steak	2
round steak, bone in	3¼
boneless	3¾
rump roast, bone in	2½
short ribs, bone in	1½
sirloin steak, bone in	2-2½
boneless	2½-3
stew beef, boneless	5

Lamb

breast and shank	2
ground lamb	3½-4
leg roast, whole	3
bone in	2½-3
boneless	3½
loin, and rib chops	3
shoulder chops	3
shoulder roast, bone in	3
boneless	3-3½
stew lamb	3

Veal

breast, bone in	2
boneless	3

Cut Of Meat	Number Of Servings Per Lb.
cutlet, bone in	3½
boneless	4
leg roast, bone in	2½
boneless	3½
loin chops, bone in	2¾
loin roast, bone in	2½
boneless	3½
rib chops, bone in	2½
rib roast, bone in	2¼
boneless	3½
shoulder roast, bone in	2½
boneless	3½

Pork

fresh pork	
blade steak	3
ham, bone in	2½
boneless	3
heart	2-2½
liver	3
loin chops, bone in	2½-3
loin roast, bone in	2-2½
boneless	3-3½
rib chops, bone in	2½-3
rib, country style	3
shoulder butt roast (Boston butt)	
bone in	3
boneless	3-3½
shoulder chops	3
shoulder roast (picnic), bone in	2
boneless	3
spareribs	1½-2
sausage	4
cured pork	
ham, fully cooked or cooked before serving,	
bone in	3½
boneless	4
center slices	4
boneless, canned	
served cold	4½-5
heated	4
picnic, bone in	2-2½
boneless	3-4
shank end	2
center slice	4
ham hocks	1
shoulder butt (Boston butt)	
bone in	3-3½
boneless	3½-4

How Much Meat Is In A Meat Product

The minimum amount of meat in a meat product is defined by U.S.D.A., and a product cannot carry the U.S.D.A. inspection label unless it meets the following standards.

Baby food

High meat dinner-At least 30% meat.
Meat and broth-At least 65% meat.
Vegetable and meat-At least 8% meat.

Bacon (cooked)-Weight of cooked bacon cannot exceed 40% of cured, smoked bacon.

Barbecued meats-Weight of meat when barbecued cannot exceed 70% of the fresh uncooked meat. Must have barbecued (crusted) appearance and be prepared over burning or smoldering hardwood or its sawdust. If cooked by other dry heat means, product name must mention the type of cookery.

Barbecued sauce with meat-At least 35% meat (cooked basis).

Beans and meat in sauce-At least 20% meat.

Beans with frankfurters in sauce-At least 20% franks.

Beans with meatballs in sauce-At least 20% meatballs.

Beef and dumplings with gravy or Beef and gravy with dumplings-At least 25% beef.

Beef and pasta in tomato sauce-At least 17½% beef.

Beef burgundy-At least 50% beef; enough wine to characterize the sauce.

Beef pot pie-At least 25% fresh beef.

Beef sauce with beef and mushrooms-At least 25% beef and 7% mushrooms.

Beef sausage (raw)-No more than 30% fat. No by-products or extenders.

Beef stroganoff-At least 45% fresh uncooked beef or 30% cooked beef, and at least 10% sour cream or a "gourmet" combination of at least 7½% sour cream and 5% wine.

Beef with gravy-At least 50% beef (cooked basis). (Gravy and beef has only 35% beef.)

Breaded steaks, chops, etc.-Breading cannot exceed 30% of finished product weight.

Breakfast sausage-No more than 50% fat.

Brown and serve sausage-No more than 35% fat and no more than 10% added water.

Brunswick stew-At least 25% of at least two kinds of meat and/or poultry. Must contain corn as one of the vegetables.

Burgundy sauce with beef and noodles-At least 25% beef (cooked basis); enough wine to characterize the sauce.

Chili con carne-At least 40% meat.

Chili con carne with beans-At least 25% meat

Chili sauce with meat or chili hot dog sauce with meat-At least 6% meat.

Chili hot dog with meat-At least 40% meat in chili.

Chop suey (American style) with macaroni and meat-At least 25% meat.

Chop suey vegetables with meat-At least 12% meat.

Chopped ham-Must be prepared from fresh, cured or smoked ham, plus certain kinds of curing agents and seasonings. May contain dehydrated onions, dehydrated garlic, corn syrup, and not more than 3% water to dissolve the curing agents.

Chow mein vegetables with meat and noodles-At least 8% meat and the chow mein must equal ⅔ of the product.

Condensed, Creamed dried beef or chipped beef-At least 18% dried or chipped beef (figured on reconstituted total content).

Corned beef and cabbage-At least 25% corned beef (cooked basis).

Corned beef hash-At least 35% beef (cooked basis). Must contain potatoes, curing agents, and seasonings. May contain onions, garlic, beef broth, beef fat or others. No more than 15% fat; no more than 72% moisture.

Corn dog-Must meet standards for frankfurters, and batter cannot exceed the weight of the frank.

Crackling corn bread-At least 10% cracklings (cooked basis).

Cream cheese with chipped beef(sandwich spread)-At least 12% chipped beef.

Croquettes-At least 35% meat.

Curried sauce with meat and rice (casserole)-At least 35% meat (cooked basis) in the sauce and meat part; no more than 50% cooked rice.

Deviled ham-No more than 35% fat.

Dinners (frozen product containing meat)-At least 25% meat or meat food product (cooked basis) figured on total meal minus appetizer, bread and dessert. Minimum weight of a consumer package-10 oz.

Dumplings and meat in sauce-At least 18% meat.

Egg foo yong with meat-At least 12% meat.

Egg rolls with meat-At least 10% meat.

Enchilada with meat-At least 15% meat.

Entrees: Meat or meat food product with one vegetable-At least 50% meat or meat food product (cooked basis). Meat or meat food product, gravy or sauce, and one vegetable-At least 30% meat or meat food product (cooked basis).

Frankfurter, bologna, and similar cooked sausage-May contain only skeletal meat. No more than 30% fat, 10% added water and 2% corn syrup. No more than 15% poultry meat (exclusive of water in formula).

Fried rice with meat-At least 10% meat.

Fritters-At least 35% meat. A breaded product.

German style potato salad with bacon-At least 14% bacon (cooked basis).

Goulash-At least 25% meat.

Gravies-At least 25% meat stock or broth, or at least 6% meat.

Gravy with beef-At least 35% beef (cooked basis).

Ham-canned-Limited to 8% total weight gain after processing.

Ham-cooked or cooked and smoked (not canned)-Must not weigh more after processing than the fresh ham weighs before curing and smoking; if contains up to 10% weight, must be labeled "Ham, water added"; if more than 10%, must be labeled "Imitation Ham."

Ham and cheese spread-At least 25% ham (cooked basis).

Ham salad-At least 35% ham (cooked basis).

Ham spread-At least 50% ham.

Hor d'Oeuvre-At least 15% meat (cooked basis) or 10% bacon (cooked basis).

Lasagna with meat and sauce-At least 12% meat.

Lasagna, with sauce, cheese and dry sausage-At least 8% dry sausage.

Lima beans with ham or bacon in sauce-At least 12% ham or bacon.

Liver products such as liver loaf, liver pate, liver paste, liver cheese, liver spread, and liver sausage-At least 30% liver.

Macaroni and beef in tomato sauce-At least 12% beef.

Macaroni and meat-At least 25% meat.

Macaroni salad with ham or beef-At least 12% meat (cooked basis).

Manicotti (containing meat filling)-At least 10% meat.

Meat and dumplings in sauce-At least 25% meat.

Meat and seafood egg roll-At least 5% meat.

Meat and vegetables-At least 50% meat.

Meatballs-No more than 12% extenders (cooked basis).

Meatballs in sauce-At least 50% meatballs (cooked basis).

Meat casseroles-At least 25% fresh uncooked meat or 18% cooked meat.

Meat loaf (baked or oven-ready)-At least 65% meat and no more than 12% extenders including textured vegetable protein.

Meat ravioli-At least 10G meat in ravioli.

Meat ravioli in sauce-At least 10% meat.

Meat salads-At least 35% meat (cooked basis).

Meat soups- Ready to eat-At least 5% meat. Condensed-At least 10% meat.

Meat tacos-At least 15% meat.

Mince meat-At least 12% meat.

Omelet with bacon-At least 9% bacon (cooked basis).

Omelet with dry sausage or with liver-At least 12% dry sausage or liver (cooked basis).

Omelet with ham-At least 18% ham (cooked basis).

Pepper steaks-At least 30% beef (cooked basis).

Pizza sauce with sausage-At least 6% sausage.

Pizza with meat-At least 15% meat.

Pork sausage-No more than 50% fat; may contain no byproducts or extenders.

Pork with barbecue sauce-At least 50% pork (cooked basis).

Pork with dressing and gravy-At least 30% pork (cooked basis).

Salisbury steak-At least 65% meat and no more than 12% extenders including textured vegetable protein.

Sauce with chipped beef-At least 18% chipped beef.

Sauce with meat, or meat sauce-At least 6% meat.

Sauerbraten-At least 50% meat (cooked basis).

Scalloped potatoes and ham-At least 20% ham (cooked basis).

Scrambled eggs with ham in a pancake-At least 9% cooked ham.

Shepherd's pie-At least 25% meat; no more than 50% mashed potatoes.

Sloppy joe (sauce with meat)-At least 35% meat (cooked basis).

Spaghetti with meat balls and sauce-At least 12% meat.

Spaghetti with sliced franks and sauce-At least 12% franks.

Spanish rice with beef or ham-At least 20% beef or ham (cooked basis).

Stews (beef, lamb, and the like)-At least 25% meat.

Stuffed cabbage with meat in sauce-At least 12% meat.

Stuffed peppers with meat in sauce-At least 12% meat.

Sukiyaki-At least 30% meat.

Sweet and sour pork or beef-At least 25% meat and at least 16% fruit.

Sweet and sour spareribs-At least 50% bone-in spareribs (cooked basis).

Swiss steak with gravy-At least 50% meat (cooked basis).

Tamales-At least 25% meat.

Tamales with sauce (or with gravy)-At least 20% meat.

Tongue spread-At least 50% meat.

Tortellini with meat-At least 10% meat.

Veal fricassee-At least 40% meat.

Veal parmagiana-At least 40% breaded meat product in sauce.

Veal steaks-Can be chopped, shaped, cubed, frozen. Beef can be added with product name shown as "Veal steaks, beef added, chopped, shaped and cubed" if no more than 20% beef, or must be labeled "Veal and beef steak, chopped, shaped and cubed." No more than 30% fat.

Vegetable and meat casserole-At least 25% meat.

Vegetable and meat pie-At least 25% meat.

Vegetable stew and meat balls-At least 12% meat in total product.

Won ton soup-At least 5% meat.

Poultry Products

All percentages of poultry are on a cooked deboned basis unless noted otherwise. When standard indicates poultry meat, skin, and fat, the skin and fat must be in proportion normal to poultry.

Baby food-high poultry dinner-At least 18¾% poultry meat, skin, fat, and giblets.

Poultry with broth-At least 43% poultry meat, skin, fat, and giblets.

Beans and rice with poultry-At least 6% poultry meat.

Breaded poultry-No more than 30% breading.

Cabbage stuffed with-At least 8% poultry meat.

Creamed poultry-At least 20% poultry meat. Product must contain some cream.

Eggplant parmagiana with poultry-At least 8% poultry meat.

Egg roll with poultry-At least 2% poultry meat.

Buying Meat For Your Freezer

Some people think they can save money by buying large amounts of meat, whether in the form of a carcass, a side or a quarter of beef, or wholesale cuts. When you buy meat in this form, whether it is beef, pork, lamb, or veal, you are also buying considerable amounts of fat, bone, and waste, maybe as much as ⅓ of the total weight. The following charts list the yield of edible meat from a carcass of beef, lamb, and pork, and for a hindquarter of beef.

Usually meat for the freezer is trimmed closer and has more bone removed than cuts of meat you buy in a retail store.

This is to save space because you can only use so much fat and bone. If a carcass or a side of beef is too much for your family, perhaps a hindquarter or forequarter will suit your needs better.

Whatever price is quoted you for the hanging weight of the meat, check to see how many pounds of edible meat you can expect and divide the number of expected pounds into the price. This figure will be the true price per pound that you are paying. In addition to the cost of the meat you also have to add to each pound of meat a proportional share of the cost of running and maintaining the freezer. This final price will reveal to you whether or not the meat you are buying for the freezer is a bargain. If you are buying the meat on credit or time, be sure to add the finance charge to the price of the meat as well.

Your family's eating habits and the time you have available to spend cooking also are considerations. You will be getting less tender cuts that require slow, moist methods of cooking as well as tender steaks and roasts. It may be more economical for you to buy either wholesale cuts or to buy the cuts you prefer on sale and store them in the freezer until needed. A beef short loin bought wholesale will include porterhouse, T-bone and club steaks, and some ground beef or stew beef. A whole pork loin will contain pork loin roasts and chops.

Meat kept in the combination refrigerator-freezer doesn't keep as well as meat kept in an ordinary freezer. When freezing meat remember that certain frozen meats do not keep as long as others. Liver keeps only 3-4 months, ground meat 3-4 months, fresh pork 4-8 months, pork sausage 1-3 months, while other meats keep for 12 months or longer. Hamburger will keep longer if it is not made into individual patties because more of the meat surface is exposed to the air which causes it to deteriorate more quickly. Be sure your meat is wrapped in freezer paper and not in regular butcher paper, which allows the meat to dry out and change color. It is possible for frozen meat to lose as much as 10% of its weight in a year due to evaporation, so don't buy any more meat than you can use in a reasonable time.

A hind quarter of beef yields more steak and roasts but it costs more per pound than a forequarter. A forequarter contains the rib roasts but it has more cuts that are less tender than the hindquarter. The yield of usable lean meat is greater in the forequarter than in the hindquarter.

Buy your meat for the freezer from a firm you can trust. Some stores substitute cheaper cuts for more expensive cuts, especially the more expensive steaks and roasts, and short weight the customer as well. When you don't see the butcher actually trimming and packing your beef how can you know you're getting fair treatment? Some stores sell what they call wholesale cuts and charge by the pound but they do not trim away the usual amount of fat and waste that would be cut

away for the usual retail cut. Winn Dixie, for example, sells 10-20 pound packages of cuts, such as beef tenderloin, sirloin, other cuts, and pork loin but do not trim the fat away as they should. The initial price per lb. may sound reasonable, but estimating the fat at ⅓ the weight raises the price of the edible meat considerably.

Be very careful when buying from a store that specializes in selling wholesale amounts of the meat to the public for the freezer. Quite a few stores take the customers' money for meat, then flee overnight without delivering the meat that has been paid for, or they deliver meat that is unsatisfactory. These stores are even more notorious for substituting cheaper cuts for more expensive cuts. Some advertise that they give you so many pounds of free chicken, pork, or ground beef with a purchase of so much meat. You are paying for this through a higher price of the meat you are buying; it is very definitely not free.

Beef carcass having a live weight of 750 lbs. and a carcass weight of 420 lbs. gives the following edible yields.

Trimmed Cuts	Yield lbs.	Live Weight %	Carcass Weight %
steaks and oven roasts	172	23	40
pot roasts	83	11	20
stew and ground meat	83	11	20
Total	338	45	80

Approximate yield of trimmed beef cuts from dressed hindquarters weighing 202 lbs.

Trimmed Cuts	Yield lbs.	Weight of Hindquarter %
steaks and oven roasts	117	58
stews, ground meat and pot roasts	37	18
Total	154	76

Approximate trimmed pork cuts from a hog with a live weight of 225 lbs. and a carcass weight of 176 lbs.

Trimmed Cuts	Yield lbs.	Live Weight %	Carcass Weight%
fresh ham, shoulders, bacon, jowls	90	40	50
loins, ribs, sausage	34	15	20
Total	124	55	70
Lard, rendered	12	15	27

Yields of trimmed lamb cuts from a lamb with a live weight of 85 lbs. and a carcass weight of 41 lbs.

Trimmed Cuts	Yield lbs.	Live Weight %	Carcass Weight %
legs, chops, shoulders	31	37	75
breast and stew	7	8	15
Total	38	45	90

CANNING

You can save money by home canning if you have fruits and vegetables from your own garden or if you have a cheaper source such as a farmers' market where you can buy produce, and if the additional ingredients such as sugar, vinegar, and spices do not add too much to the cost. Any equipment purchased for canning does add to the cost of the food.

When choosing the fruits and vegetables, stick to firm, sound fruits and young tender vegetables. They must be sorted according to size because large and small fruits or vegetables cook at different rates.

The less time between the harvest and the canning the better, because less of the organisms that cause spoilage are present. When canning, the food must be processed for the time suggested in order to kill all these organisms and to stop the action of the enzymes to keep the food from changing color or flavor, or becoming tough.

There are several types of canners you can use. There are the steam pressure canner, a pressure saucepan used for low acid foods, and the water bath used for high acid foods. In order to kill organisms which survive at boiling temperature it is important for the food to cook at a temperature above 212°F. Failure to cook at this temperature can result in botulism

Steam Pressure Canner

This is used for all low acid foods, including vegetables, meats, poultry, and fish. Low acid foods are always processed with the pressure canner or pressure saucepan.

The steam pressure canner is a heavy kettle with a cover that can be closed air-tight. This enables the temperature inside the canner to rise to temperatures easily above boiling. The cover has a petcock or vent, a pressure gauge, a safety valve, and gasket. If open, the petcock allows air in and steam to escape, but if closed it holds steam inside. The pressure gauge registers the pressure inside the dial type of cover. The safety valve blows out when the steam becomes dangerously high. It is made of rubber or metal and is replaceable. The rubber gasket around the edge of the cover helps to seal the steam in.

Before using the pressure canner, wipe the kettle part clean with a wet cloth (don't put the canner in water) and check the safety valve to be sure it is in good operating condition. The petcock opening should be cleaned by pulling a narrow string or piece of cloth through it to make sure the steam can escape.

Pressure Saucepan

The pressure saucepan has a gauge or indicator for controlling pressure at 10 lbs.

(240°F.) and is used for canning vegetables in pint jars and No. 2 cans. Add 20 minutes to the processing time listed under each vegetable processed in the steam pressure canner.

Water Bath Canner

This is used for acid foods which do not require such high temperature during canning, including fruits, tomatoes, radishes, pickled vegetables. Jams, preserves, conserves, marmalades, and fruit butters should be processed in this at a temperature of 212°F. for five minutes. Any large pan or tub will do as a water bath canner. It should have a snug fitting lid and a rack to keep jars from touching the bottom. This keeps the jars from breaking. There should be room enough for an inch of water over the top of the jar and several inches to allow for boiling above the jar. The jars should not touch each other, and the canner should not be overloaded or the temperature will not get as high as it should be.

If the steam pressure canner is deep enough it can be used as a water bath canner. The cover is placed over the top but it is not fastened in place. The petcock is left open so that all the steam escapes and does not build up.

The water must be hot before the jars are put into it, and the jars must also be hot. This keeps the jars from breaking. Count time from the time the water comes to a hard boil after the jars are put in. After the processing time is up, remove the containers from the hot water immediately.

Containers For Canning

Glass jars and tin cans are the two types of containers that are used.

Jars and lids must not be defective, otherwise they will not form a seal. The jars must be clean and hot when the food is placed in them. Used jars must be sterilized by boiling for 15 minutes. There are two types of lids that are used, the porcelain-lined zinc cap, and the two piece cap.

Porcelain-lined Zinc Cap-It must not be cracked, broken, or loose, or have slight dents at the seal edge. Most of the damage to these caps is done by prying them open with a knife or other sharp edge. These caps can be used more than once, using a fresh rubber ring each time. Wet the rubber ring and fit onto the jar shoulder. After the jar is filled with food and liquid wipe any food from the rubber ring and rim of the jar. Screw the cap on securely, then turn it back ¼ inch more. After the food has been processed seal the lid by screwing the cap on as tightly as it will go.

Two-piece Cap-The metal cap with sealing compound can be used only once (the metal band can be used again if in good condition). Fill the jar with food and wipe the rim of the jar clean. Place the metal lid on the jar with the sealing compound next to the jar. Screw the metal band very tightly. The lid has enough natural give to let the air escape during the processing. Do not screw the cap on any tighter after taking it from the canner. After 24 hours the metal band can be removed and used on another jar.

Tin Cans

There are three types of tin cans used in home canning: the plain, the C-enamel, and the R-enamel. Plain tin cans can be used for most foods. C-enamel cans with a dull gold colored lining is used for corn and hominy. R-enamel cans which have a bright gold lining are used for beets, sauerkraut, winter squash, red berries, cherries, plums, and rhubarb. The C-enamel and R-enamel are not absolutely essential but will prevent the discoloration that takes place in plain tin cans.

Only perfect cans, lids, and gaskets can be used. The cans are washed, scalded and placed upside down to drain. Do not wash lids, just wipe with a damp cloth before placing on the can. Use a sealer to seal the lids onto the cans. Hand sealers and automatic sealers are available. The sealer should be tested to make sure it is doing the job correctly. To test it, place a small amount of water in a can, seal, then place the sealed can in boiling water for a few minutes. If the seal is not tight, air bubbles will rise from the can. To adjust the seal follow the manufacturer's directions.

Pressure Canner

It is important that your gauge be accurate because otherwise the food will not be cooked at the proper temperature. If your gauge is off more than four lbs., you need to buy a new gauge. If it is less than four lbs. off you can correct it by using the following chart.

If 1 lb. high-process at 11 lbs.
If 2 lbs. high-process at 12 lbs.
If 3 lbs. high-process at 13 lbs.
If 4 lbs. high-process at 14 lbs.
If 1 lb. low-process at 9 lbs.
If 2 lbs. low-process at 10 lbs.
If 3 lbs. low-process at 7 lbs.
If 4 lbs. low-process at 8 lbs.

The water should reach the shoulder of the jars, and will be enough to keep the kettle from boiling dry. The steam it creates will cook the food.

The jars should not touch each other or the sides or bottom of the cooker. If the cooker is tall enough to hold two rows of jars, place a rack between the two rows and stagger the second row.

After closing the cover on the cooker close the petcock and heat until the pressure registers slightly under the required number of lbs., then lower the heat. When the gauge registers the exact number of lbs., adjust the heat to keep the pressure steady. When you are using tin cans loosen the safety valve slightly to allow a little steam to escape. Do not loosen the safety valve when using jars.

Begin timing from the time the gauge reaches the pressure required. When processing time is up, turn off the heat and remove the pressure cooker. When using glass jars let the cooker cool until the gauge reaches zero. Opening the cooker when still hot causes jars to break or draws liquid from the jars. When using tin cans open the petcock gradually so the steam escapes slowly. Then open the cooker when the gauge measures zero. The cover of the cooker cannot be removed until the steam stops coming out of the cooker. Lift the back of the cover first so the steam will not burn your hands or face.

Checking The Seals

After the containers cool thoroughly, the seal should be checked. Test the lids of jars by removing the screwbands and pressing on the center of the lid. If the lid stays down and doesn't move, the jar is sealed. Jars with porcelain-lined caps and tin cans can be checked by turning them over in your hand. If a container is leaky or is not sealed, it can be emptied into another container and reprocessed for the full time. You may however wish to eat the food immediately because some foods become overcooked if reprocessed.

Exhausting Tin Cans And Jars

The air should be removed from the jar and can before the lids are put on. To remove air from a jar run a knife gently between the jar and the food.

Tin cans need to be sealed when they are at 170°F. or higher so the can ends will not bulge, and the seams break. You can either pack the food when it is hot or heat it in the open cans and then seal them. Even after packing the food it may need to be reheated if the temperature falls below 170°F. To check the temperature, place the bulb of your thermometer at the center of the can.

FREEZING

You can save money by freezing your own food if you have home grown fruits, vegetables, and meats, or if the food is available at a low price.

You should keep your freezer full because it takes just as much money to run a freezer that is half full, and the cost is divided between less food.

Only equipment that is made of aluminum, earthenware, enameled ware, nickel, glass, or stainless steel can be used when preparing food for the freezer. Galvanized ware should never be used because zinc becomes poisonous when it oxidizes with the fruit. Metallic off-flavors can also result in the fruit if iron, chipped enamel or tinware are worn or not well tinned.

Use a stainless steel knife for preparing fruits. Wash fruits and vegetables before they are peeled, sliced, and hulled in order to preserve the flavor and color better.

You can save as much as ⅓ of your freezer space by using square containers.

Tips On Using Freezers

The temperature of the freezer should be set at 0°F. or lower, never higher. When the temperature is higher than 0°F., changes in the flavor, color, and texture of the food can occur.

Fruits and vegetables packaged ready for freezing can be held in the refrigerator for a short time at 38-45°F, if necessary. But they can only be kept at this temperature for several hours before freezing.

If your freezer does not defrost automatically be sure to defrost it at least once a year. Partial defrosting can be done several times a year as needed to keep the operating cost down.

A cubic foot of freezer space holds 35-40 pint cartons of food, 35-40 pounds of fruit and syrup, 25-30 pounds of vegetables, or 35-40 pounds of meat. More space per pound is required for holding bulky items such as whole chickens or turkey.

Precooked foods should be thawed, reheated quickly and served; leftovers should not be reheated and used, to keep certain bacteria to a minimum that would cause food to spoil.

Containers For Freezing

A variety of containers can be used including jars, cans, and waxed cartons lined with plastic bags. If the plastic bag is placed inside a carton it will be protected from being damaged and from drying out. When packaging fruits in syrup or liquid, plastic bags alone cannot be used.

Plastic cartons, whether rigid or flexible, are good because they are moisture-vapor proof and can be reused. The rigid type ones may break or crack if mishandled. The containers show the filling line, allowing for proper head space. Since air is destructive to the food, crush a piece of cellophane, foil, or plastic to put over the top of the food in the container.

Non-flexible aluminum containers with lids and those made of aluminum foil are reusable. Allow ¼ inch head space for each container. The foil type can be damaged if mishandled.

Air should be pressed out of bags before sealing to keep the air from being sealed in.

Sheets of plastic or aluminum foil can be used to wrap corn on the cob, asparagus spears and whole green beans, and are then wrapped in a plastic freezer bag, or freezer wrap.

The unwaxed or highly waxed cartons that ice cream and cottage cheese come in are not completely moisture and vapor resistant and cannot be used because the food can become damaged. If you line these containers with plastic liners and seal the top after filling it with a rubber band the quality of the food can be maintained.

Glass jars can be used over and over again, but they are easily broken and are bulky. Jars with a separate rubber, metal screw top with separate rubber, or lid with metal band lined with freezer paper may be used. Fill only to the shoulder of the jar to allow for expansion during freezing. If a jar is filled too full it will expand and break during freezing.

Both friction top and regular canning tin cans are usable. They are filled leaving ½ inch head space at the top. Enameled cans are necessary for fruits and asparagus while plain tin can be used for vegetables. The disadvantage of cans is that they cause a loss of space in the freezer.

To exhaust the cans, place the filled open cans in the water-bath with water reaching 2 inches below the can tops. Cover the kettle, then bring the water back to a boil and boil until the thermometer reaches 170°F., about 10 minutes. Remove the cans from the water one at a time, replacing the liquid lost from the cans during the heating. Place a clean lid on the can and seal. Then process.

If you are sure the temperature of the food was 170°F. or above when the cans were filled you don't have to exhaust the cans but instead just add boiling liquid to fill the cans to the top. This gets rid of the air bubbles. Then seal and process.

Methods Of Packing

There are two methods of packing the food into the containers, raw pack and hot pack.

Raw Pack-Most fruits and some vegetables are packed cold and raw into the containers. Most raw foods are packed tighter into the containers since they shrink during cooking. The exceptions are peas, corn, and lima beans which expand during cooking.

Pack the fruit or vegetable into the container. Then cover with the boiling syrup, juice or water. Fruits are usually packed with syrup, while vegetables are packed with water. Tomatoes are pressed down into the container so they are covered with their own juice. No other liquid is needed.

Hot Pack-Food is packed at or near the boiling point when filling the containers. The fruit or vegetable is cooked or steamed in syrup, water, or juice. Juicy fruits can be heated without adding juice. Low acid vegetables are packed either in the water from the heated vegetables or in fresh boiling water. The food is packed fairly loosely into the container.

Head Space

A small amount of head space is left between the packed food and the top of the container. Under each food is listed the head space suggested.

Canning Without Sugar Or Salt

It is not necessary to add salt or sugar when canning because it does not help to prevent spoilage, or preserve the quality of the food. Use the same processing time suggested whether sugar or salt is added or not.

Liquid

It usually takes about ½ to 1½ cups liquid to a quart jar to cover the solid food.

Preparing Vegetables And Fruits

Prepare only enough food for one canner load at a time so that the flavor is not lost and the food doesn't darken.

Work as quickly as possible between preparing the food, placing it into the container and processing it.

Produce should be processed as quickly as possible after harvesting. But if you do have to delay, discard any pieces that are bruised or decayed because the damage will spread to the rest of the produce. Store the food in a cool, well ventilated room until you are ready to prepare it.

Wash the produce a small amount at a time, changing the water until the water is clear with no dirt or residue. Then hull the produce, and remove the seeds, pits, and peels.

For less firm fruits such as tomatoes and peaches hot water peeling is recommended. Place the fruit in a wire basket in boiling water for ½ minute, or until the skins pull off easily. Then plunge the fruit into cold water for a few seconds. Drain and peel quickly.

Canning Fruits In Syrup

The water or juice and the sugar is boiled together for five minutes to make the syrup.

Sugar is not essential when canning fruits but it does help to preserve the color, texture, and flavor. If sugar is not added, you will need to add water, or if possible fruit juice. Dry fruits such as apples and pears will need more liquid than fruits that are naturally juicy.

To extract fruit juice to use as canning liquid, crush the fruit. Heat until it begins simmering. Then strain through a cloth or jelly bag. If you are making syrup, juice may be used instead of water.

For very juicy fruits such as blackberries that are packed hot, sugar can be added directly to the fruit without making it into a syrup. Usually ½ cup sugar is added to every quart of prepared fruit, depending more or less on taste and the acidity of the fruit. Simmer the fruit and sugar over low heat. This saves time because the syrup is extracted and the sugar dissolved in one step. Pack into containers and process.

Corn syrup or mild flavored honey such as regular table honey or clover honey can be used instead of sugar. Strong tasting honey, such as sourwood, brown sugar, molasses, sorghum or other strong flavored syrup should not be used because these may darken the fruit and mask its natural flavor. The type of syrup you use depends on the natural sweetness of the fruit and your own personal preference. Artificial sweeteners may be used when canning fruit. Just follow the directions of the manufacturer for the amount needed to substitute for each cup of sugar.

Type	Sugar	Water or Juice	Yield
very thin	1½ cups	4 cups	4½ cups
thin	2 cups	4 cups	5 cups
medium	3 cups	4 cups	5½ cups
heavy	4¾ cups	4 cups	6½

FOODS NOT SUITABLE FOR FREEZING

Food	Usual Use	Condition After Thawing
cress, cucumber, watermelon, lettuce, green onion, endive	as raw salad or raw relish	limp, becomes water logged, much of aroma and flavor are lost, oxidizes and turns dark
egg whites, cooked	creamed foods, sandwiches, sauces, gravy or desserts	soft, spongy and rubbery
Irish potatoes, cooked-baked or boiled	in soups, casseroles, sauces	soft, water logged, crumbly
overmature vegetables	cooked dishes	tough, stringy, too starchy, lose flavor

In Case Of Power Failure

If your freezer stops, do not open the door unless necessary. Food in a full freezer will stay frozen for as long as 24 hours. If you have advance warning of a power failure turn the freezer up to the coldest setting. If the power is to be interrupted for more than 1-2 days, dry ice can be placed in the freezer to keep the food frozen. 25 pounds of dry ice is sufficient for a 10 cubic foot cabinet freezer. If the freezer is half full it will keep the food frozen for 2-3 days; if the freezer is full it will keep the food frozen for 3-4 days. Be careful when handling dry ice; do not handle it with bare hands and use only in a ventilated room. Place the dry ice on neavy cardboard or on boards on top of the frozen food.

When the power is resumed check all the food packages carefully to see if they are still frozen. Packages that contain some ice crystals can be refrozen but the quality of the food may be affected. Fruits and vegetables may be refrozen but the quality will not be as good, vegetables may become tough, and fruits may become mushy and soft. Usually fruits thaw more quickly than other foods but do not spoil as quickly because of the acid content.

Meats, poultry, fish, and vegetables are subject to spoilage by bacteria, and are not good candidates for refreezing. But they can be refrozen if there seems to be no bad odor, and if you are certain the temperature did not rise above 32°F. and did not remain at the highest point for longer than a few hours.

Freezing Vegetables

For best results, overmature or starchy corn and peas should not be frozen, and green beans should be picked when the immature pods are only two thirds full so the pod is nice and tender.

Vegetables must be blanched to stop the actions of the enzymes which are involved in the flavor. If vegetables are not blanched they will lose their color and flavor and may become tough while frozen within 4 weeks. Blanching also makes the vegetables shrink and become easier to pack. Some vegetables, including beets and winter squash are precooked rather than blanched before freezing.

You can blanch with boiling water or with steam. Some of the vegetables that are steamed are broccoli, pumpkin, sweet potato, and winter squash. Green leafy vegetables are never steamed. Vegetables must be blanched for the required time since under-blanching will not affect the enzymes while over-blanching will cause the vegetables to lose their flavor, color, and nutritional value.

Prepare and blanch only the vegetables that you can pack in a reasonable time, no more than 5-10 packages. This will ensure freshness.

Blanching In Boiling Water

A large kettle with a cover or a kettle with a blanching basket may be used. If a blanching basket is not available, use a wire basket or a boiling bag.

Blanch only one pound of vegetables at a time so the water doesn't take too long to return to a boil when the vegetables are added. If the pot is large enough, 2 pounds of vegetables can be done at a time in 2 gallons of water. Heat the water to a full boil in the kettle. Place the vegetables in the basket or bag, then lower them into the boiling water. If the water takes longer than a minute to return to a boil add less vegetables the next time. Lift the basket or bag up and down to shake the vegetables and make sure they are evenly heated for the recommended time. Begin timing when you put the basket into the boiling water. The water can be used continually, just replace any that evaporates and bring to a boil again. If the water becomes dirty or discolored, replace it.

Blanching With Steam

For this you need a kettle with a tight fitting lid and a rack that will hold the steaming basket at least 3 inches above the bottom of the kettle. Pour water in the kettle to a depth of 1-2 inches, then bring to a boil. Place the steam basket in the kettle then spread a single layer of vegetables in the steam basket. Place the cover on the kettle and time.

After the vegetables are removed from the water or steam they are cooled by placing in ice, or under running water. They cool by being spread in a thin layer on a wet towel in front of a fan. Stir several times during the cooling which should take as long or perhaps a little longer than the blanching process.

The vegetables should be cooled as quickly as possible, and not allowed to set in the cold water or they will become washed out and lose flavor and nutrients as well as color.

Warm vegetables should never be packaged for freezing so test the center of the vegetable to be sure it is cool. You can test by biting into several pieces to see if it feels cool to the tongue. After cooling, then drain on paper or cloth towels.

Selecting Vegetables

Vegetables should be frozen on the same day they are picked for maximum freshness. Otherwise they can become tough and over-matured. If it is necessary to store vegetables for a short time before freezing, store them in a well-ventilated place. They may be cooled in ice water and then stored in the refrigerator. Almost all vegetables will keep for a year in the freezer. After washing the vegetables in several changes of cold water until the rinse water is clear, peel, trim, and cut the vegetables into pieces.

Vegetables are usually packed dry or solid but they may be packed in brine if desired. This helps to maintain the color and texture. ½ teaspoon of salt is added to each cup of water and is added to a pint of vegetables.

Individual Vegetables-Instructions For Freezing

Asparagus

For top quality asparagus, freeze it within 2-3 hours from the time of harvest.

Only young, tender spears with compact heads should be used. Discard any tough spears, and break off and discard the woody part of the stalk. Wash the spears. Then sort the spears according to size, small, medium, and large. The spears can be sliced into pieces 1 inch long.

Small spears are blanched for 1½ -2 minutes, medium for 3 minutes, large for 4 minutes. Altitudes above 4000 feet the blanching will be 1 minute longer for each size.

Beans, Snap

Very young beans should be chosen with tender pods when the seed is just beginning to form inside the pod. Mature ones should not be frozen. ⅔-1 pound of fresh beans will make 1 quart of frozen beans. The stringless beans require less work. Wash and drain, then snap the ends off. Cut the beans into 1-4 inch long pieces or slice them lengthwise. Larger pieces are considered better. Then blanch the pieces for 2-3 minutes. The blanching time for altitudes over 4000 feet is 3 minutes for small beans and 4 minutes for large beans. Drain, cool, and package. For French style beans they are cut lengthwise and blanched only 1 ½ minutes.

Beans, Lima

They should be harvested while the seed is still green. The pods should be filled with tender, young beans. The beans should be green, not starchy and mealy. The beans are shelled from the pod and sorted according to size because the different sizes require different blanching times.

The small beans should be blanched 1 minute, medium 2 minutes, large 3-4 minutes. For altitudes above 4000 feet blanch the small beans 3 minutes, medium 4 minutes, and large 5 minutes.

Beet Greens

The young tender leaves should be washed. The tough part of the stalk is cut off. Then they are blanched for 2 minutes. Drain, cool and package.

Beets

They should be tender, with a deep, uniform, red color. Older beets may be used if you slice them first. Wash the beets, then leave the roots and one inch of the beet top on them. Cook in boiling water until tender. For small beets cook 25-30 minutes, medium and large beets cook 45-50 minutes. For altitudes above 4000 feet cook small beets 40 minutes, and medium and large 50-55 minutes.

Drain and cool the beets. Peel, and either slice or dice.

Beets that are under 1½-2 inches in diameter can be blanched rather than cooked. Blanch for 3 minutes, then cool, peel, and freeze whole or sliced.

Broccoli

Dark green, firm, young tender stalks with compact heads and no blossoms should be chosen. Leaves and woody portions of the stalk should be removed. The heads should be split lengthwise into pieces that are no more than 1 inch across. The pieces are then placed in a brine mixture of 4 teaspoons of salt to a gallon of water to kill any insects, and allowed to set for 30 minutes. Then rinse the broccoli and drain.

Blanch the smaller pieces 3 minutes and the larger pieces 4 minutes. However steaming for 5 minutes is preferred to blanching. Drain, cool and package the broccoli. It should be packed with half the heads in one direction and the other half in the other direction so they fit compactly into the package.

Brussels Sprouts

Fairly small, solid sprouts that are compact, firm and a dark green color are considered best. Discard the outer leaves. Wash the sprouts, checking carefully for insects. Sort them by size. Larger ones may be cut in half and blanched as if they were medium sized. Blanch the small ones 3 minutes, medium 4 minutes, and the large 5 minutes.

MAKING IT

62 MAKING IT

Cabbage Or Chinese Celery

Discard any discolored, wrinkled rough outside leaves. For Chinese celery cut through the center halfway down the stalk for faster cooking, then cut both the stalk portion and upper leafy portion into 2 inch wedges. Cabbage should also be cut into 2 inch wedges. Then blanch the cabbage or leafy part of the Chinese celery 1 minute. For stalk portions of the Chinese celery blanch for 2 minutes. Drain, cool and package.

Cabbage is frozen only when there is an over-abundance. Since cabbage is available year-round you might buy fresh when the price is reasonable and use the frozen when the price is too high.

Carrots

Carrots should be young, tender, coreless, and mild flavored, of medium length. Remove the tops, then wash and scrape if desired. Small carrots can be frozen whole. Others should be cut into ¼ inch thick slices or lengthwise slices. Whole carrots are blanched for 5 minutes, carrot slices are blanched for 2-3 minutes. For altitudes above 4000 feet the small carrots are blanched 6 minutes and the slices are blanched for 3 minutes.

Cauliflower

Choose firm, tender, and compact snow white heads. Cut the heads into pieces 1 inch across, discarding the leaves and center core. Then wash the pieces. If you suspect insects to be inside the heads soak in a solution of 4 teaspoons salt to a gallon of water for 30 minutes. then rinse.

To help retain the white color add 4 teaspoons salt to the blanching water. Blanch for 3 minutes. For altitudes over 4000 feet blanch for 4 minutes. Then drain, cool, and package.

Celery

Frozen celery can only be used in cooked dishes and only crisp tender celery should be frozen. Separate the celery stalks and discard the bottom core. Then wash and drain. Break or cut into serving size pieces. Blanch for 3 minutes. Drain, cool and package.

Corn

Corn that has tender plump kernels with sweet milk is considered best. If the milk is very starchy and thick (which happens as the corn becomes mature), it freezes better as cream style. But both corn on the cob and whole kernel corn should be young.

For corn on the cob, husk the corn, remove the silk and wash it, then sort the ears according to size, and blanch. Only 8 medium ears should be blanched at a time. For small (up to 1¼ inches in diameter) 7 minutes, medium ears (1¼-1½ inches in diameter) 11 minutes. For altitudes above 4000 feet the corn should be blanched 8 minutes for small, 10 minutes for medium, and 12 minutes for large.

For whole kernel corn or cream style corn, blanch the corn before cutting it off the cob. Blanch small ears 5 minutes, medium 6 minutes, and large 7 minutes. For altitudes above 4000 feet blanch the small ears 6 minutes, medium 7 minutes, and large 8 minutes. Drain and cool. Then for whole kernel corn cut the corn only ⅔ the depth of the kernel. For cream style cut the corn once or twice no deeper than the center of the kernel. Then scrape the cob with the back of the knife to remove the milk and the corn hearts.

Another way to prepare cream style corn is to cut the corn from the cob without blanching. Then place the corn in a double boiler and heat for 10 minutes, stirring constantly, until it thickens.

Eggplant

This should be harvested when color is fairly dark and before the seeds become mature. Wash, drain and peel the eggplant, then slice into ½ inch thick slices or dice. Prepare only enough eggplant for one blanching at a time since it turns dark easily.

Blanch for 4 minutes, adding ½ cup lemon juice or 4½ teaspoons citric acid to the blanching water. Then cool, drain, and package.

Greens

Greens that may be frozen include collards, kale, mustard, spinach, turnip greens, beet greens, and swiss chard. For any greens, use only tender young leaves.

Wash and drain the greens. Remove any stems and defective leaves, and leave whole or cut into pieces if desired. Discard the tough midribs of the leaves.

For all greens except spinach, blanch by using 3 gallons of water, and blanch for 2 minutes. For altitudes above 4000 feet blanch for 3 minutes. Spinach is blanched only 1½ minutes. Blanch in small batches to keep the leaves from matting together. Cool, drain and package.

Kohlrabi

This should be picked when the stems are fully grown but still tender. Trim the top and bottom and peel off the touch bark. Then slice the tender centers crosswise into ¼ inch thick slices. Blanch the slices for 2 minutes. Cool, and drain. Then package.

Mushrooms

The tender button or medium-size ones are best, and can be frozen uncooked or cooked.

If they are to be frozen uncooked wash and trim. Then wash in a brine solution, containing 1½ tablespoons of salt to 1 quart of water. This is to keep them from discoloring.

Blanch the button size ones for 3 minutes, and the medium size 5 minutes.

If you are cooking them before freezing, wash and either slice or leave whole. Cook in margarine or butter for 3-5 minutes, but do not overcook. Cool the mushrooms and package.

Okra

Ones that are smooth freeze better because there is less chance of splitting along the ridges.

The okra should be young, tender, and green. Wash, trim, then remove the stems without cutting open the seed cells. Divide into 2 groups: under 4 inches, and four inches and over. Slice the larger okra into 1 inch pieces. Blanch the small pods and the 1 inch pieces for 3 minutes, and the large pods for 4 minutes. For altitudes over 4000 feet blanch the small pods and pieces 4 minutes and the large pods 5 minutes. Cool and drain.

Onions, Bulbs

Onions that are frozen can only be used for cooking and will keep only 2 months. Green onions are not frozen because they lose their crispness and become tough. Freezer space should not normally be used for onions except as a convenience in having peeled and chopped onions ready to add to food during cooking.

Peel and chop the onions, then freeze in very small packages without blanching. If you prefer the bulbs, peel and leave whole. Then blanch the bulbs for 3-7 minutes until the center of the bulb is heated. Cool and drain. Then freeze.

Parsley

Dark green, tender stalks are best. Wash and drain. Remove any wilted discolored leaves. Chop it if desired or leave whole. Place enough for a single use in each container.

Parsnips

Cut the tops off. Then wash and peel. Slice lengthwise into slices ¼ inch thick. Blanch the slices for 2 minutes. Cool before packing into containers.

Peas, English

These should be harvested when very young and tender before the peas become starchy. The pods should be bright green, plump and firm.

Wash the peas, discard any that are overmature or immature, then hull and sort according to size.

Blanch small peas for 1 minute, medium for 1½ minutes, and large for 2 minutes. For altitudes over 4000 feet blanch the small peas for 1½ minutes, medium for 2½ minutes, and large for 3½ minutes. Then cool and package.

Peas, Field (southern peas, black eye peas, crowder)

These should be picked when pods are well filled with tender peas. Shell the peas, discarding any that are immature or show insect damage. Sort them according to size. Blanch small ones for 3 minutes, larger ones for 4 minutes. At altitudes above 4000 feet blanch the smaller ones for 4 minutes, and the larger ones for 6 minutes. Then cool, drain and package.

Peppers, Green

These should be firm, crisp, tender, brightly colored, and thick walled with no bruises or blemishes.

They should be washed and drained. Cut out the stems and remove the seeds. They can be frozen whole, in halves, strips or diced.

The frozen peppers can be used in both cooked and uncooked dishes. They can be frozen either blanched or unblanched. Blanching makes them easier to pack. If blanching is done, blanch whole peppers 1½ minutes, halves for 3 minutes, and pepper slices for 2 minutes. For altitudes above 4000 feet blanch the halves for 3 minutes, the whole for 2½ minutes, and the slices for 3 minutes. Cool, drain, and package.

Pimentos

Choose well ripened, firm, crisp, thick walled pimentos with deep red color. Wash and dry. Place in a shallow pan in a single layer and roast at 400°F. for 3-4 minutes until the skin is charred, but do not burn. For altitudes above 4000 feet roast for 4-5 minutes. If desired wash off the charred skin or peel. Drain, core and remove the seeds. They can be left whole, or cut into halves, or pieces. Cool, drain, and package.

Potatoes, Irish

Small new potatoes can be frozen whole; older ones can be cut into french fries and then frozen.

Small new potatoes 1-1½ inches in diameter are best. Wash, then peel and scrape. potatoes under 1½ inches in diameter are blanched for 4 minutes, those 1¾ inches in diameter or larger, for 6 minutes. Cool and drain, then package.

For french fries, wash the potatoes, then scrape or peel. Cut into ¼ inch thick sticks. Blanch for 2 minutes, cool, drain, then package.

Potatoes, Sweet

Only medium to large potatoes that have been cured for at least a week are frozen. Wash and cook the potatoes in water, in a pressure cooker, or in the oven until almost tender. Let stand at room temperature until cool. If they are cooked in water pour the boiling water off and then cool. Peel, and mash or cut into halves, or slices. The halves or slices can be dipped in a solution of ½ cup lemon juice to 1 quart of water to keep the potatoes from turning dark.

2 tablespoons of orange or lemon juice can be added to each quart of mashed potatoes.

If desired the pieces of potato can be rolled in dry sugar before packing, or 50% syrup can be added. The potato puree is packed with 1 part of 50% syrup to 5 parts puree, adding a little lemon juice. Put through a sieve, then package and freeze.

Pumpkin

Fully mature ones with a hard rind are best. Peel, remove the seeds, cut into wedges. Cook until tender, using steam, boiling water, pressure cooker or the oven. Drain, then cool by setting the kettle over a pan of ice water. Put through a sieve. Package and freeze. If desired add 1 part sugar to 6 parts of puree.

Soybeans

Soybeans should be harvested when the beans are just developing and still in the green stage. Wash the pods, then blanch for 5 minutes. Drain and cool. Squeeze the beans out of the pods. Rinse the beans, drain, and package.

Squash, Summer

Young squash with a tender rind is best because it has smaller seeds and is more tender.

Wash and drain, then slice in ½ inch thick slices or into pieces. Blanch for 3 minutes in boiling water, then cool and drain. For altitudes above 4000 feet blanch the small pieces for 4 minutes and the larger pieces for 5 minutes.

The squash pieces or slices can be cooked in boiling water until done to make a puree. Drain the cooked squash and put through a sieve. Cool, then package and freeze.

Squash, Winter

Choose fully mature ones with a hard rind and prepare as for pumpkin.

Tomato Juice

Only firm, well ripened tomatoes with a good color should be used because the underripe ones lack flavor and nutrition.

Wash, cut the stems out, then cut into quarters or slices. Simmer for 8-10 minutes adding no additional water. For altitudes above 4000 feet allow 10-12 minutes for cooking the tomato. Press through a sieve or other strainer and add salt if desired. 1 teaspoon of salt is added per quart of juice. Allow head space.

Tomatoes, Cooked

These are only used in cooked dishes.

Dip the tomatoes in boiling water, then peel and remove the core. Cook until tender, adding no additional water. Then pass through a sieve, cool and package.

The puree can be concentrated by boiling until half the volume is reduced. Then cool and package.

Vegetable Puree

Prepare each vegetable separately. Cool and drain. Put all the vegetables through a food chopper. Package and freeze.

Vegetables, Mixed

These may be made up to put into soups, stews, or as vegetables. Prepare each vegetable separately, cool and drain, then mix together, package and freeze.

Fruits

Fruits that are packed with some form of sugar keep their flavor, color, and texture better than those packed without sugar. Follow the directions listed under each individual fruit because some can be packed satisfactorily without sugar while others cannot.

The amount of sugar or syrup depends on the acidity of the fruit. Juicy fruits, such as **strawberries will make their own syrup when dry sugar is added** but less juicy fruits need a **syrup pack**. Apricots and peaches use a syrup pack, while blueberries and cranberries do fine with dry sugar.

Fruits packed with dry sugar or unsweetened will be more suitable to use in cooking because there is no liquid in the fruit, while those packed in sugar syrup are more suitable for dessert.

Head Space

For fruit packed without sugar or liquid allow ½ inch head space for all containers. For those packed with sugar, syrup, or liquid allow the following head space:

container with narrow opening; pint ¾ inch, quart 1½ inches

container with wide opening; pint ½ inch, quart 1 inch

Making Syrup

Dissolve the sugar in either hot or cold water. If hot water is used cool the syrup to 70° F. before adding to the fruit. Syrups made ahead of time can be refrigerated for a day or two until used. Each pint of fruit usually takes about ½-⅔ cup syrup.

After the fruit is placed in the freezing container it is covered with syrup, and if the fruit floats to the top of the syrup use a piece of crumpled parchment paper or other moisture-vapor resistant paper on top of the fruit to hold it down under the syrup. In some cases the fruit is sliced directly into the syrup in the freezing container to keep the fruit from discoloring.

Sugar Pack

You can sometimes use as little as 1 part sugar to 5 or 6 parts fruit by weight, depending on the acidity of the fruit. For most fruits, one part sugar to one part fruit is sweet enough and sufficient in preserving the fruit. The amount can vary according to taste but should never be more than one part sugar to three parts fruit.

Combine the fruit and sugar and let stand for several minutes until the sugar draws the liquid out of the fruit. Stir the fruit gently but do not crush. Then pack the mixture in the freezer container. To keep from crushing the fruit, prepare only 2-3 quarts of fruit at a time for freezing.

Formulas For Sugar Syrup

The recipes for freezing fruits call for a percentage syrup. The following chart will tell you how much sugar and water it takes to make the formula needed.

Type Of Syrup	Sugar, Cups	Water, Cups	Yield of Syrup, Cups
30%	2	4	5
35%	2½	4	5⅓
40%	3	4	5½
50G	4¾	4	6½
60G	7	4	7¾
65G	8¾	4	8⅔

If desired ¼ -½ cup of cane syrup can be used instead of ¼ -½ cup of the sugar listed in the formula. This is suggested for bland, light colored fruits.

Unsweetened Pack

Light colored fruits that discolor have ascorbic acid added. The fruits may be sliced or crushed in its own juice if desired, or water may be added. Hold the fruit down in the water or juice with a crumpled piece of parchment paper.

Preparing The Fruit

Only sound ripe fruit, with good color and flavor should be used. Avoid mushy soft or bruised fruit. A uniform shape and size is also desirable. Immature fruit when frozen becomes tasteless and pale while overripe fruit becomes dark.

To retard discoloring, slice the fruit directly into the syrup in the container or the liquid containing ascorbic acid.

Use the size of container that will be used at one time with no waste or leftovers.

The fruit should be kept cool from the time it is picked until the time it is processed. Some fruits are better if processed immediately after picking while some others improve in flavor if they are held until the next day. Apples and pears can be held over for several days, while peaches, plums, figs, and most berries can be held overnight. But when the fruit is being processed and prepared for freezing, prepare only a few quarts at a time, or whatever amount you can finish within an hour.

Some fruits are frozen whole; others are peeled and sliced, pureed, or made into juices.

Some fruits such as youngberries and boysenberries make better jellies if they are first frozen. Freezing releases the natural juice and makes a better color juice because the color has time to dissolve.

Using Frozen Fruits

When using frozen fruits in cooking be sure to allow for the sugar and liquid added.

Most fruits with syrup should thaw just enough to allow for eating raw, with some ice crystals still present.

Apples

A pound of apples roughly equals 3 medium size apples or 2 cups of sliced apples. 1¼ pounds of apples usually makes 1 pint of frozen apples.

Crisp, firm apples are best; avoid those that are mealy. Wash, peel, trim, core, and slice the apples into slices or thicker than ½ inch. The slices may be blanched in steam for 1½-3 minutes depending on the variety to prevent discoloration. After blanching, the apples can be packed dry without liquid. Keep the apples under water until sliced. Cover with 40-50% syrup. Ascorbic acid will prevent discoloring. The apples should be sliced directly into the syrup in the container, starting with ½ cup syrup to a pint container. Press the apples down and add more syrup as necessary.

For pie, the slices are frozen dry.

Applesauce

Slice the apples into eighths. Add ⅓ cup water to each quart of apples and cook until tender. Cool and strain. Then add ¼-¾ cup sugar to every quart of applesauce. Cool, pack into containers, and freeze.

Apple Juice

Pack the freshly made juice into jars, tin cans, or plastic containers. It should have ¼ inch head space. Seal and freeze.

Baked Apples

The freshly baked apples are cooked, then wrapped individually in freezer paper. Place as many as necessary for one meal to a container. Seal and freeze. Defrost when ready to use. Heat in the oven at 350°F. for 30 minutes, basting with a little butter.

Apple Pie Filling

The uncooked pie filling can be mixed up and frozen. Spread in a pie pan lined with

Saran wrap and freeze. When frozen, remove the pan and wrap, and place in the freezer. The filling will keep for 12 months. Place the unthawed filling between the unbaked pastry of a double crust and bake.

Apricots

The fruit should be fully ripe but not soft. Wash, halve and pit the fruit. If you wish to peel it, place in boiling water for 30 seconds. Then peel, and slice if desired. If apricots are not peeled, place them in boiling water for 30 seconds to keep the skins from toughening during freezing. Cool in cold water and drain. Add ascorbic acid to prevent discoloring. Cover with 40-50% syrup or add ½ cup dry sugar to each quart of fruit.

Blackberries (including youngberry, boysenberry, and dewberry)

Berries should be plump, fully ripe and firm with glossy skins. Discard any berries that are soft, underripe or defective. Handle as little as possible to prevent crushing. It is better if you wash them in a large container where the berries can float to the top as you scoop them out. Then drain well. Remove all leaves, stems, and hulls.

A syrup pack is considered best for dessert purposes. 40-50% syrup is satisfactory.

If the berries are to be made into pie and jam, the dry sugar pack can be used rather than syrup. For each quart of whole berries ⅔ cup sugar is suggested. For crushed or pureed fruit, 1 cup sugar to each quart of fruit is used. If desired 1 cup syrup can be added to each quart of crushed or pureed berries.

Blueberries (also huckleberries and elderberries)

Only ripe, full flavored, tender berries should be used. Fruits that are soft, immature, or defective should be discarded. Leaves and stems should be removed.

They should be sorted, then washed and drained. If desired, the berries can be blanched for 1 minute to improve the flavor and tenderize the skin. Wild berries may need more blanching than cultivated ones. Blanch by immersing the berries in boiling syrup for 1 minute. Then cool both the berries and syrup. Replace the berries in the syrup and freeze.

The syrup pack is recommended for use in desserts and salads; the dry sugar pack is recommended with cereals, gelatin molds and fruit salads. The berries can also be packed dry without sugar or liquid for use in baking pies, muffins, pinwheels, and in sauces.

Berries must be used within 12 months and should be kept at 0°F. since they become tough and develop a woody flavor if the temperature fluctuates. The syrup pack can be from 40-50%.

For crushed or pureed fruit add 1¼ cups sugar to each quart of fruit.

If blueberries are to be used in cooking, only thaw them enough to separate the berries. For other uses, thaw just until the ice crystals disappear.

Blueberry sauce may be made and frozen until needed for ice cream, cakes, cream puffs, puddings, custard, waffles, or pancakes. Pack the cooked and cooled sauce into jars, leaving ½ inch head space.

Blueberry Pie Filling

The uncooked pie filling can be mixed, spread in a pie plate lined with Saran wrap, and frozen until solid. Then remove from the pie plate, wrap in freezer paper, and freeze. Place unthawed between pastry crusts of a double crust pie. If the filling is frozen in a pint or quart plastic container it must be thawed slightly to spread in the unbaked pastry shell.

Cantaloupes (Also Watermelon, Honeydew, Casaba, Persian)

Only high quality, really ripe but firm fruit should be used. Cut in half, remove the seeds. Then peel and either slice in ¾ inch slices, cubes, or cut into balls. Place the melon directly into the syrup as you slice it. It can be packed with or without sugar. This is served when only partially thawed to retain the shape and firmness of the fruit. It is usually better when combined with other fruits. Syrup from 30-50% may be used, depending on the natural sweetness of the fruit. It can also be packed with dry sugar with 1 part sugar to 4 parts melon.

Citrus

Peel the fruit, remove all the white membrane and fiber. Separate into segments and remove the seeds. For pink grapefruit use only 35% syrup. For other citrus use 40% syrup. Ascorbic acid should be added to prevent discoloring. Juice may be used instead of water in making the syrup.

Citrus only keeps for 2-3 months.

Citrus Juices

Use a juicer that does not extract oil from the rind.

Then if you wish, sweeten the juice with 2 tablespoons of sugar to a quart of juice. This may be frozen without ascorbic acid, but the addition of ½ teaspoon to each quart of juice is suggested.

Cherries, Sour

Use firm ripe fruit. Wash and drain. Then remove the stems and pit if desired.

If the cherries are to be served uncooked, 60% syrup is recommended. For pies, pack the cherries in dry sugar ¾ cup to a quart of cherries.

Cherries, Sweet

Firm, tree-ripened cherries with good clear color are recommended. Remove the stem, and discard any defective or unripe ones. Wash, drain and remove pits if desired. Avoid handling the fruit too much. Ascorbic acid is suggested to retain the full color and flavor. 40-50% syrup is used.

Cranberries

Many pre-packaged cranberries advise that the package may be put in the freezer. But some of these berries are immature, underripe, or crushed, and some still have their stems on. Only bright, deep red, shiny, glossy, firm berries should be chosen. Then wash and drain.

They may be frozen without sugar or liquid, with dry sugar, or a 50% syrup may be added.

They may also be crushed or pureed before freezing. Add 2 cups of water to every quart of fruit and cook until the skins pop. Then press through a sieve to remove the seeds if desired. Cool and add sugar to taste, about 2 cups to each quart of puree. Seal and freeze.

When you are making cranberry sauce, relish, or adding cranberries in a cooked dish, such as a pie or a dessert, do not thaw out the berries first.

Currants

These should be bright red, firm, and fully ripe. Wash, drain and remove the stems. Pack with dry sugar, ¾ cup sugar to a quart of currants.

Fruit Cup

Fruits may be mixed to the desired combination. Dry sugar may be used if it is suggested for the fruits in the fruit cup. But if dry sugar is not suggested then use sugar syrup of the desired sweetness.

Fruit Juices

Grape, apple or cider, and berry juices are all excellent frozen.

The fruit should be crushed slightly and then heated slightly over low heat to start the flow of juice from the fruit, but don't have the heat so high that the fruit will boil. A small amount of water may be added. Strain the juice from the fruit through a jelly bag and let the juice stand overnight to clear so it will not be cloudy. Add sugar to taste, then freeze. If the juice is to be made into jelly later, use a mixture of slightly ripe and underripe fruit to make the juice and do not add sugar. Then freeze until you are ready to make it into jelly.

Figs

Fruit should be soft and fully ripe. Check the center of the fruit to make sure it is not soured. Sort the figs, then wash and drain. Cut off the stems, peel if desired, and cut in half or leave whole. Then freeze them without sugar or roll the individual figs in sugar. A sugar syrup may be used, from 35-50%. Use ascorbic acid to keep the figs from turning dark.

Gooseberries

The berries can be green or ripe. Wash and drain, then remove the stems. Cover with 60% syrup.

Grapes (Other Than Muscadine Type)

Use firm, sweet, and fully ripe grapes, discarding any soft or bruised grapes. Wash and drain, then remove the stems. If the seeds are removed, grapes are usually frozen as puree, unless the seeds are removed by hand.

Pack the whole grapes in 40% syrup. After thawing, cook or eat as fresh grapes.

To Seed Grapes

Place the grapes in a saucepan and heat to boiling. Then put through a colander to remove the hulls and seeds. Add 1 part sugar to 5 parts puree by weight and freeze for use in pies and desserts.

If the seeds are removed by hand by cutting the grapes in half, and the hulls are left on, the grapes can be packed as whole grapes above.

Grape Juice

Heat the grapes to boiling, then strain or press out the juice through a jelly bag. Add sugar to taste. Fill containers, leaving ¼ inch head space. After thawing use as you would fresh grapes.

Seeded Grapes

Squeeze the grapes from the hulls. Place the pulp in a saucepan and heat to a boil so the seeds will separate from the pulp. Remove the seeds. If desired, the hulls can be removed from the grapes before the grapes are heated, then cooked with the pulp for 15-20 minutes until tender. Otherwise the hulls toughen during freezing. Add 1 part sugar to 6 parts grapes by weight, stirring until the sugar is dissolved. Cool and pack in containers and freeze.

For muscadine grape juice follow the regular grape juice directions.

Peaches

The white varieties are best because the flavor is always uniform, very sweet with a perfume-like aroma; the flavor of the yellow and orange varieties may vary from one variety to another.

The fruit should be well ripened and firm, with no green color on the skin. If the peaches are held in a cool place for 1-3 days after picking this improves the flavor.

Peaches may be packed in syrup, dry sugar, or in water, but if packed in water the fruit may be mushy when thawed.

Wash the peaches, being careful not to bruise them. Then peel by hand with a knife, or place in boiling water for 30 seconds to remove the peel by hand. If the peaches are packed in a syrup, slice them directly into the syrup as you peel.

A 40-60% syrup is used and ⅔ cup syrup is usually sufficient for a pint of peaches. To keep the peaches from turning dark, add ascorbic acid.

For dry sugar pack, peel and slice the peaches quickly so they don't discolor. Sprinkle the peaches with a solution of ascorbic acid in water before adding the sugar-use ¼ teaspoon of ascorbic acid to ¼ cup of water for each quart of fruit. Add ⅔ cup sugar to each quart of fruit. Peaches may also be packed in water with no added sugar. Cover the peaches with water and add 1 teaspoon ascorbic acid to each quart of fruit. Then seal and freeze.

For crushed or pureed peaches press the sliced fruit through a sieve or heat the peeled pitted peaches for 4 minutes in just enough water to keep the fruit from scorching. Then press the fruit through a sieve.

Add 1 cup of sugar and ⅛ teaspoon ascorbic acid to each quart of crushed peaches. Pour into containers and freeze.

Pears

Pears will have a more mellow flavor if they are tree-ripened. They may be held for several days until they ripen if necessary, but keep in a cool place. They should be crisp and firm, but never mealy in texture.

Wash, peel and core the pears, then cut them into halves, quarters or ½ inch thick slices. To keep the pear slices from discoloring blanch in boiling water for 2 minutes, then

drain and cool in cold water. They may be heated in syrup, and cooled before freezing.

They can be packed in 40-50% syrup, leaving ¼-½ inch head space. They are used for salads, pies, and desserts.

Pears may be baked, then individually wrapped and frozen. To use, place them in the oven while still frozen and heat at 350°F. until tender, about 20-30 minutes.

Pears are excellent when frozen with melon balls.

Pear Pie Filling

The uncooked pie filling is mixed, adding ¾ teaspoon of ascorbic acid to each pie. Remove the frozen filling from the pie plate, and wrap in freezer paper, then freeze. Place the filling in the center of an unbaked double crust pastry.

If the pie filling is packed in a quart container, it should be thawed partially so it can be spread in the unbaked pie crust.

Pecans

Shell the nuts then dry them for 24 hours by spreading them in a thin layer in a pan. Pack into freezer bags and seal. They may be chopped or left in halves. Syrup may be added if desired.

Pineapple

This should be firm and ripe for a good flavor. Peel and remove the eyes. Then slice, remove the core, and dice, crush, or cut into wedges.

It may be packed in syrup using 30-40% syrup, or it may be packed with dry sugar, using 1 part sugar to 1 part pineapple by weight. If desired, it may also be frozen without sugar or liquid.

Plums (Red And Prune Varieties)

All firm fleshed plums are recommended. Plums that are slightly soft can be frozen; those that are still firm can be canned.

The fruit should have a deep color, and should be ripe enough to yield to slight pressure.

Allow the fruit to mellow in a cool place for several days before freezing but don't allow to overripen.

Wash the fruit. Then drain and cut in halves. If you wish, remove the pits and slice the larger plums.

They can be packed in syrup from 40-50% depending on the tartness of the fruit. Add ascorbic acid to keep the fruit from turning dark.

The plums may be frozen, either peeled and whole without sugar. Do not leave any head space in the container.

They may also be packed in dry sugar, using 1 part sugar to 5 parts fruit by weight. Soft plums may be made into a puree by pressing through a sieve or colander. Sugar syrup may be added to the puree if desired.

Plum sauce may be made by boiling the whole ripe fruits (adding no additional water). Then remove the pit and skin, return the pulp to the heat, add spices if desired. Cook until the pulp thickens slightly. Add 1 part sugar to 1 part pulp by weight, and cool before packing and freezing.

Raspberries

Berries should be firm, plump, fully ripe, with glossy skins with even good color. The purple ones have a better flavor than the black ones. Those that are green, partially ripe or defective should be removed. Wash the berries in a large container in water so that you can scoop out the berries as they float to the top of the water. Then drain.

The syrup pack is considered best; 30-50% syrup would be used for dessert.

Packing with dry sugar is recommended if the berries are to be made into jam or pies, using ⅔ cup sugar to each quart of berries.

Rhubarb

Tender, crisp and firm, well colored stalks with very few fibers should be chosen. Wash and drain, then trim and cut into 1-inch pieces. Blanch in boiling water for 1 minute, then drain and cool. Blanching helps maintain the flavor and color of the fruit. After heating, pack the pieces with 40% syrup. If desired, rhubarb can be packed raw without blanching, with no sugar or syrup.

Strawberries

It takes about ⅔ quart of fresh berries to make 1 pint of frozen berries.

Strawberries should be firm, yet fully ripe with a deep red color (the color varies from variety to variety). Discard all immature or defective berries. Wash the berries a few at a time in a large pan of cold water. Drain in a colander, then remove the hulls and slice.

Berries can be packed in a dry sugar pack either whole or sliced. Use ¾ cup sugar to each quart of berries. Whole berries may need a little more sugar to make enough juice for freezing, as much as 1 part sugar to 4 parts fruit by weight.

For syrup pack a 40-50% syrup is used.

Crushed or pureed fruit may be frozen using ⅔ cup sugar to each quart of puree. The strawberries may be frozen in water by adding 1 teaspoon ascorbic acid to each quart of water and covering the berries with the water.

Freezing Meats And Poultry

A slaughter house will usually package pork, beef, lamb, and veal, trimming away the amount of bone and fat you instruct. The more bone that is trimmed away the less freezer space it will take. Only place 2 pounds of meat in the freezer at a time for every cubic foot of space in the freezer. This insures that the meat will freeze quickly to prevent off-flavor and spoilage. Packaged meat is frozen at the slaughter house and is ready to put in your freezer.

Kind Of Cut	Amount Per Person In Lbs.	Comments
ground meat	¼-⅓ lb.	do not salt
steaks and chops, club or t-bone steaks pork, veal, and lamb chops	½-¾ lb.	Separate with 2 sheets of waxed paper
steaks, sirloin or round	½-¾	Package each one separately
bony cuts, such as spareribs	¾-1 lb.	
liver, kidney, heart, tongue	¾-1 lb.	Liver is sliced and will keep for only 3 months.
roast	¾-1 lb.	Use leftovers within 2 days.

Packages should not be very large. Larger packages take longer to freeze and thaw and are awkward to handle.

Pack the meat in heavy moisture-vapor resistant paper. Freezer paper or locker paper is good. Moisture proof cellophane, polyethylene and aluminum foil that is .0015 gauge can all be used. The packages can be taped or wrapped in a stockinette. When using freezer paper place the shiny side next to the meat.

If you are wrapping the meat yourself close the wrap tightly to exclude all air. To wrap, place the meat in the center of the paper, allowing enough paper so you can fold both edges down 2-3 times in 1-inch folds. This is done by first bringing both edges together and making a folding crease. Repeat until the fold nests tightly against the meat. Press down hard to expel all air at both ends. Fold the ends securely and either tape or tie. Label, using a crayon or grease pencil.

Possum, rabbit, venison, and squirrel can all be frozen. Possum may become rancid within 6 months.

Beef And Pork

If ground meat is made into patties, make the patties small because air space between them will cause them to become rancid. Sausage will keep for about 2 months. Try to make up your own salt-free spice mixture because salt shortens the storage life of sausage. If you are freezing ham, a whole or half a ham keeps better than slices.

Poultry

Whole or halved chickens keep longer than the cut up chicken, but the cut up chicken is more compact and takes up less space. For wrapping whole chickens, use aluminum foil or other paper that will mold itself to the shape of the chicken. Freezer paper is least desirable for this because loose fitting wrap will cause more air to be sealed in and make the chicken dry out. When packing cut up chickens or halves of chickens, place waxed paper between the layers. If necessary, older chickens can be tenderized by chilling for 6 hours before freezing.

Frozen cooked poultry will keep longer if packed with broth or gravy. Fried chicken and poultry packed without gravy or broth have a shorter storage life. If the cooked meat is removed from the bones and packed solidly, this helps protect the meat from developing a rancid flavor. Adding broth or gravy also helps to preserve the flavor by preventing contact with the air.

Freezing Fish And Shellfish

Only freshly caught fish or seafood should be frozen. Do not freeze fish from the market.

Scale, dress and wash the fish, then leave whole, or cut into fillets or steaks. Fatty fish such as mackerel are treated with ascorbic acid. Add 1 tablespoon of ascorbic acid to a quart of water and dip the fish in this mixture for 30 seconds. This helps to preserve the flavor and keep it from turning rancid.

DRYING, SMOKING, AND PICK-LING FRUITS AND VEGETABLES

Drying is a good method of preserving fruits and vegetables and it's cheaper than freezing or canning because you don't need canning jars or freezing containers and you don't use as much energy as freezing and canning.

Vegetables that can be dried include peas, okra, butter beans, tomatoes, cabbage, onions, celery, green and hot peppers, green beans, whole kernel corn cut from the cob, carrots, winter squash, pumpkin, beets, and sweet potato.

Almost any fruit can be dried.

Blanching

Blanching vegetables before drying is a good way to preserve vitamins, if you wish. Do not blanch juicy fruits. If you blanch apples, add ascorbic acid to the water to keep the apples from discoloring.

You can use a blanching basket, strainer, or a boiling bag to hold the food in the blanching water. Bring a gallon of water to a boil in a large kettle. Place about 4-5 cups of prepared vegetables or fruits in the boiling bag or basket. Lower into the boiling water. Cover and blanch for the time suggested. Place the food in a pan until it is cool, and you're ready for drying.

Most vegetables are blanched for 5 minutes. Carrots, corn, beets, pumpkin, and sweet potato are blanched for 10 minutes. Apples are blanched for 3 minutes.

Preparing The Fruits Or Vegetables

Peel, core and slice the fruit, leaving berries and grapes whole. Some fruits (grapes, blueberries, cranberries) should be pierced with a fork so the moisture will escape more easily.

Cut corn from the cob; peel and slice squash, pumpkin, beets, sweet potatoes, and tomatoes; slice carrots, celery and cabbage; remove peas and butter beans from the pod. Green beans should be broken into 1 inch pieces if they are to be dried flat. Beans and okra may be left whole and strung to dry on heavy string using a needle. Beans dried in this manner are called shuck beans.

Drying The Vegetables And Fruits

Spread the prepared food on a large clean, cloth-covered tray that you can move in and out of doors as needed. Spread the food on top of the cloth so the pieces of food do not touch each other. Cover the food with a clean cloth to protect it from insects and soil. The top cloth must be raised so that it does not touch the food but allows the air to circulate freely. Place clean rocks or tin cans around the edges of the cloth and at the center of the bottom cloth. Now spread the top cloth over the rocks so that it covers the food but doesn't touch it. Place a rock at each corner of the top cloth to keep it from blowing off.

Place the tray in a very warm shady place. Direct or excess sun is bad because it will dry the food too quickly and cause excessive shrinking. Warm sunny dry weather is the best for drying, because overcast wet days can cause the food to spoil since it doesn't dry as quickly. Turn the food several times a day until dry.

Then place the food on a cookie sheet and dry it in the oven at 175°F. for 10 minutes. This insures that all moisture that could cause spoilage or mildew is removed. Remove from the oven and let cool. The food can be stored in scalded clean jars or plastic bags.

Smoking And Pickling Fish At Home

Smoking

Fish that can be smoked include salmon, trout, carp, chub, buffalo, and catfish.

The fish must be kept very cold from the time they are caught until the time they are prepared for processing. A dressed fish will keep slightly longer than a whole fish, and larger fish will keep longer than smaller ones.

There have been some cases of botulism in home prepared smoked fish but if you follow the procedure outlined here you should not have any trouble. For safety, remember these inflexible rules:

(1) use the recommended amount of salt in making the brine

(2) test the temperature of the brine at 40°F.

(3) use the correct amount of brine for the amount of fish you are processing

(4) use the same size and similar kinds of fish because different fish absorb salt at a different rate

(5) when smoking the fish remember to have the chamber heated to the proper temperature and keep this temperature constant throughout the whole smoking process

Pickling Fish

Pickling is a good way to preserve any surplus fish you have that you may not wish to freeze. Almost any type of fish can be pickled at home: soak the fish in brine, then combine the fish with vinegar and spices and cook until done.

The factors involved in the flavor of the pickled fish include the water, salt, sugar, vinegar, and herbs used:

Water-Hard water and water with magnesium, calcium or iron are unsuitable, so hard water must be softened before making the brine.

Vinegar-Distilled white vinegar with a guaranteed acetic acid content of at least 4% is needed to prevent bacterial growth. Cider, fruit or wine vinegars are not used because they can color the fish and give it an off color.

Salt-Non-iodized canning salt or granulated dairy salt is considered best.

Sugar-Use granulated sugar.

Spices and herbs-Buy these whole, as fresh as possible, and mix at the time of use.

Preparing The Fish

Soak the fish for 1 hour in a brine containing 1 cup salt to 1 gallon of water.

Then drain the fish and place in a heavy plastic, glass, or enamel container. Cover the fish with brine made up of 2½ pounds of salt to a gallon of water. Keep the fish in this brine for 12 hours in the refrigerator at 40°F., not below. The fish is now ready to pickle.

The following pickle mixture is enough for 10 pounds of fish:

1 ounce white pepper

1 ounce allspice

1 ounce mustard seed or 2 ounces mixed pickling spices

½ ounce bay leaves

1 ounce hot, ground or dried red pepper, optional to taste

½ pound onions, sliced

2 quarts distilled vinegar

2½ pints water

Remove the fish from the brine and rinse well. Then bring the pickle mixture to a boil. Add the fish and simmer for 10 minutes, or until the fish is tender enough to be pierced with a fork. Remove the fish from the pot, place in a shallow pan in a single layer and refrigerate until cool. Pack the cooled fish in a scalded clean jar, adding bay leaf, other spices, sliced onions and lemons to taste. Bring the hot pickle mixture to a boil, and cover the fish with the boiling mixture. Cover the jar and seal. Store in the refrigerator at 40-45°F. and use within 4-6 weeks.

Chapter 3
Clothes

SEWING YOUR OWN CLOTHES

Yes, you can save money by making your own clothes, and what's more, home made clothes usually last longer and wear better than store bought clothes.

Since the price of fabrics and sewing accessories has kept pace with everything else, you will save money if you buy your fabrics on sale rather than at the regular prices. You can also keep pattern costs down by buying the less expensive brands of patterns and by buying patterns that can be used several times.

If you are a beginner and are buying your first sewing machine, remember you will have to sew a lot to make the machine pay for itself. So if you are uncertain whether you will have the time and patience to sew a lot, reconsider before investing a lot of money in a fancy machine.

Making neckties has become very popular because ties can be made for a fraction of the cost of a ready-made tie and the same pattern can be used over and over. Before undertaking any project check the sale price of the item ready-made to be sure you will truly save money by sewing your own.

Choosing your fabrics

It takes the same amount of work to make a garment with a poor quality fabric as with a good quality, better lasting fabric. Cheap fabrics or remnants of unknown quality can fade, shrink, or ravel, and will not wear as long or as well as a good quality fabric. You can always judge the quality of a fabric just by looking at it but here are some ways you can reduce your chances of getting a bad buy.

When the fabric is bought from the bolt, the bolt contains the fiber content as well as care instructions, and whether the fabric is preshrunk. Any fabric that is more than 1% shrinkage must be washed or dry cleaned first before using. Some stores such as department stores will have remnant sales to get rid of pieces left over from the ends of bolts. Even woolens and linens can be bought for as little as $1.00 a yard at such sales. These remnants are safe to buy only if you know and trust the store.

The prices of identical or similar fabrics will vary from store to store, with discount stores offering the cheapest prices. As long as the fabric is on the bolt with a manufacturer's name you trust, don't hesitate to buy from discount stores.

Remember that fabric has sizing that makes it stiff. Keep this in mind when matching your pattern to your fabric. It may be a good idea to wash the fabric first before choosing your fabric because the sizing can make a difference in how the material hangs.

The least expensive fabric you can buy is unbleached muslin. It can be bought for as little as 78¢ a yard in some stores. You can dye it any color you wish before cutting your pattern out. Don't sew before dyeing because the thread will dye a different color than the muslin.

Some mail order catalogues sell bundles of fabric that are real bargains. The bundles are priced according to the quality and fiber content of the fabric as well as the number of yards the bundle contains. The catalogue lists the number of pieces of fabric in the bundle and the size of each piece. You can choose a bundle for fall, winter, or summer, but here don't have a choice of color or pattern. These pieces are left over from the ends of bolts and are top quality materials for a very low price.

By buying your material out of season you can also save at least 50%. In the spring, stores get rid of the previous winter's fabrics to make room for the spring and summer stock. The same is true of summer stock, on sale in the fall or winter. By anticipating your needs you can save a lot of money on good fabrics. Even the most expensive Pendelton woolens go on sale! You can buy your fabric out of season, and wait until later for your high fashion pattern.

To help you choose your fabrics, the major synthetic and man-made fibers are listed here with their care requirements and durability. The kind of the fabric, whether it is denim, broadcloth, or pile, and the types of fabric finishes also are factors that influence the durability of a fabric.

Synthetic Fibers

Polyester-may be called dacron, fortrel, kodel or vycron.

This is probably one of the major fibers in use now. It is high in wrinkle resistance when both wet and dry, and is abrasion resistant. It builds up static electricity, and is difficult to dye. It is not very absorbent and may feel cold and clammy or hot and uncomfortable. Considered one of the better fibers to use in blends it resists shrinking and will hold permanent pleats. It is also considered one of the best for permanent press finish.

CARE-Because it will absorb body oils, all stains should be treated immediately, or before washing. Items made of white polyester should be washed separately. Polyester should be washed in lukewarm water and ironed at low to medium settings because it cannot take high temperatures. It washes easily and dries quickly. It is difficult to remove pleats or creases that are ironed in and it is also hard to alter because the old pleat or hemline will show and will not wash out as in other fibers.

Nylon-may be called nylenka, caprolan, antron, cudon, quiana, and cantrece

Fabric Width Conversion Chart

FABRIC WIDTH	32"	35-36"	39"	41"	44-45"	50"	52-54"	58-60"	66"
YARDAGE REQUIRED	1⅞	1¾	1½	1½	1⅜	1¼	1⅛	1	⅞
	2	2¼	2	1¾	1⅝	1½	1⅜	1¼	1⅛
	2½	2¼	2	2	1¾	1⅝	1½	1⅜	1¼
	2¾	2½	2¼	2¼	2⅛	1¾	1¾	1⅝	1½
	3⅛	2⅞	2½	2½	2¼	2	1⅞	1¾	1⅝
	3⅜	3⅛	2¾	2¾	2½	2¼	2	1⅞	1¾
	4	3¾	3¼	3⅛	2⅞	2⅝	2⅜	2¼	2⅜
	4⅜	4¼	3½	3⅜	3⅛	2¾	2⅝	2⅜	2¼
	4⅝	4½	3¾	3⅞	3⅝	3¼	2⅞	2¾	2⅝
	5	4¾	4	3⅞	3⅝	3¼	2⅞	2¾	2⅝
	5¼	5	4¼	4⅛	3⅞	3⅜	3⅛	2⅞	2¾

If the pattern lists a 36 inch fabric and you are buying a 50" width, look under the 36" for the amount the pattern calls for, then directly across the line under 50" will be the yardage you need. For certain fabrics, such as one way prints, plaids, and nap, and for knits, you need to add an extra ¼ yard. For a style such as kimona or dolman sleeves where the body and sleeve is cut in one piece, add an extra ¼ yard. If there is a wide spread conversion, for instance from 32" to 50" or from 36" to 54" add an extra ½ yard.

It is the strongest and most durable man made fiber and will take a lot of wear. It has natural resilience and elasticity that causes it to be wrinkle resistant and have permanent shape retention. Knitted nylons hold their shape well.

CARE-It is washable and dries quickly. White nylon should be washed separately from colored items. It produces static electricity and is sensitive to strong sunlight. It requires little pressing. The antron or multilobal is more absorbent. The cantrece or bicompent looks like crepe. Quiana has elegance yet is durable.

Acrylic-may be called acrilan, creslan, zetkrome, orlon, or zefran

It is soft and lightweight yet warm, and has high bulking power. It is resistant to wrinkling and shrinking and is excellent for holding pleats. It is resistant to both sunlight and stains. It tends to pill and develops static electricity.

CARE-It can be washed in warm to fairly hot water, and dries quickly. It is easily cared for, and can be ironed at low temperature if necessary. Any stains should be removed before washing.

Modoacrylic-may be called dynel or verel

It is warm, soft, resilient, strong and retains its shape. It is wrinkle resistant. It is also resistant to fire, acids, and alkalines. It accumulates static electricity.

CARE-It is very sensitive to heat, so a low temperature is used when pressing. Those with 100% modoacrylic should not be ironed. Oily stains should be removed immediately or before washing. Dry cleaning or fur cleaning is recommended for deep pile.

Acetate-may be called celanese, estron, chromspun, celasperm, acele, and colorsealed

It is soft, crisp and silky, and has resistance to abrasion and soiling. It drapes softly and has fair resistance to wrinkling. Used as silk substitutes, it has many of the qualities of silk at a low price. All except the solution died, chromspun, colorsperm, and col-

orsealed are sensitive to fading from sunlight, atmospheric gases, perspiration and washing.

CARE-Pretreat all oily stains before washing. It is usually best to dry clean unless the label says otherwise because washing will cause fading. The fibers are washable but the finish may not be. Use low temperatures in washing, drying, and pressing because it is sensitive to heat. Acetone, fingernail polish remover, and paint remover will all damage the fiber.

Triacetate-may be called arnel

It is similar to acetate but is less sensitive to heat and has greater wet strength. It can be given permanent pleats and creases by the permanent press process, which also makes it resistant to shrinking, stretching, and wrinkling. It blends well with other fibers.

CARE-It does not require as much care in handling as acetate. It may be washed at a low to high temperature and pressed at higher temperatures. Water-borne stains wipe off easily.

Rayon-may be called bemberg, colorspun, cupioni, fortison, jetspun, viscone, coloray, and avisco

It is cool, comfortable to wear, and has good absorbency. It is moderately durable. It is weak when wet and when exposed to high humidity. It has poor resistance to abrasion and soil. It lacks resilience and wrinkles easily, and may shrink or stretch unless it has a special finish. Because it is easily dyed and drapes well and softly, it is used in blends. It is weakened by long exposure to sunlight. Coloray, colorsperm and jetspun are highly resistant to fading from sunlight, washing, and perspiration because they are solution dyed.

CARE-Handle very carefully when washing, do not wring or twist the fabric because it is weak when wet. Do not use chlorine bleaches unless the label says you can. Oily stains should be removed immediately. When ironing and washing a blend use the care required for the most delicate of the two.

Modified Rayon-may be called avril, avon, carval, lirelle, and zontrel

It is often used in blends because in some ways it is superior to rayon. Many are treated to be wrinkle resistant. It is more shrink and stretch resistant than rayon, and stronger when wet and dry.

CARE-Avoid chlorine bleaches. It may be washed and ironed without special care; follow the directions on the label.

Natural Fibers
Wool

It is comfortable to wear because it has good insulating qualities that retain warmth and are absorbent. It is very durable, resilient, and naturally wrinkle resistant. It is dry cleaned unless the label says it can be washed. Even washable wools will shrink and felt less if dry cleaned.

CARE-Avoid excessive agitation when hand or machine washing. It must be protected from moths, carpet beetles and other insects. Do not use chlorine bleach. Always press with a cloth but avoid high temperatures because it also causes felting and shrinking. Dry heat can damage the fiber.

Cotton

It is cool, soft, highly absorbent, and comfortable for summer wear. It does not build up static. It is durable, economical, and dyes easily. It is attacked by mildew. If cotton has a wrinkle-resistant or wash-and-wear finish it will wrinkle less. If buying a blend of cotton with other fiber the cotton must be at least 30% of the fiber content to have any of the characteristics. For example, if a shirt is only 20% cotton and 80% polyester it will not have any of the characteristics of cotton.

CARE-It is easily washed and ironed without special care. It can be washed and ironed at high temperature because it has good resistance to high temperature. Use chlorine bleaches only if the label says so. Special finishes are used because wrinkling and shrinkage can be problems.

Linen

It is durable, has high strength and absorbency. It has natural beauty and luster that gives it a look of elegance. It feels and looks cool and crisp. It does not shed lint, and is susceptible to mildew. Because it creases and wrinkles easily it should be treated with a wrinkle resistant finish.

CARE-It will withstand frequent hand laundering. Check the label before using bleach. Remove any oily stains before washing. Those finished with a wrinkle or wash-and-wear finish may set the stains permanently if the stain is not removed before washing.

Silk

It is beautiful, luxurious, has a high luster. Because it is naturally resistant and elastic it sheds wrinkles and returns to shape readily. It is lightweight, yet absorbent, has a smooth finish and good strength. White silk may tend to yellow with age.

CARE-It should be treated with the greatest of care. Follow instructions on the label, but most of the time it is dry cleaned. It can waterspot easily. It can also be damaged by chlorine bleach, sunlight, and perspiration. If the label says it is washable use lukewarm water and iron at a low temperature to prevent yellowing.

Fabric Finishes

If a fabric is treated to be permanent press, wash-and-wear, or wrinkle resistant, it will require less care when washing. Items that are wrinkle resistant and wash-and-wear may require light pressing. Items that are permanent press have a shorter life, will not wear as well or take abrasion as well as the identical fabric that is not permanent press. Alterations are difficult in permanent press clothing because the old lines will show and the new seam or cuff will not hold a permanent press crease and may require touching up to make it look better.

Permanent press can be washed in warm or cold water, preferably using the permanent press or wash-and-wear cycle on the machine, and a cool rinse. They are tumble dried and hung up immediately. They will wrinkle if allowed to remain in the dryer.

For permanent press fabric you need to use a polyester core thread, or size 50 or 60 mercerized cotton thread. There should be 10-12 stitches per inch, using a fine sharp needle and a relaxed stitch tension to avoid puckers in the seam, because these puckers will not iron out.

Check permanent press fabric to see that the printed designs, crosswise stripes, and plaids are all finished at the right angle to the selvage because you cannot straighten off-grain permanent press fabric.

Since permanent press fabric is preshrunk, make sure your interfacings, linings, and zippers are preshrunk. Preshrink the zipper by soaking it in water for 10 minutes, then allow it to dry before sewing into the garment.

Choose a pattern that has as few seams and details as possible, and avoid topstitching if possible. Topstitching will usually show puckers.

Denim

Denim has a firm body and is suitable for pleats and gathers. Choose a pattern that does not have extreme bias or extreme curves, since denim is a heavy-weight material. Interfacing is usually used for belts, waistbands, and buttonholes, but is optional for collars and cuffs.

If the denim is 100% cotton use a mercerized cotton thread; if it's a blend of cotton and synthetic fibers, use a polyester thread or polyester core thread with cotton warp.

Because denim ravels easily the seams will have to be finished. You will want to finish hems, using pinking or scalloping shears to trim the edge and blindstitch the hem, or apply seam binding to the edge and use a hemming stitch.

Corduroy And Velveteen

Narrow wale corduroy is better for children's wear while the wide wale is used for sportswear and coats with simple lines. When selecting a pattern to make with corduroy choose one with as few seams as possible.

Clothing from corduroy and velveteen must be made with the grain or nap running the same direction. If you want the garment to last longer, cut it with the pile running down because this enables the material to withstand abrasion better. If you want a richer deeper color cut the pattern with the nap running up, or toward the top of the garment.

When you are cutting the pattern pieces out, be sure that all the pieces are pointing in the same direction. Make any folds with the right sides together lengthwise.

Darts are slashed and pressed open to make them lie smoothly. Make facings from a lightweight material, do not make them of corduroy or velveteen.

Seam finishes are needed because the edges of the seams tend to ravel.

Always press corduroy and velveteen on the wrong side, do not press the nap or pile of the material.

Lace

For lace you should choose a pattern with few seams, simple lines, and very little detail. It is sometimes lined with taffeta, net, or other thin, sheer lining.

If you are lining your garment, baste the lining and lace together with the wrong side together. Then machine stitch to hold the two layers together. If you are not using a lining, you will want to baste tissue paper along the seam lines on the right side of the lace, then sew the garment together as usual, and tear the paper from the seams after you stitch the seams. The tissue paper keeps the two layers of lace from slipping while you sew them together. If the garment is unlined you will want to use French seams for a neater look—⅛ to ¼ inch wide. For the armhole use a whipped French seam. Always press lace on the wrong side.

Sheer Fabrics

Sheer fabrics require certain handling techniques because the seams, hems, and darts all show through the fabric.

Many sheer clothes need lining which can be stitched directly to each piece of the sheer fabric or sewn together before placing with the sheer fabric.

Make sure your pattern is suitable to be made of sheer fabrics. When cutting out a pattern in sheer fabric, place a piece of tissue paper on top of the material under each pattern piece. Cut through the tissue paper, and sheer material at the same time and make any markings on the tissue. Before you begin any sewing, staystitch all the edges to keep them from stretching. Sheer garments often have hems that are three layers thick, so add enough to the length to allow for this extra hem. Tucks and unstitched darts show less and are preferred to ordinary darts.

When using a lining or underlining use a French or double bias fold to finish the edge of necks, sleeves and hems, rather than facings.

Use a small needle, and a stitch with 14-18 stitches per inch, and a loose tension on your machine to avoid puckering. Leave the tissue paper on the material until you stitch the seams together, then tear the paper out. Use French or double seams only ¼ -⅛ inch wide.

Deep Pile Fabrics

Deep pile fabrics are fur-like and are used in coats and jackets. The closer and denser the pile the better the quality, although fabrics with less pile are cheaper.

Since this is primarily a winter fabric it goes on sale in the spring at bargain prices. By buying on sale at the end of the season you can save 50% or more.

Use warm water and a short machine cycle when washing and spinning. The pile usually looks better if you line dry it or hang it on a hanger. After drying the pile may need to be brushed to restore the fluffiness. Do not steam or press because this causes the pile to mat or cramp.

If the fabric has a knit-back construction it may shrink badly. If it is not preshrunk, allow a little extra and preshrink by machine or hand before cutting the pattern out.

Be very careful when choosing your pattern for deep pile. Choose one that has few seams; avoid collars, set-in sleeves, and buttonholes. Use loops rather than buttonholes.

Place all the pattern pieces on the back or wrong side of the material so that the pile goes in one direction, down. Avoid extra seams, such as center back seams by cutting as one piece. Cut facings in one piece to eliminate extra seams, or use braid on the edges. If the fabric is very thick cut one thickness at a time.

Use a medium sized machine needle, size 14 and 10 stitches per inch. Use a heavy duty thread. The tension and pressure should be normal, but try on a scrap piece of material first.

Seam tape should be used to reinforce on all points of strain. To finish the seams, sheer the pile on the seam allowance and then machine stitch ⅛ inch from the edge. All darts should be slashed and pressed open with the fingers.

After stitching turn the garment to the right side and use a long needle to lift the pile that has been caught in the edge of the seam. This helps hide the seam.

Bonded Or Laminated Fabrics

A bonded fabric may be foam backed or fabric-backed, the fabric backed has more drape and flexibility.

Bonding has certain advantages. It gets rid of layers of lining and underlining, is more wrinkle resistant and holds pleats well. Seams are smooth and do not ravel. It drapes better and makes it possible to have delicate fabric such as lace hang well.

Bonded fabrics with very loose weaves or large open knits are more likely to blister and separate as the fabric layer shrinks more easily.

There are several problems that can occur with laminated or bonded clothes. The layers can separate, or one of the layers can shrink, it may form puckers or bubbles, or the foam may peel away in spots.

Some dry cleaners will not take responsibility for cleaning bonded fabrics because they tend to be damaged easier than other fabrics.

Choose a pattern with few seams and very few details; avoid set-in sleeves—dolman or raglan sleeves are better.

The fabric with thinner layers of foam will be easier to work with, and woven fabrics that are bonded are easier to cut on the grain than knits that are bonded.

Be sure that your fabric has straight grain because it cannot be straightened.

If possible, cut the facing and the garment in one piece to avoid extra seams.

Bonded fabrics are not cut on the fold as pattern pieces would indicate. Instead place the pattern piece on a single thickness on the right side of the material, allowing for the other half on the other side of the fold line. Then cut one piece, flip the pattern over on the fold line, and cut the opposite side.

For foam backed materials hand baste together because the machine will not sew over pins when foam is used. To get the machine started, turn the wheel by hand for the first five or six stitches because the machine may clog up over the foam. To make stitching easier over foam, use seam tape or place tissue next to the stitching line so the machine goes smoothly. Baste the seam tape or a 1 inch strip of lightweight cotton on the seam line. Experiment first to see which placement of the tape is best. Leave this tape in place to reinforce the seam. You may do better if you have paper on top and a strip of material on bottom, or the reverse. Practice on a sample strip of material until you find what is best for you. Staystitch all curves and bias seams. Slash darts and stitch by hand so they lie flat.

Stretch Fabrics

Stretch fabrics may be either woven or knitted, and they can stretch in only one direction (a one-way stretch), or they can be made up of all stretch yarns (a two-way stretch).

Woven stretch fabrics are usually used in sports and casual wear, and in children's clothing. These fabrics include corduroy, velveteen, shantung, seersucker, twill, and denim.

Knitted stretch fabrics are used in clothing that requires elasticity and action allowance, such as slacks and sweaters.

Clothes made of stretch fabrics should be comfortable. not tight, and they should not sag at heavy points of wear, such as the knee and seat.

When sewing, use a lock or chain stitch with 14 stitches or more per inch. If slacks have only lengthwise one-way stretch they require a bootstrap, ones with horizontal stretch do not need a bootstrap. Clothes with lengthwise stretch will stretch less if you fold and store them in a drawer.

If a pattern is designed for stretch it will say so. You can adjust a standard pattern by making the following allowances:(1) for slacks turn 1 inch up at the hem and make a ½ inch tuck across the crotch line (2) for a skirt make a lengthwise tuck from ½ to 1 inch equal to the amount of ease.

Be sure that the fabric you are buying will stretch in the right direction for your pattern: pants and skirts need fabric that stretches two way or in the direction needed; blouses and jackets need a fabric with a crosswise or horizontal stretch.

If the fabric is not preshrunk, steam it carefully without burning the material, and allow to dry. Spread the fabric out and let it rest for 24 hours to let it relax. This insures that the garment will fit better. Then pin the pattern onto the fabric, placing pins at right angles to the stretch every 6 inches. Be careful not to stretch the material.

Use a textured nylon thread that will have the necessary stretch. The tension should be loose and should make 14 stitches per inch. If the thread breaks when the seam stretches loosen the tension. You can baste the pieces together or place the pins as you did when pinning the pattern on. To finish the seam you may zigzag the edges or stitch ⅛ inch from the raw edge.

Do not use lining since it will not give with the fabric. When making buttonholes reinforce with interfacing. Use a pressing cloth when pressing stretch material.

Knit Fabrics

Knits are comfortable, lightweight yet warm, and are perfect for travel because they do not wrinkle easily.

There are two types of knits; the warp knits which stretch crosswise, and filling knits which stretch lengthwise.

A double knit is a jersey that is knitted on both sides so it is heavier and holds its shape better than jersey.

Filling knits are more common and more elastic than warp knits. It may be difficult to tell the right and wrong side of a single knit apart unless there is a pattern or texture on the right side. Knits may also be bonded. Single knits are made up of one yarn and are lightweight, soft and supple. Raschel knits are a type of warp knit that has a long loose or loopy appearance.

Firm double knits can be hung on hangers but other knits should be folded and stored in a drawer. Knits should be allowed to rest at least a day between wearings so they can get their original shape back.

Choose a fabric with few seams, and clean simple lines. Gored and flared skirts that have bias seams should be avoided. Be sure to choose a pattern that is recommended for knits. Be sure your knit has no flaws, pulled loops, or is offgrain. The grain line should be along the rib of the fabric. Bonded knits cannot be corrected if they are offgrain.

If your fabric is not preshrunk, do this before cutting your pattern. Wet a sheet in warm water, then wring out as much water as possible. Lay the wet sheet out flat, place the fabric on the sheet and fold loosely. In about 2 hours when the fabric is wet, remove from the sheet and spread out on a flat surface to dry.

Be sure to preshrink all zippers, interfacings and seam tapes before sewing.

Sewing Techniques

Underlining

Underlining is used to help a fabric hold its shape and to cushion seams. Underlining in a skirt back should reach below the hip line. It is sewed to each piece of fabric, and treated as one piece of material when making the seams.

Lining

Lining gives a neat appearance to the inside of the garment. It is designed to help clothing keep its shape, body, and it prolongs the life of the garment. The quality of the lining you use should correspond with the quality of the fabric you are using. For example, don't use the best quality lining on a cotton dress because the lining will outlast and outwear the cotton. On the other hand you don't want to use a cheap nylon lining with a fine woolen, because the lining will wear out, ravel, and pucker. If your fabric is permanent press make sure that your lining is also. Otherwise the lining will become wrinkled and uncomfortable to wear while the permanent press is smooth and comfortable.

The lining is made separately and attached to the garment. The seam and hem of the lining is turned toward the body of the seam if the imprint will show on the right side of the garment.

Interfacings

Interfacings should not be heavier than your fabric, but they may be lighter. They should have the same give as the fabric and should be a color suitable for the fabric. They should require the same care as the fabric, and must be washable if the fabric is washable.

Staystitching

For parts of the patterns that are hard to fit together, such as collars, sleeves, and sewing corners, the staystitching should be closer to the seamline. A wrinkle resistant fabric will probably need staystitching only at the neck and other difficult areas.

Collars

The upper collar must be larger than the undercollar to keep the seam and undercollar from showing. For thicker fabrics the top collar should be a little larger than usual. Sew with shorter stitches so that you can trim the seams closer.

Grading the seams with the larger side next to the upper collar will help the seam lie flat. Notching the seam and trimming close to the corner also helps the collar to be smooth.

Neck facings

After stitching the facing in place, clip the seam to make the facing lie flat. Turn the seam toward the facing and stitch through the seam and facing. This helps the seam to lie flat and prevents the facing from peeping out and showing.

Tack the facing only at the shoulder seam and the zipper. Do not sew it down all the way around with stitches showing on the right side of the garment.

Sleeves

The set-in sleeve should be hemmed after it is sewn in. The underarm seam of the sleeve and bodice are sewn before the sleeve is put in. The underarm part of the seam should be stitched twice because it takes a lot of strain. Usually sleeve seams are not trimmed. Be sure to finish the edge of the seam if necessary because the sleeve seam is one of the first places to start raveling.

On dimona type sleeves the curve along the underarm seam needs to be reinforced with tape. Place the tape directly over the open seam. Stitch in place on each side, stitching through the seam and the tape on the wrong side. Then clip the seam to where the tape begins.

Waistline seams

Waistline seams take a lot of strain, so stitch the seam twice. You can use tape no wider than the seam to finish the edges of the seam to keep it from raveling.

Belts

The fabric used for covering a belt should be cut lengthwise on the fabric.

Hems

Finish the raw edge of the hem so it will not ravel. The stitches should be loose because this discourages breaking. The stitches should not show on the right side, and should be straight with the grain, not over ½ inch apart. Pass the needle straight under 1 or 2 threads of the fabric so the stitch will catch but be inconspicuous on the right side.

Sewing Machines

For economy, choose a machine that has only the features you need. An automatic zigzag machine is good for embroidery, decorative stitchery, seam finishing and buttonholes, and may use templates to produce different designs or patterns. If you are buying a zigzag machine test it to be sure that it will make the designs you want. Some zigzags have needles which swing in both directions, while others may swing only to the right or to the left. A wider variety of patterns and designs are possible when the needle swings both ways.

If you decide that you do not need the zigzag stitch, you can buy a straight stitch machine which usually costs less. You may need to buy separate attachments for button holes.

If you are short of room you may want to buy a portable which you can store when you aren't using it. A portable is also an inexpensive machine for a beginner who doesn't expect to sew a lot. Usually a sewing machine cabinet does not offer you a lot of storage space, but it brings the machine to a comfortable height and gives you a flat sewing surface.

Choose a machine with a smooth, glossy surface that will not cause glare. Check the position of the sewing machine lamp to make sure that it does not cause glare. Some portables may not have a lamp, but remember a supplemental source of light is needed in any case.

Your sewing machine should last for years and normally requires very little servicing. Choose the brand and dealer carefully so that if you do have problems you will be able to get service and spare parts. If you buy from a store in a nationwide chain you can be assured that there will be a dealer if you have to move to another town.

Check for these easy-to-use features before buying.

(1) Does the machine stitch backwards, and does the stitch-length control lock into position?

(2) Does the machine have a foot rest on the foot control?

(3) Are the upper tension markings easy to read?

(4) Is the lamp in an awkward position that it will burn you?

Check the machine for smooth operation.

(1) Is the bobbin easy to remove and replace?

(2) Does the machine start and run smooth and quietly?

(3) How easy is it to guide the material when stitching curves?

Check the design of the machine for long life.

(1) Is the cabinet well constructed?

(2) Are service and parts available?

(3) Is the wiring located where it will be pinched, is it protected against wear and oil drip?

(4) Are the cover plates easy to remove to clean and oil?

Care of your machine

Your machine will work better and last longer if you clean it and take good care of it.

A machine should be oiled every 8 hours of sewing. Apply one or two drops of machine oil in the points that are indicated in your instruction manual that came with your machine.

Check the belt to be sure that it is not too tight or loose. If the belt is too tight, it will wear out more quickly, if the belt is too loose shorten a little. Dust the area around the bobbin and under the inside of the machine, because dust and lint and even thread catches inside the bobbin case and causes the machine to operate inefficiently.

If the bottom and top stitch do not match, or if your thread keeps breaking, check the tension. Make sure that you are using the same size thread on both the top and bottom of the machine. Adjust the upper tension until the stitch is corrected, adjust the bobbin tension screw as a last resort.

Adjust the size of your stitch to suit the material, small stitches for sheer material, longer stitches for heavier fabrics.

You may find a seam guide attachment helpful because it helps you to keep all the seams the same size.

Always keep your instruction manual handy. If you don't have a cabinet drawer, keep it with your sewing accessories, or if you have a portable you might tape it to the inside of the machine cover. This manual contains important information that you might need and helpful information if you are having trouble with your stitch and tells you how to adjust it differently for different kinds of problems.

Pattern Selection
Select your pattern
Every pattern you buy adds to the cost of your clothing, so choose your patterns with care. Choose one with a style that will last for several years, has several variations, or one that you plan on using several times. Perhaps you can borrow patterns from a friend or neighbor, or share the costs of a pattern.

Choosing your figure type
Before choosing your pattern size first determine figure type. Patterns come in about seven figure types, young junior teen, junior, misses', misses' petite, women's, and half size.

Many patterns now come in several figure types, so be sure the pattern you choose is in your figure type. Poorly fitting clothes and alteration problems can arise when the pattern comes in the wrong figure type. Try to stick to your figure type. By choosing a pattern out of your figure type you are more likely to have to make alterations and the garment may not hang as it should. It is easier to add extra width at the hips than to make alterations at the bust, so if you have to choose between pattern sizes where one fits in the bust and is too small in the hips, choose the one that is too small in the hips. A total of 2 inches can be added in the hips without even slashing the pattern.

Young junior teen
This is designed for the pre-teen and teen with a developing figure whose waist is large in proportion to the bust. She is slightly taller than the junior petite but is shorter than the junior. The shoulder and hip widths will be about equal, and has just the beginning of bust development.

Junior
This is designed for a fully developed figure with a high firm bust. It is shorter and shorter waisted than misses', with narrow shoulders. It is slightly less narrow through the hips.

Junior petite
This is designed for a well developed figure that is smaller and shorter in scale than the junior size. The waist is small, and the waist length is shorter. The hips and bust are full. The shoulders are normal in width.

Misses'
This is designed for a fully developed, well proportioned figure with normal waist length and shoulder width. Lengths are short, medium, and tall, and styles range from the youthful to the mature.

Misses' petite

This is designed for the shorter misses' figure. It has a shorter waist length than misses' but larger than junior petite.

Women's

This is also designed for a fully developed, well proportioned figure with normal waist length and shoulder width. These styles are more suitable for the fuller figure and the older woman.

Half sizes

This is designed for women who have a misses figure but who are shorter. The waist and hips are larger, and the waist is shorter. The shoulders are also more narrow.

Choose your size on the following charts before you go shopping for your pattern.

Young junior teen sizes

size	5/6	7/8	9/10	11/12	13/14	15/16
bust	28	29	30½	32	33½	35
waist	22	23	24	25	26	27
hip	31	32	33½	35	36½	38
back waist length	13½	14	14½	15	15⅜	15⅜

Misses' petite sizes

size	6mp	8mp	10mp	12mp	14mp	16mp
bust	30½	31½	32½	34	36	38
waist	22½	23½	24½	26	27½	29½
hip	32½	33½	34½	36	38	40
back waist length	14½	14¾	15	15¼	15½	15¾

Women's sizes

size	38	40	42	44	46	48	50
bust	42	44	46	48	50	52	54
waist	34	36	38	40½	43	45½	48
hip	44	46	48	50	52	54	56
back waist length	17¼	17E	17½	17⅝	17¼	17⅞	18

Half sizes

size	10½	12½	14½	16½	18½	20½	22½	24½
bust	33	35	37	39	41	43	45	47
waist	26	28	30	32	34	36½	39	41½
hip	35	37	39	41	43	45½	48	50½
back waist length	15	15¼	15½	15¾	15⅞	16	16⅛	16¼

Junior sizes

size	5	7	9	11	13	15
bust	30	31	32	33½	35	37
waist	21½	22½	23½	24½	26	28
hip	32	33	34	35½	37	39
back waist length	15	15¼	15½	15¾	16	16¼

Junior petite sizes

size	3jp	5jp	7jp	9jp	11jp	13jp
bust	30½	31	32	33	34	35
waist	22	22½	23½	24½	25½	26½
back waist length	14	14½	14½	14¾	15	15¼

Misses' sizes

size	6	8	10	12	14	16	18	20
bust	30½	31½	32½	34	36	38	40	42
waist	22	23	24	25½	27	29	31	33
hip	32	33½	34½	36	38	40	42	44
back waist length	15½	15⅝	16	16¼	16½	16¾	17	17¼

Pattern Alterations

Minor alterations such as adding extra width at the hip, correcting the waist length in a dress, or moving darts, are usually possible without having all your body measurements. But if for some reason you are difficult to fit, if your measurements are different than those listed on the pattern, if you have a small bust or are short-waisted you may need to take more care in checking your pattern for proper measurements and fit. It is easy enough to check if darts are in the correct position just by holding the pattern piece up to your figure.

Before making any pattern alterations keep certain things in mind. The amount of ease allowance is not printed on a pattern, but this ease is necessary to allow for freedom of movement and comfort.

A pattern is cut on a perfect line matching the grain needed. This perfect grain is necessary to make sure that the fabric, seams, and garment will hang correctly.

The center back and center front are straight and at right angles to the floor.

The shoulder seams need to be at the proper slant and length in order to fit at the armhole without wrinkling, and strain lines.

The underarm seams must also be vertical and straight and the sleeve should be from the edge of the shoulder to the elbow and hang vertical and straight.

The hem should be straight and parallel to the floor unless the style is one with a curved hem, such as a gored skirt.

Bustline darts, when located at the side and front waistline point to, but do not extend beyond, the fullest part of the bust. Sleeve darts should be located at the elbow.

The waistline of the garment is at the natural waistline of the figure unless the design puts the waistline elsewhere. Strain lines and wrinkles will result if the waistline is incorrectly placed above or below the natural waistline.

All pattern alterations either add fullness or take fullness away. This means that if a pattern is too full through the bust, remove the fullness at the bust area of the pattern rather than at the side seam.

Alterations are better if not carried into the center back or center front because this affects the balance of the garment as well as the neckline. Avoid carrying alterations into the armholes and neckline unless absolutely necessary.

Width is added or subtracted through seams and darts, but if a pattern piece needs the length altered check to see where it indicates the change should be made.

The altered pattern piece must be flat when finished. The original pattern outline should be preserved if at all possible, otherwise the design may be affected.

When altering a pattern piece be sure to check what effect the change has on other pieces. For instance, if the bodice of a dress is made wider at the side seams it will also be necessary to make the skirt seams wider as well.

You can add up to 2 inches in the side seams, but if more is required you will have to use slash lines. Slash lines are drawn at right angles and parallel to the grain line.

You can determine if pattern pieces need alteration by comparing your body measurements to those of the pattern, or by fitting the pattern directly on your figure. But usually a combination of both methods are used since fit is also influenced by the placement, slant, and curve of seams and darts.

Once you have made alterations in a pattern for a specific brand of pattern, these alterations will be the same or similar to other styles of pattern in that brand for only that particular figure type. You can't go from junior to misses and make the same alterations.

Comparing your measurements with the measurements of the pattern

This is necessary if you are not fitting the pattern piece directly on your figure. Make only those measurements that are needed. For instance the sleeve measurement will not be needed as long as you are sure the sleeve is wide enough around the upper arm.

Measure the pattern pieces to be sure that enough ease allowance is allowed after seams and darts are made. Your body measurement plus ease allowance should equal the pattern measurement after space is taken for seams, darts, and tucks. If there is a difference between the pattern measurement and your body measurement the extra space will be the part that needs to be taken up or added during the alteration.

For proper fitting over the hips it is necessary to know if extra fullness is needed through the thighs or through the hips. If extra fullness is needed for hips through thighs, add it there. But if extra hip width is needed because of large buttocks or a large back hip curve then begin the alteration at the hips and extend it down past the buttocks.

The following is a guide for the ease allowance normally needed, although it will vary of course with the style and from pattern to pattern.

EASE ALLOWANCES

Bust - 3-4 inches total, with half in the front and half in the back.

Chest - the front usually has ¼ -½ inch, the back ½ -1 inch.

Bodice length - ¼ -½ inch.

Upper sleeve width - 2 to 3 inches.

Elbow - 1 inch.

Lower sleeve length - 1 inch for a slim sleeve, more for a full or larger sleeve.

Wrist - ½ inch for a slim sleeve, more for a fuller or larger sleeve.

Arm Length - ½ inch divided between the upper and lower arm.

Waist - ½ to 1 inch.

High hip circumference - 1 to 2 inches.

Full hip circumference - 2 to 3 inches.

Body measurements for this purpose are taken over a slip, not over a dress as other measurements are taken. The three basic measurements used in choosing your pattern size are waist, bust, and hips. These measurements are divided into front and back measurements for you to compare with the front and back pieces of the pattern. All measurements are taken snugly. Ease allowances are added later to the body measurement before comparing with the pattern measurements.

Make a table and measure all of the following measurements including the front bust, back bust, front hips, back hips, front waist and back waist.

Body Measurements

Shoulder length

Find the base of the neck by placing a cord around the neck so that the cord rests easily in a comfortable position. The neck base will be at this point at the side of the neck. The shoulder ends at the point where the top of the arm begins. The top of the arm will be the point that remains stationery when the arm is raised and lowered. Measure from the neck base to the end of the shoulder to get the shoulder length.

Front waist length

This is made in two ways. It is made at the center front of the neck down, allowing for the curve of the bust to the waist. The other measurement is made from the middle of the shoulder to the fullest point of the bust. Then measure from this fullest point of the bust down to the waise, allowing for bust curve.

Underarm waist length

This is made with the arm slightly raised, measuring from the armpit to the waistline. Then subtract 1 inch from this measurement.

Chest widths

This is made to measure the crease lines formed when the arms are down at rest at the sides. For the front measure 4 inches below the center front base of the neck; for the back measure 4 inches below the neck base at the center back.

Sleeve measurements

Upper arm - This is made over the fullest part of the arm. It is made halfway between the shoulder and elbow while the elbow is bent all the way up.

Elbow - Measure around the elbow while the arm is bent all the way up.

Lower arm - Measure around the arm at the point halfway between the elbow and the wrist.

Wrist - Measure around the wrist at the wrist bone.

Arm length - There are two measurements involved (1) from the end of the shoulder to the elbow bone. This is made on the outside edge of the arm while the elbow is bent slightly. (2) This is made from the elbow bone to the wrist with the bones bent slightly in.

High hip circumference

This is made 3 inches below the center front waistline and on a line parallel to the floor.

Skirt lengths

You need the front, back, and side skirt measurements. Wearing shoes of the same height that you normally wear, tie the tape measure around your waist with one end of the tape hanging down to the floor. Place the knot at the center front, and note the measurement of the tape hanging from your waist to the floor. Then move the knot to the left side, right side, and center back, and make the same measurement. Subtract from the length of that measurement the distance from the floor that you wish for your skirt length.

Now compare your measurements with the measurements of the pattern.

First locate the hip line and the bust line on the pattern pieces. Locate the hip line of the pattern piece by measuring 3 inches below the mark noting the natural waistline of the pattern. Do this also for the back piece. To locate the bust line first draw lines through the center of the waistline dart and then through the center of the underarm dart. Do the same on the front and back pieces.

The bust line of the pattern will be the point where these two lines intersect. For the back, place the pieces together at the side seam correctly, then draw the bust line marked on the front pieces through onto the back pieces.

Now add ease allowances to your body measurement, compare that to each corresponding pattern measurement. Any difference between the two measurements will be what is taken up or added by alteration.

Fitting the pattern onto your figure

Armhole and neckline pieces should be reinforced with scotch tape on the inside of the seam allowance to keep them from tearing. These two edges are then trimmed on the cutting line and clipped into the seam allowance but not into the pattern itself. Other pattern pieces are not trimmed. If the waistline of the skirt is curved it should also be taped and trimmed. Pin the pattern pieces together on the stitching line. All darts should also be pinned on the stitching line. The top two inches of the underarm seam are left unpinned to keep from tearing the pattern. Sleeves are not pinned into the pattern.

Wear the underclothes that you will be wearing with the garment. When fitting a jacket wear whatever you will be wearing under the jacket.

Check the fit of the bodice at the shoulders. If you see wrinkles or if the armhole is the wrong size, adjust the bodice.

Check the darts to be sure they point to the fullest part of the curve. If they have to be moved mark the actual point where the dart should end, then redraw the dart later. Check to make sure there is enough ease allowance. If the pattern is too large you can move the seamline to take up the extra. But if the pattern is too small make a mark exactly where it is too small.

Check the skirt to make sure the waist is in the right position and is the correct width.

If a side seam tends to be too tight or pull to the back through the hip line area, the skirt is too tight in the back. You can add extra allowance to the back seam for this.

If the darts poke out in the back where they taper and end, then the darts are too deep for the figure. The darts should be repinned to make a slightly more narrow dart and the extra fullness can then be taken off at the side seam.

REPAIRING CLOTHING

Mending rips, tears, and frayed seams can save a garment and prevent uneven wear. Do not delay the repair or you may ruin the garment. Underarm seams, pocket edge, buttons, buttonholes, and hems receive more wear than other spots and are most likely to wear out first.

Specific repair problems are discussed here as well as different kinds of repairs and their use.

Patches

There are several kinds of patches—hemmed, lapped, inset, three-cornered, machine, straddle, and rewoven. Each patch is designed for a different type and shape of hole or worn area. Some are sewn by machine while others are done by hand.

Patches should be cut on the straight of the goods, or if you are patching a faded worn article cut a patch from a hem or facing straight with the thread. Try to match the design of the fabric carefully when cutting the patch so that it sill not be noticeable. Iron-on patches may be used as well as sewn-on patches. If you cut or trim an iron-on patch, cut the corners on a curve to help them to adhere more securely to the fabric. A square corner doesn't last as long. For heavy duty use the iron-on patch can be stitched in place.

Hemmed patch-This is used for dresses, blouses, and work clothes. The stitching may be done on the machine if the stitches will not show much, for example on a patterned fabric.

Trim the torn area of the hole, cutting on lengthwise and crosswise threads. Clip each corner diagonally ¼ inch deep. Then turn the edge under ¼ inch to the wrong side, being careful not to stretch the material. Cut a patch of matching fabric 1 inch larger on all sides than the hole. Place the patch on the wrong side of the garment under the hole with the right side of the patch toward the wrong side of the garment. Pin the patch in place. Turn the garment right side out. Hem the edges of the hole to the patch. Use small stitches in matching thread so the stitches don't show. Now turn the garment to the wrong side. Turn under the edges of the patch ¼ inch and hem with fine stitches.

Three-corner patch-A small three-corner shaped tear can be patched in washable fabrics. If the fabric is not washable use a reinforced hand darn rather than a patch. Do this just like the hemmed patch. Just trim the tear to the smallest right angle possible. For larger three-corner tears, cut a patch that is 1 inch larger than the tear on all sides and shaped in a right angle. The patch is then applied just like the hemmed patch.

Machine patch-This is recommended for jeans, work clothes, and shirt sleeves as well as garments that require a strong patch.

Trim the hole on the crosswise and lengthwise yarns to form a rectangle or square. Clip the corners ⅜ inch. Then fold ¼ inch of the raw edge to the wrong side. The creases must meet neatly at the corners. Cut a patch about 2 inches larger on each side than the hole.

Center the patch under the hole with the right side of the patch against the wrong side of the garment. Place the patch so that the lengthwise direction matches that of the garment. Then pin or baste the patch in place. Machine stitch along the outside of the hole about ¼ inch from the creased edge of the hole. Be sure the stitch is deep enough at the corner to prevent further tearing or wear (Figure 54). Then make another row of machine stitching ¼ inch further in on the garment from the first row of stitching.

To reinforce the corner make a diagonal row of stitching just inside the corner as illustrated.

Turn the garment to the wrong side and trim the excess material away from the raw edges of the patch. Cut the corners at right angles. Press.

Iron-on patches-Be sure to buy the correct color, size, and the right material to suit the garment. For jeans and other items that receive heavy and rough wear or frequent washings, the iron-on patch can be sewn in place around the edges. Be sure to trim the corners in a curve if you cut or trim the patch.

Inset patch-This is used for finer fabrics and may be sewn in by hand or machine. Turn the patch to the smallest possible square or rectangle. Clip each corner diagonally ¼ inch. Turn the edges under ¼ inch and press, being careful to not stretch the fabric.

The patch is cut ½ inch larger on all sides than the hole. Then press ½ inch on all sides of the patch so that it fits the hole perfectly. Place the patch on the wrong side of the hole, with the right side of the patch showing on the outside of the garment. Then sew the edges of the hole and the patch along the folded line where you creased the patch. You may stitch by hand or machines. Then press the seams open, and overcase the raw edges of the seam to keep them from raveling. The seam does not show on the right side but looks very neat.

Darned-in patch-This inconspicuous patch is fairly sturdy, and good for large tears in wool and other heavy wool-like fabrics.

Cut the patch to fit the hole exactly. Baste a piece of net or other fabric as a lightweight reinforcement to the back of the patch. Fit the patch in the hole with right side up and baste to the garment. Then using either a dull matching thread or yarns from the garment, darn each of the sides of the patch in the direction of the fabric grain. Darn over the corners twice to reinforce the corners. If the stitches do not begin and end in a straight line they will be less conspicuous. Trim away the excess material along the edges of the reinforcement. Remove any basting stitches that show on the right side of the garment.

Woven-in or reweave patch

This is suitable for tweedy, loosely woven fabrics and wools because the patch is difficult to find. It is good for cigarette burns and moth balls.

On the garment to be patched place a pin at each corner to form a square or rectangle of the area to be patched. Then clip out and pull one yarn on each of the sides of the area marked by the pins. Make sure the pulled yarns meet at the corners to form a square or rectangle (Figure 1). Then cut a patch from matching fabric that is 1 inch larger on all sides than the hole to be patched. Be sure the lengthwise and crosswise yarns of the patch match those of the garment. Ravel the yarns from the edges of the patch until the patch matches the hole perfectly. Pin the patch on the right side of the garment to cover the hole. Using a small crochet hook pull the raveled yarns of the patch through to the wrong side, drawing the raveled yarns through the hole left by the yarn that you pulled from the garment. Begin by drawing one yarn at each corner to hold the patch in place. Take fine hemming stitches along the line the yarns were pulled through to hold them in place, using a thread that is a shade darker than the fabric.

Darning by hand

There are several kinds of darns including the diagonal darn, straight darn, three-cornered darn, plain darn, and patterned darn, but all types of darns have the same general principles.

The thread used must blend into the fabric without showing. Pull yarns from the garment's seams or hems, or from matching scraps of material. Use lengthwise yarns for darning lengthwise and crosswise yarns for darning crosswise. This helps the yarn to blend into the fabric so the darn doesn't show. If no matching yarns are available, use a dull darning thread or embroidery thread a shade darker than the fabric. Sweaters often come with yarn and extra buttons; store these in a safe place because you may need the yarn for darning.

You may want to put a piece of material on the wrong side of the tear to reinforce the area of strain.

Use a short thread when darning because a long thread as it is pulled through may wear holes in the fabric or wear out the thread.

Start and finish ¼ inch beyond the end of the tear in each direction.

Work on the right side of the fabric using fine stitches that aren't pulled too tight or too loose. The fabric should always be flat underneath the stitch, and should not be allowed to pucker. Keep the rows of stitches in line with the threads in the fabric. When you change directions do not pull the thread so tightly that you stretch the fabric. Notice in Figures 2-6 how the needle is inserted under and over the threads in the fabric for each stitch. This makes the stitch less conspicuous.

The end and beginning of the darn should run unevenly into the fabric so that the darn is not so conspicious.

Steam press the darn when you are finished.

Different kinds of darns are used for tears and cuts than for snags and small holes. For tears and cuts use the straight, diagonal, and three-cornered darn. Use the diagonal darn for diagonal tears, the straight darn for straight tears and cuts, and the three-cornered darn for L shaped tears and cuts.

For snags and holes use the plain or patterned darn (Figure 5 and 6) and leave the hole round but trim off any jagged edges. Your choice of a plain or patterned darn depends on the texture and pattern of the fabric you are repairing. For a nubby, more textured fabric the patterned darn is better because it will come closer to matching the texture and weave of the fabric. Fill in the lengthwise threads as illustrated. Then fill in

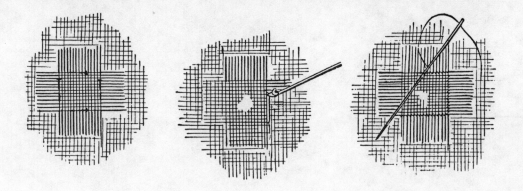

Fig. 1

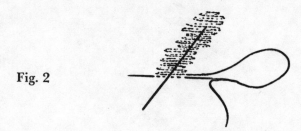

Fig. 2

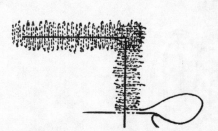

Fig. 3

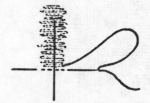

Fig. 4

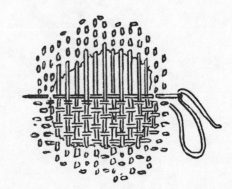

Fig. 5

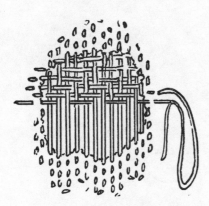

Fig. 6

the crosswise threads. In the plain darn go under every other lengthwise thread alternating from one row to the next; in the patterned darn go under every other group of two threads, skipping one more or less so that the weaving is uniform on the lengthwise thread.

Try to repeat the weave of the material as you finish the crosswise threads.

Chain stitch darn for sweaters and knits

Use a fine matching color yarn a little smaller than the sweater. Do not trim the hole. Work crosswise, filling in the rows similar to the rows used in the knitting. Then beginning at the top of a knit rib to the left of the hole make chain stitches, catching each crosswise yarn a little beyond the end of the hole. Now make lengthwise rows of stitches over the hole. Then repeat the chain stitching as you did crosswise, but going in the lengthwise direction this time.

Seams

If you notice a seam is narrow, crooked, or poorly stitched, you can keep it from wearing out by running a row of machine stitching about 1/16 inch deeper than the original seam. If the edge of the seam is frayed or raveled use a zigzag stitch to keep it from raveling any more, or make a row of stitches near the cut edge of the seam.

Buttons and buttonholes

If a button has worn a hole underneath, you will want to repair this hole before sewing the button back on.

If the area underneath the button is worn or thin, you can sew an extra layer of material by hand behind the button before sewing the button in place. If a button was sewn on using a thread shank be sure to use one when you sew the button back on.

You can use a stay button on the back of the fabric under the button to protect the fabric from wear where the button is sewed on.

If a button receives excess strain, the fabric underneath the button can be reinforced with tape. This often happens at the bottom of a shirtwaist dress or a coat. Remove the buttons that need to be reinforced. Place a strip of tape from ½-⅝ inch wide on the underside of the material. Stitch the tape in place by machine so that the stitching does not show on the right side of the garment. Resew the buttons back in place.

If a buttonhole is raveling or showing wear, repair it using a buttonhole stitch. If the buttonhole has completely raveled out, machine stitch about ⅛ inch from the cut edge of the hole. Then finish the edge with the buttonhole stitch by hand.

A button can also be reinforced by using a thread shank to prevent puckering. Use a stay button on the back of the fabric. Then form your thread shank by holding the button up far enough to make the shank. Wind the thread round and round the threads that holds the button to the fabric. Fasten the end of the thread in place with several stitches.

Sleeves

Repairing the worn edge of a sleeve-This is done using the trimmed part of the sleeve as a facing so the sleeve will not be too short. If the sleeve has a lining, cut the stitches holding the two fabrics together. Carefully remove any sleeve buttons and any interfacings and set aside to reuse. Then trim the edge of the sleeve carefully on the line where it is showing wear, cutting straight with the threads in the fabric. Trim off any worn part on both the sleeve and the strip of material you trimmed off the sleeve. Use this strip of material as a facing and sew it back on

the sleeve. Pin the right side of the sleeve to the right cut of the facing. Match the seams and grain. Then machine stitch the sleeve and the facing together using no larger than a ⅛ inch seam. Press the seam open. Stitch on the right side of the sleeve through the facing and sleeve close to the seams. This will keep the seam from rolling. Replace any interfacing on the wrong side of the sleeve edge. Then fold and finish any vent corners as they were before. Tack the loose edge of the facing to the sleeve, stitching so the stitches do not show on the right side of the sleeve. Sew the lining back in place and replace any buttons.

You can also finish the edges of sleeves of sport coats and jacket with a contrasting fabric. For wool a suede-like fabric may be used. Cut a strip of the contrasting fabric, usually no wider than 1 inch. Handstitch the right side of the material to the right side of the sleeve on the bottom edge so the worn edge is hidden. Turn the raw end of the material to the inside of the sleeve, and stitch by hand. It looks very neat, and it looks more like a trim than a repair. Leather and leather-like fabrics are often too heavy to be used for this.

Repairing a rip in the placket of a sleeve-
The placket and the cuff are the first areas to show wear on a shirt. Rips in the placket should not be neglected because it will cause the sleeve to rip even more. Sew the tear up as a dart. If the ripped area is very small a straddle patch or a machine darned patch can be used.

Hems

If a hem is only coming loose part of the way, tie the threads to keep it from coming loose any further. Use matching thread to hem the loose area. If the whole hem has to be redone, stitch so that the stitches do not show on the right side. The needle should not pick up more than 1-2 threads of the fabric for each stitch.

Rumpled and lumpy hems in coats-
As lint collects in the corners and hem of a coat it causes the coat to have a lumpy hem. The fabric will become worn thin over these lumps, so the lint must be removed to prevent this from happening. Carefully open the hem, and remove the lint. Sew the hem back in place carefully.

Dangling threads

Do not pull and break any dangling threads. Use a needle to pull the thread to the inside of the seam or hem. Fasten the end of the thread securely in place with several small stitches.

Underwear

The fly placket in men's shorts will often tear at the bottom of the placket.

Cut a piece of iron-on interfacing to cover the tear, allowing a ½ inch allowance on each side. Then pull the two edges of the tear together and machine darn with the interfacing on the wrong side. Baste the placket end back in place and resew the crotch if torn. You can use ¼ inch wide cotton tape on the crotch seam and on the end of the placket before stitching back together. This tape will reinforce the seam.

Repairing elastic on underwear-
When elastic tears out in places it can be stitched back in place. Stretch the elastic as you stitch, and make as many rows of stitching as the rest of the elastic has. There will usually be at least two rows of stitching on narrow elastic, and perhaps more on wider elastic.

If elastic has completely lost its stretch, remove the old elastic, and replace it with a new piece. If underwear begins to fray at the edges, with threads hanging loose, finish the edge of the seam under the elastic. Clip the stitches holding the elastic to the material from the area that is frayed. Use a zigzag or a straight stitch, turning the raveled edge under ¼ inch. Sew the slastic back over the edge. Keeping all edges repaired should make the underwear last a very long time.

Straps on slips and bras-Broken straps on slips and bras can be either replaced or be repaired. To repair the broken ends of the strap place the right sides together, and stitch using a ¼ inch seam. Then using a zigzag or straight machine stitch, stitch ⅛ inch from the edge of the seam. This will keep the seam from raveling.

If a strap becomes twisted in the strap holder, clip the seam holding the strap around the holder. Straighten the strap. place through the holder and stitch back in place. If the holders are broken or bent out of shape remove the holder and sew the end of the strap to the top edge of the garment. The strap will not be adjustable but will be wearable. Worn or broken straps can be removed and replaced with a new strap. Straps are available at most dime stores.

Bras often become too small as the elastic bands shrink and wear out. If a bra becomes too small you can add extra length or fullness by buying one of the extensions sold in dime stores to add to the bra. The extension has hook and eyes and fastens to the end of the bra.

Mends in T shirts or undershirts-Rips and holes in T shirts and undershirts can be patched. The patch will show but at least the shirt will be wearable. Old shirts with rips or worn areas should be saved to be used as patches for other shirts.

Cut the patch ¼ inch larger on all sides than the hole. Place the patch over the hole and turn the edge of the patch under. Baste the patch in place by hand. Place the tissue paper under the edge of the patch as you sew to make it glide smoothly in the sewing machine and to keep it from puckering. Use a zigzag stitch. Rip the tissue paper out after the patch is sewn in place.

If the underarm seam of a T shirt is terribly worn with several holes you need an extensive patch in the form of a shield. Cut the patch to fit the underarm seam exactly in the shape of the seam, allowing for ¼ inch of seam to turn under. Then continue as for a regular patch on a T shirt.

Slacks

Repairing fly tears-This is usually not done on dress slacks, because the machine darning will show too much, but for work clothes or wearing around the house the slacks will be fine.

Clip the stitches in the seam so you can repair the torn or frayed edge of the pants. You may have to remove the stitches in the placket as well. Place iron-on interfacing to the back side of the hole. Then machine darn over the torn area. Following the grain of the material so the darn doesn't show very much sew the seam back up and tack the end of the placket back in place.

Men's trouser guard-These guards protect the bottom of the slacks from the wear and tear of rubbing against shoes. A guard is usually the same fabric or the same color in another fabric. Heavy cotton twill is good because it will take a lot of wear. If the fabric ravels easily press the edges under ¼ inch before stitching onto the slacks. The trouser guard is cut ⅝ inch wide, so add an extra ½ inch if you plan to turn the edges under. It should be long enough to reach around the edge of the trouser leg, adding extra if you turn the two ends under. Pin or baste the guard on the wrong side of the leg next to the edge where you will fold the hem or cuff up. Machine stitch the guard in place if you are using a cuff; hand stitch if you are only hemming the slacks.

Waistline adjustors on men's slacks and shorts-When the edges and ends of these tabs become frayed or ripped by metal prongs they can usually be repaired. Remove the tabs from the slacks, being careful not to rip the waistband. Trim the frayed and worn edges of the tabs. Turn the trimmed edges in to form a seam, and turn the two ends of the tab under to form a V shape. Stitch the tab on the edges and ends. Stitch the ends of the tabs back to the slacks. Install snap fasteners to the slacks and to the tab.

Repairing cuffs on slacks

The cuffs on slacks can be repaired four times without severely shortening the slacks. The fourth time the cuff is eliminated completely.

The first time the wear is on the bottom edge of the cuff, the second and third time make a false or French cuff.

First repair-Cut the tacking threads that hold the folded cuff in place. Remove the hem in the cuff and trim the worn fabric, cutting away as little as possible of the worn edge. Take the piece of material you have cut off and trim the worn area from it. Do not use the cut piece as a facing to sew back on the cuff to make the cuff longer. Place the facing with the raw edge toward the raw edge on the slacks with the right sides together. Stitch together, using a seam no wider than ⅛ inch. Turn the seam toward the facing and stitch

through the thickness of the seams and the facing. This prevents the seam from rolling. Machine stitch the top edge of the cuff back in place using a guard on the top edge of the hem as you stitch. This guard helps prevent wear on the hem of the cuff.

Second and third repairs-For these you are really making a half cuff on the back side of the cuff with a whole cuff on the outside.

Remove the tacking thread holding the cuff in place and the hem on the inside of the cuff.

You will then have three crease lines. Mark a chalk line 1¾ inches above the top crease. This chalk line will be the top of the new cuff. Form a fold along the top crease and baste to the chalk line. Then fold and baste along the second crease line to form the lower edge of the cuff. Press along these two basted lines. Turn the cut edge in so that it just meets the basted insife fold line. Do not let the two folded lines overlap because this will cause a ridge when the cuff is pkessed. Stitch the two folds together using a slipstitch. Tack the cuffs in place and sew a guard on by hand on the lower edge to protect it from wear.

Fourth repair-Now when the edge of the cuff wears out you must eliminate the cuff altogegher. Remove the stitches holding the cuff in place. Mark and trim the edge for a 1¾ inch hem. Sew a trouser guard in place to protect the hem from wear.

Worn Areas in Elbows, Knees and Seats

These can be reinforced before holes actually appear using a tailor's stitch called retreading. It can also be used in new clothing to prevent wearing and stretching.

Press the area to be repaired, then turn to the wrong side. Cut a piece of soft material, such as rayon lining, the shape and size to cover the area. Match the lengthwise and crosswise yarns with those of the garment. For knees of slacks press a crease to match the crease in the slacks. Beginning in the center, and working toward one side and then the other side, tack the end of your thread in place. Then make your retreading stitches ½ inch apart and rows ½ inch apart. The stitches should go diagonally with the rows in pairs. The direction of the stitches should follow the lengthwise grain of the fabric. Only tiny stitches appear on the right side. For the seat of slacks use one piece for each side of the seat. You may tack the reinforcement at the seam or take the seam apart and sew it up in the seam. To sew in the seam it is necessary to take the back seam apart, sew the reinforcement in place, then sew the seam back up.

Jackets

For the worn front edge of a jacket, clip the machine stitching holding the front edge to the facing a little above and a little below the worn area. Baste and turn in the frayed edge of the coat and the facing separately. This new line should be as straight as the original; it must not curve. Slipstitch the two layers back together and press. Then machine stitch on the exact line where the original machine stitching was. The new stitching should overlap with the old to make it less noticeable.

Pockets

Worn side pocket edge
If you repair the pocket before it is too frayed, it will be much easier than if you wait until the whole edge is frayed.

Clip the stitches holding the pocket and its facing together. Clip about ½ inch beyond the frayed edge. Turn the frayed edge back on the pocket and then on the pocket facing, keeping a straight pocket edge. Baste the pocket and facing back together. Slipstitch them together, and then press. Machine stitch, overlapping the new stitching with the old to make it less noticeable.

Holes in pocket linings
If the hole in the lining is small and at the bottom just make several rows of stitching to close the hole up. But if the hole is too deep or is not at the bottom, you need to patch the hole.

Pocket corners
Pocket corners should be backstitched at the end so they are held in place by two rows of stitching. If necessary you can reinforce the area under the pocket corner with seam tape before stitching or if it becomes worn.

Shirts

Mending the worn edge of a shirt collar
The worn line at the fold of the neckband is hidden because the height of the band hides it. Rip the collar from the neckband. If the top collar area is extremely worn, machine darn it to a piece of interfacing. Reverse the collar to the neck side of the band so the darned edge is hidden on the underside. Stitch the collar back in place. Press the collar with the seam side down inside the band. Stitch the inside neckband and back to the collar with top stitching.

Mending knit shirts
When a knit shirt tears or gives at the seams, the seam can be restitched about ⅛ inch in from the edge of the old seam. Stretch the fabric very slightly as you stitch so that the thread will be less likely to rip out. Refinish

the edge of the seam with a zigzag stitch or overcast the edge by hand. Knit collars and cuffs can also be repaired. Rip the neck edge and the top of the cuffs open. The worn or torn edges can be repaired by sewing a seam that will take in the worn edge so it doesn't show. Narrow elastic is set in the seam as you stitch so that the sewn edge will retain its elasticity. Stretch the material slightly as you stitch. Turn the collar or cuff right side out. Pull the seamed edges of the cuffs and ease the seamed edges underneath slightly so that it doesn't show. Press, then hand hem the bands back into place at the neck edge or cuff.

Plackets and pleats

Placket

A thread tack placed at the end of a continuous placket will help take strain off the placket and keep it from tearing. Make the thread tack so it doesn't show when the placket closed. The thread tack goes through the two edges of the placket that don't show when the placket is closed. Bring the thread up from the wrong side of the garment through the stitched edge of the placket, leaving about ¼ inch thread loose between the two edges of the placket. Cut the thread and tie in a secure knot in the end of the thread tack.

ALTERING CLOTHES

Before buying something that needs to be altered, examine it carefully to be sure that it can be altered and that you have the skill to do it. Altering should not be confused with remaking clothes. Clothes are remade if the style is to be changed or if the garment is much much too large and has to be taken apart completely and remade. All alterations must be made through seams and darts, so check to make sure there is enough fabric to work with. Will the old stitching line show if you let the seam out? Does the alteration go along with the design and lines of the garment? If at all possible buy a garment that fits correctly through the shoulders and bustline because this is one of the hardest places to alter. The width of the garment at the hips can be let out as long as the seams are large enough.

When a garment fits properly there should be no bulges, unwanted wrinkles or strain lines. All of these are indications of poor fit. Check the location of these wrinkles, bulges, and strain lines to determine where the alteration is to be made. If you can't find any indication of what is producing the problem then the garment is not fitted properly for your figure. To correct an improper fit you must let out seams and darts or take them up, using basting stitches until the garment fits properly.

Making alterations

If a one piece dress such as an A-line, or princess line has wrinkles at the waist this means it is too small through the upper hips. Let the seam out through the hips but make sure the dress hangs straight with the new seam.

If a one piece dress is too large, take in equal amounts in each side seam, basting and trying the dress on before stitching. It will probably be necessary to loosen the hem at the seam so you can take the seam up all the length of the dress.

Skirts and slacks waistline

If the waistline is too small or too large remove the waistband. If too small let out the seam, tapering almost to nothing over the hips. Then replace the waistband. If too large take the seams up equal amounts at each side until it fits. Do not let darts out or take them up to make a skirt or slacks fit; the darts are designed to taper from the waist where they take in the extra fullness needed down to the hips. If the zipper is in the side it will usually be necessary to remove the zipper to adjust the seam.

If the skirt or slacks are too small after letting out the seams, it may be possible to raise the skirt to get more fullness through the hips, if the hem is long enough to let out because this will shorten the skirt. If you raise the skirt, extend the darts to the new area to fit at the hips, move the zipper down, and trim the extra fabric from the top of the skirt. Then sew the waistband back in place. Slacks can be raised only if they are long enough in the crotch to allow for this since raising them will shorten the crotch. Make sure the side seams hang straight, and do not curve.

The darts must be in the correct place for you, and the correct width. If the darts are too deep they can be let out, so the side seams will take up the extra fullness. The darts should point to but not extend beyond the fullest part of the hips. If they are out of position they should be moved.

Hems

After altering a garment check the hem to be sure it is the correct length. If the garment has been taken in this will often make it shorter, and it may be necessary to let the hem out. The same thing is true of a dress. A matching binding may be used to lengthen the hem if necessary.

Shoulder seams

When altering the shoulder seam it is necessary to remove neck facings, sleeves, sleeve facings, and collars. If you are letting a shoulder seam out the collar must be large enough to cover the new area. Usually it is not

a good idea to let a collar out because it will not look very neat.

The slant of the shoulder seam can be incorrect or can be too long if it reaches over the edge of the shoulder to the arm. A shoulder seam may be but seldom is too narrow.

If the slant of the shoulder seam needs to be changed be sure there is enough allowance at the sleeve for your alteration. Be sure that taking up the shoulder seam will not shorten the garment too much. Check the neckline to be sure it will not be too tight when you take up the shoulder.

If the shoulder seam drops over the edge of the shoulder, use chalk to mark the edge of your shoulder, tapering to nothing at the underarm. Then rip out the sleeve, and repin on the chalk line you drew.

If the shoulder is too narrow, let the shoulder seam out about ¼ inch. Doublestitch the seam and finish the raw edge to be sure it will not rip or ravel out. You can also take the extra length of the shoulder seam up into any seam that runs lengthwise between the shoulder seam and the waistline. In blouses it is possible to make a row of gathers on the front seam, but not on the back, then take the back up in a shoulder dart. In some dresses this is possible but make sure it fits the design of the dress.

If you are taking up a shoulder seam, be sure to resew the shoulder dart to the correct length.

The Bodice

If the back is not wide enough the seams can be let out at the point where it is tight if the seam is wide enough. Be careful about letting out darts in the back of a one piece dress because the back dart runs from the widest part of the upper back to the beginning of the hips. Be sure to keep this balance if you alter this dart.

If the waist length is too short, it can be let out at the waistline seam. If too long it can be taken up, but check the finished length to make sure the dress will not be too short.

If a dress is too tight at the waist it can be taken apart at the waistline seam and let out evenly between the seams. but if the dress is too large at the waistline be sure to divide the space taken up into the seams. Avoid altering darts that have the correct shape, to preserve the design and balance of the dress.

If the front of the dress pulls tightly over the bust or has strain lines running diagonally from the bust to the waistline, adjust it at the side or waistline darts. First check the darts in the side to make sure they are placed correctly and are the right depth for you. If they are the right depth for you they will not be too full at the point where the dart ends and your bust begins. If there darts are correct, then let out the side seams, and take up the fullness in the waistline dart.

Sleeves

If sleeves are too short the hem can be let out, or the edge can be faced if necessary. In long fitted sleeves check the elbow darts to be sure they are in the correct place for your elbow.

Strain lines at the upper cap of the sleeve indicate it is too narrow, so the seam has to be let out. Rip out the seam, move the raw edge of the sleeve in from the edge of the shoulder seam as much as the sleeve seam will allow, about ¼ inch or more. Be sure the new stitching line on the sleeve is in line with the old stitching line of the bodice because if you move the seam line of the bodice and shoulder they will fit improperly. Stitch the new seam,

finishing the edges if necessary to keep it from raveling or ripping out.

If the armhole is too tight you can let it out in one of two ways. In the first method rip the sleeve seam out and reser the sleeve back in the opening. Stitch the new seam as close to the caw edge as possible, perhaps ¼ inch wide seam. Then stitch a second time to reinforce. This lets the sleeve and bodice out enough that it shouldn't be too tight. If the garment is wide enough across the shoulder and chest you can try a second method which makes a deeper seam. Rip the sleeve out from the armhole. Set the sleeve deeper into the armhole of the garment, and stitch, clipping the seam to help it to lie flat. Some of the gathers and ease can be let out at the top of the sleeve so that the sleeve fits the larger armhole.

If wrinkles occur from the shoulder seam to the underarm at the armhole, this means that the sleeve cap is too low. Rip out the sleeve seam in the upper half of the sleeve and reset the sleeve in the seam, using a smaller seam allowance. Be sure to make the new and old seam overlap evenly so there will be no gap where one seam is larger than the other.

REMAKING CLOTHES

There are two reasons for remaking clothes: if the garment is too large to be altered; if it is out of date or to change the style.

Skirts and slacks are difficult to update. Now skirts are made wider, usually without kick pleats. Slacks too are much wider and straighter in the legs and are no longer tapered. Narrow slacks cannot be made wider or straight unless they are several sizes too large.

Remaking a skirt

Take the waistband off. It is usually necessary to take the zipper out also. Then fit the front and back of the skirt, making seams and darts to take up the extra fullness. If the skirt has a center front and center back seam some of the extra fullness can be taken up there also. Baste the darts in place and trim the edges until each piece fits. Be sure you allow enough for seam allowance and for ease allowance in fitting. Half the extra fullness should be trimmed off each seam of each piece, or ⅛ off each seam if the center front and back seams are taken up. Be sure you keep the original shape of the garment. Then sew the pieces back together. Sew the zipper back and replace the waistband. If the skirt has side pockets, be very careful about taking too much off the sides, because this will throw the pocket off balance.

Remaking slacks

The remaking of slacks is the same for skirts except the slacks must fit at the crotch. Be careful about taking too much fullness in the side seams and darts because this can cause the slacks to pull higher and cause the crotch to be too short. Slacks should not poke out across the hips or at the darts.

If slacks are too long in the crotch, the hem will need to be ripped at the inside leg seam. Then rip the inside leg seam out, and baste on the new seamline. Try the slacks on to be sure you have the crotch the correct length. Then stitch on the new seamline and trim the seam to ⅝ inch. Finish the edges of the seam if they are likely to ravel. Restitch the hem at the inside leg seam.

If the slacks are too short in the crotch you can let them out a little, only as much as the seam allowance allows. You can sew an insert between the seam at the crotch, but it may show, depending on how wide the insert is and how well it matches the slacks. The insert method is only for work pants and slacks worn around the house, not for dress slacks because of its tendency to show. The insert should be of matching fabric if possible, or the same color fabric, and should be cut on the bias. It should be wide enough to allow for a ⅝ inch seam on each side plus about 2 or 3 inches to widen the crotch, making it 4¼ -4½ inches wide. It should be long enough to extend comfortably through the crotch area and several inches down the leg seam. The length depends on the size of the slacks but should be 6 inches at least.

Rip the crotch seam an inch beyond where you will be sewing the insert in Working on one seam at a time, pin the insert over the ripped edges of the crotch seam. The insert tapers from the crotch seam to almost nothing further down the side seam, with the right side of the insert and the slacks together. Pin along the other seam. Then sew one side of the insert in place at a time, tapering the seams so the insert ends neatly where the seam is ripped open.

Remaking a dress

If the dress fits through the neck and armholes it will not be necessary to remove the collar, neck and sleeve facings, or sleeves. A neckline can only be made smaller by taking a center back or center front seam up as long as that doesn't make the dress too tight through the bust or back. A neckline can be made larger by taking a larger seam at the neckline. A neckline that is too deep, wide, or low cannot be corrected. If the dress is too large in the armhole and at the underarm seams you need only take the side seams up if the dress doesn't have sleeves. Rip the tacking holding the sleeve facing in place at the underarm seam and the hem at the bottom of the dress. Then take the side seams up equal amounts on both sides. Trim the side seams to ⅝ inch wide. Do not take the side seams up so much that it changes the shape of the dress. Remember that the seam must be straight, not curved. Finish the seam edge if it is likely to ravel. Tack the facing back in place and restitch the hem.

If it is necessary to take up extra fullness into the bustline darts you will need to rip out the underarm seam enough to do so. Then when the new dart is completed, restitch the underarm seam.

If the back neckline of a dress is too large and gapes open, it can fit better by adjusting the center back seam. This is often necessary when a dress is very large because all the extra width cannot be taken up in the side seams. Rip the collar or neck facings loose at the center back seam. This is possible with blouses also. The zipper will have to be taken out if it is in the center back seam. Take up the center back seam enough to keep the neckline from gaping, but don't take up the seam so much that the dress will be too tight through the upper back and shoulders. Replace the neck facings and zipper. If the collar ends at the front of the dress you will have to rip the collar loose and restitch it because it will now be too large to fit the back neck opening. Restitch the collar or replace the neck facing at the back center seam.

For dresses with a fitted waist the waistline is often too long or the dress may be too wide at the waist. Take the dress apart at the waistline and then fit the bodice of the dress to your figure, making any changes that are necessary. If the bodice needs to be made shorter, allow for the seam before trimming and the ease allowance recommended. Then fit the skirt to the bodice, taking it up as needed. Usually you take the side seams of the skirt up as much as the bodice to keep it balanced.

Restitch any tucks, pleats, or gathers in the skirt to fit the new waistline. Then restitch to the bodice of the dress. Check the length of the dress because it will probably be shorter now. Make any changes in the length of the hem as needed.

If the sleeves and armholes are too large, the dress is usually much too wide and you can remake the dress at the armhole and underarm side seams. Rip the sleeves or armhole facing out of the dress. Then take up the underarm seam the amount needed, but remember to leave enough room for the ease allowance recommended. Try the dress on to make sure the new armhole is comfortable. It should be loose enough to allow for movement, and the underarm seam should not dig into the skin or be tight.

Long sleeves with cuffs

If a blouse or dress is too long you will need to rip the cuff out. You cannot just turn the cuff under since this would interfere with the buttons. Trim the edge of the sleeve the amount needed, leaving ⅝ inch seam for a seam allowance. Stitch any gathers or pleats back in the edge of the sleeve. If you cut as much as 3 or 4 inches off the sleeve you may need to move the placket opening up because the opening will not be as long as it was. Resew the cuff back on the edge of the sleeve.

Remaking blouses

A blouse is remade like a dress, and the method you use depends on how large the blouse is. If it is too wide in the sleeve and under the arm, follow the method for dresses. If the blouse is too large all over, try to make it smaller at the center back seam or the front opening.

If a blouse overlaps too much at the front opening and is too large in the front at the neck, it is possible to make it smaller if the buttonholes can be moved over. Loosen the collar or neck facing at the front edges. Remove the buttons on the front opening, turn the raw edge back the needed amount, and press the edge in place. Trim the edge with the buttonholes, leaving ⅝ inch for a seam allowance. It must be trimmed enough to completely remove the old buttonholes and still have room for new buttonholes without the blouse being too tight. Then take a piece of facing, placing the right sides together on the edge where the buttonholes were and sew a ⅝ inch seam. Then sew the edge of the collar or facing back in place at the neck edge, before turning the facing to the back side. Press the facing flat. Make new buttonholes on the front edge. Sew the buttons back on.

Ladies' suits, jackets, and blazers

Usually if a jacket is much too large it has excess in the front and back shoulders and the neckline.

Remove the lining and neck and front facings carefully from the jacket. Then take the jacket apart at the seams required to adjust the fit. Remember to divide the amount of fullness that you take up equally between the two sides. Be careful to preserve the cut and original design of the jacket . Make the armhole and neck facings larger or smaller as needed. Trim all the seams to ½ inch. Then finish the edges of the seam as needed. Do not make sleeves too tight, allowing for the bulk of the dress or blouse that will be underneath it. When you have completed the jacket try it on to be sure it fits well. Replace the sleeves and facings. Restitch the hem as needed. Take the lining up so that it fits the jacket, then sew the lining back.

REMOVING STAINS

Stains should be removed while they are fresh if possible, they become more difficult to remove as they set. The type of stain determines the type of strain remover you will use. There are greasy stains and non-greasy stains, although some stains are a combination. Some commercial stain removers handle both kinds of stains. Instructions for removing these types of stains as well as removing individual stains are given.

Even though a stain remover does not damage the fiber or fabric finish it may leave the stained area looking noticeable even after the stain is gone. It may cause bleeding or fading of dyes, shrinkage, or stretching of the fabric, or a loss of luster in the fiber. Fabrics that are difficult to treat include velvet, crepe, silk, gabardine, and rayon moires.

Before you apply a stain remover to a garment first test it on a sample of the material or if possible on a hidden section of the garment such as a seam, hem, the tail of a shirt or blouse, or the inside of a pocket. If the stain remover causes damage to the fabric or changes the appearance of the fabric, have the garment treated by a dry cleaner.

Heat will set many stains so that they are impossible to remove, so check for stains before you do laundry. Soiled areas should be pretreated before placing in the laundry. Make a paste of detergent and washer and rub or brush onto the soiled area. Full-strength liquid detergent can also be used to pretreat soiled areas. The same detergent that you use in the washer should be used. Detergents should not be mixed.

Using absorbent materials to remove stains

Some fresh stains (grease for example) can be removed using cornmeal, talc, cornstarch, or powdered chalk. Spread the powder over the stain before it has a chance to dry. Then as the powder absorbs the stain, remove the soiled powder and replace with fresh powder until the stain is absorbed. You can brush, shake, or vacuum the powder off the stain. This is a difficult method to use on some dark colored items because the white powder cannot be completely removed and leaves an area as conspicuous as the stain.

Absorbent cloth, paper, and sponges can be used to soak up a fresh stain before it soaks into the fabric. The more staining agent that is soaked up, the smaller the stain will be and easier to handle. This is good for fabrics that absorb stains slowly, such as heavy coats and even upholstered furniture and rugs.

If the stain is a greasy one you can remove the stain by adding a little water to the stain and repeating until the stain is removed, using an absorbent material.

Using soaps and detergents to remove stains

For surface stains rub soap, detergent or liquid detergent into the stain. Then rinse the stained area or wash as you usually would. If the stain is deeply imbedded, work the soap or detergent into the stained area. This is done not by rubbing but by bending the yarns or fibers of the stained area so the detergent works into the stain. Hold the fabric in both hands and work the stained area back and forth between your thumbs. On items that cannot be bent easily or on wool that must be treated gently, work the detergent into the stain with the edge of the bowl of a spoon.

Nonwashable articles can be treated with soap or detergent in the same way. Use as little soap or detergent as possible because the excess will be difficult to wash out. Dilute liquid detergents with an equal amount of water before applying to a non-washable item.

After working the detergent or soap into the stain, rinse the area with a sponge dampened in cool water or by forcing water through the stain with a syringe. If alcohol is safe to use on the fabric, use it instead of water to rinse the stain. Alcohol dries quicker and rinses the soap or detergent out easier.

Using a solvent

Solvents must be used with care. They are poisonous if swallowed or if the vapors are inhaled. Some are also flammable.

Be careful how you dispose of clothes and paper that contain solvents and other chemical removers, since they can be poisonous. Do not place them in a strash can incinerator. All dishes or utensils used with these should be stored and labeled, where small children will not get to them and you will not forget and use them for cooking or other purpose.

Work out of doors if possible when using solvents, or open as many windows and doors as possible to allow the fumes to escape because they settle unless there is adequate forced ventilation. A fan can be used to blow the fumes towards a window or door. Children should not be allowed in a room where solvents are being used.

Use only a small amount of solvent at a time. Do not pour the solvent into an open bowl. If you spill solvent on your skin, wash it off immediately because it is caustic and burns.

When using flammable solvents do not store or use near open flames, gas pilot lights, and gas equipment, or where electrical equipment or static electricity might ignite a fire. Articles treated with a flammable solvent should not be placed in a washer or dryer.

These solvents will not damage or dissolve the fabric but may change the appearance of the stain so that it is still noticeable.

General methods of removing stains

Greasy stains

Washable fabrics-Soap or detergent will remove most greasy stains on washable articles. It may be necessary to let the detergent soak into the stain for several hours or possibly overnight before rinsing. Some greasy stains need the use of a grease solvent which will remove the stain even after the garment has been washed. Fabrics with special finishes (permanent press for example) require more work because the stain is harder to remove. If the stain has been set by age or heat, a yellow stain may remain with the use of a grease solvent. Chlorine or peroxygen bleach is used to remove yellow stains. Or if the fabric will not be damaged use a strong sodium perborate solution.

Nonwashable articles-On nonwashable fabrics the stain is sponged with the grease solvent and then dried. Repeat if necessary. If a yellow stain remains use one of the bleaches for washable fabrics.

Nongreasy stains

Stains set by age or heat may be impossible to remove. On washable garments sponge the stain with cool water or soak in cool water for 30 minutes or longer. Some stains may need soaking overnight. If soaking does not remove the stains, apply soap or detergent. If the stain is still present use a chlorine or peroxygen bleach. For nonwashable items sponge the stain with cool water or apply water to the stain with a syringe.

If the stain persists use soap or detergent. Chlorine or peroxygen bleach can also be used if the detergent doesn't remove the stain.

Combination stains

A combination stain is caused by both greasy and nongreasy substances. For washable articles treat as discussed under greasy stains. If a colored stain remains after the spot dries, use a chlorine or peroxygen bleach. For nonwashable articles treat like a nongreasy stain. If a colored stain remains after the spot dries use a chlorine or peroxygen bleach.

Using a chemical stain remover

Chemical stain removers include bleaches and color removers. Try a mild treatment first. Dampen the stain with cool water and place the stained area over a sponge, absorbent pad, or bowl. Dry removers are sprinkled over a stain while liquid ones should be applied with a medicine dropper. If the article is washable the stained area can be washed in a solution of the remover. Do not let the remover dry on the fabric. Keep the stain moist while the remover is on it. Then rinse the remover by sponging or rinsing in clear water. Nonwashable fabrics should be sponged (although they can be rinsed with a syringe) but do not let the wet area spread. If this mild treatment doesn't remove the stain, try a stronger treatment. For this, lengthen the treatment time, use a more concentrated solution of the remover or raise the temperature of the water or solution. The use of the stronger treatment increases the chance of damage to the fabric.

Bleaches are the most widely chemical stain remover but they are likely to damage fibers and fade dyes. Bleaches should not be placed in metal containers because they react with the elements in the metal and can cause damage to the fabric. There are three kinds of bleaches—chlorine, peroxygen, and color removers. Chlorine and peroxygen generally remove the same type of stains.

Chlorine bleaches are sold in liquid, powder or tablet form. Peroxygen bleaches include sodium perborate, potassium monopersulfate, and hydrogen peroxide. Sodium perborate is available at drug stores as a powder. Powdered bleaches sold under trade names contain sodium perborate and potassium monopersulfate. Hydrogen peroxide, 3% strength is sold in drug stores. Color removers are sold under trade names.

Using bleaches

Chlorine bleaches must be used with caution because they are harmful to some fabrics. It should not be used on silk, wool, spandex fibers, polyurethane foam, or fabrics with a special finish (including fabrics with shrinkage resistance, wrinkle resistance, crispness, sheen, or durable sculptured or embossed designs). If the label states that chlorine bleach is safe then it can be used. But fabrics with these resin finishes, including permanent press and wash and wear, often absorb and retain chlorine, causing them to weaken and turn yellow. Test all dyed fabrics for colorfastness before using chlorine bleach.

For washable fabrics combine 2 tablespoons liquid chlorine bleach with 1 quart of cool water. For powder or tablet form use the directions on the package. The solution is applied to small stains with a medicine dropper while large areas are soaked in the solution. Leave the bleach on the stain for 5-15 minutes, then rinse well with wate. Repeat if necessary. For a stronger treatment combine liquid bleach to 1 cup of cool water. For powder or tablet bleaches follow the directions on the package. Strong treatment for non-washables is not recommended. But the strong treatment outlined above can be used.

CHECKING THE QUALITY OF CLOTHING

It is important to check the quality of clothing before you buy because you can find both well-finished and poorly finished clothing in the same price range. Choosing the one that is well made will insure that it will last longer.

Be sure that you buy the proper size and allow for shrinkage when necessary. All knit undershirts and T-shirts shrink considerably, so buy a size larger than is needed, and it will shrink to the correct size. Another item that can always be expected to shrink is blue jeans, or any other item made of cotton denim. Blue jeans do not shrink quite as much crosswise from the crotch up, but the legs shrink considerably lengthwise. Buy a half or a full size larger than you need to be sure they will fit after shrinking. The legs should be longer than needed to allow for expected shrinkage, or you can buy those with a large hem so you can let the hem out later. If you buy a denim jacket make sure it has a little extra give around the chest area and closes easily without being too snug. The sleeves and bottom edge should have a hem that you can let out because the shrinkage is greater lengthwise than crosswise.

Remember that you cannot expect clothing to last well unless you give it the care it requires. Washing sweaters, cotton flannel, and nylon in hot water at a high temperature will shorten their life span because they will become pilled sooner and look shabby. The same thing happens when blue jeans and other denim items are washed in hot water and dried in a dryer—they shrink more than in the proper cool temperature.

The fiber content is also important in how well an item of clothing can be expected to wear. To check the wearability and durability of a fiber, check page 78· for the quality of fibers.

The cut of the garment

Patterns in fabrics should match at the seam lines. The nap or pile of corduroy, velvet, and other fabrics with one way nap, should run in the same direction in all pieces of the garment. If a pocket, belt, or waistband runs a different direction, the other pieces will reflect the light differently. All the pieces of the garment should be cut so that the yarns or ribs of the fabric hang straight rather than going uphill.

Seams

Seam allowances should be wide enough to withstand wear without fraying and coming apart. Many seams are now finished with a zigzag stitch, and the seam will not always be ⅝ inch wide. But the seam finish will keep the seam from ripping out. Certain seams on garments will not be finished. On many pairs of slacks all the seams are finished except those along the zipper opening. If the fabric is likely to fray, finish this seam yourself before wearing. Sheer fabrics may have French seams which will only be ⅛ to ¼ inch wide. If you choose a garment with wider seams you can let the seam out if necessary. But don't plan on letting any seams out of a permanent press item because the old seamline will always show and will not wash out as in other materials. Some fabrics such as velvet and satin will show the old stitch marks of a seam.

With loosely woven fabric and knits, the shoulder and waistline seams should be reinforced with tape. If the seams are not finished then finish them yourself at home, and don't put it off because the seams may fray badly in the wash.

Stitching

Check the stitches in the seams to make sure they are not too long. If the stitches are longer than they should be the seam will gape open and will wear out sooner. Check to make sure the seams are not sewn with a chain stitch, which is only satifactory for hems. If there is space between the stitches when you pull two pieces of the garment apart at the seam, the stitches are too long.

Linings

Check to be sure the lining fits comfortably within the garment. If the lining is not large enough to fit properly it will be uncomfortable. A lining in a dress or skirt should not be skimpy, and should come below the hipline, preferably to the hemline, although it is hemmed separately from the garment. The seams of linings, especially rayon, should be finished to prevent raveling. The lining of stretch fabric must also stretch.

Plackets and closures

Buttonholes should be cut with the grain of the fabric, and should have deep, close stitches so the edge will not pull or ravel out. Vertical buttonholes are commonly used because they are cheaper and faster to make but those made horizontal will stay closed better. If the pieces are cut on the bias or if the fabric has a diagonal weave the buttonhole should be horizontal.

Buttons, hooks and eyes, and snaps should be sewn tightly with no loose threads. If necessary, tighten these yourself before wearing the garment.

Snaps are not very practical for the front opening of a dress because they are likely to pop open easily.

Hems

The hem on a straight skirt should be 2½ inches wide. A flared skirt hem can be more narrow, about 1½ inches. Permanent press fabric hems cannot be let down, but in othere fabrics look for a large hem that can be let down if necessary.

Before buying

Before buying clothes check these points carefully to make sure the garment fits well.

All vertical seams must hang straight, without pulling or twisting.

Darts should be in the correct place for your figure. They should point toward but not beyond the fullest part of the body curves, the bust or the hips.

The waistline should be at your natural waistline unless the design is one that places it elsewhere.

The shoulder seams should fall at the center of the shoulder curve off into the arm. The slant of this seam should follow the slant of your shoulders.

The sleeves should be roomy enough to allow you to raise your arms comfortably. If it is too small under the arm, the seams will probably rip out. The sleeve should also be wide enough across the cap of the sleeve so that it doesn't bunch up when your arm is raised.

An ease allowance is provided to allow body movement although some designs and fabrics require less than others. Usually there should be about 3-4 inches in the bust including both front and back, ½ inch in the waist, 2-3 inches in the hips, and ¼ -½ inch in the length.

When buying knit garments try them on first. Check the label to be sure it is preshrunk. Check the loops on the garment to be sure that they are round and not stretched long and narrow—such stretched loops indicate that the garment has been strained out of shape.

The cuff placket should be wide enough to cover the opening when buttoned and should be cut on the grain.

Buying sweaters

It is a good idea to buy sweaters one size larger than your shirt or blouse size.

Seams and joinings should be closely stitched with no loose yarns or bulkiness and should be neat. They should be straight and even, not puckered and twisted.

A full fashioned sweater may not be any better quality than a fake full-fashioned one but perhaps you should understand the difference. The fake full-fashioned has threads that are added at the seams, such as the sleeve seam, while the full-fashioned has stitches that aren't separate but are part of the knit. Good quality usually has a card with extra yarn and buttons that may be needed for making a repair.

The knit of the yarn should be close and firm, loose ones will not last as well. The ribbing on the sleeves, neck, and body should be firm, even when you stretch it.

Buttonholes should be evenly spaced, finished well with no loose thread, and have deep stitches close together. Check the construction of the sweater to make sure it fits well at the shoulders. In poor quality sweaters the seam at the sleeve may be bulky.

Sweaters are made of wool or man-made fibers, usually acrylic. Wool is more likely to stretch during wear and while wet, while acrylic is likely to pile. A sweater with fuzzy yarn will become more fuzzy with age.

A moderately twisted yarn is more longer wearing than a loosely twisted one because it resists abrasion better. It also helps the yarn to resist pulling but may make the garment less soft. To remove severe pilling from a sweater place the sweater on a flat soft surface, take a straight razor or depilling tool and run over the pilled area. Don't press down on the razor as you move it.

Buying socks

Socks seldom have a chance to wear out before they either shrink or the tops stretch out of shape, with loose or pulled threads. Wool shrinks less than other fibers but it still stretches out of shape at the top. Washing or drying some synthetic fibers as well as wool will cause them to shrink, so check the washing instructions. If you buy a brand that offers a guarantee, be sure to save the sales slip. Nylon socks get runners which look unattractive but do not affect the wear. Support hose do not shrink as much as ordinary socks although the tops do stretch out of shape. Support hose are recommended by doctors for men with a lot of varicosity, and they do not cost anymore than other socks.

Wool socks can be darned when holes wear in them, but be sure you are buying 100% wool. Socks with 80% wool and 20% nylon are common because nylon is long wearing, sturdy, and shrinks less than wool. Check the label for the fabric content.

Socks should be at least ½ inch larger than the foot at the longest toe. If the socks do not have shrinkage control, buy a larger size to allow for shrinkage. Small children should have absorbent socks, such as cotton, rather than stretch socks.

Don't buy socks that are too bulky and thick to fit into the shoes.

Buying clothes at thrift shops

All thrift shop clothes are not bargains. The clothing may be stained or worn, and the quality may not always be the best. But with careful shopping you can find really good buys and buy more expensive clothes than you could otherwise afford.

There are two kinds of thrift shops, the ones run by charities and the ones run privately for profit. Usually the pcices in the privately owned stores are more expensive and are not as good bargains. In some of the larger thrift stores the stock changes with the season, with winter clothes on sale only in the fall and winter, and summer clothes only in stock from spring to summer. So become familiar with the thrift shops in your community. Prices vary from store to store, so become familiar with the stores and shop in several stores if you have to.

The sales people in thrift shops are extremely helpful. They know their stock and can help you find the best buy if you tell them what you are looking for.

Thrift stores run sales just like any other store, but they do not advertise their sales. You can sometimes save as much as 50% of the price marked on the clothes at sales.

The thing to remember is that the item must be worth what you are paying for it. The clothing market is now flooded with cheap, poor quality clothing, so naturally many of these items are showing up in thrift shops, but even at cheap prices these clothes aren't worth it. When buying clothes at thrift shops inspect for quality just as you would new clothing. Check for any stains, ripped or worn areas, especially at the seams. Try the garment on and be sure it fits. If major alterations are necessary, be sure you are prepared to take the time and care to do them. If alterations are necessary check the label to be sure it is not permanent press. If possible try to buy clothes that still have the tags on them. Without the tags you can only guess at the fiber content and the care the clothes require. You can also get a better idea of what the clothing is worth if the tag tells you the manufacturer's name. Check sweaters, knits, and woolens for pulled threads, pilling, or signs of matting.

Sometimes thrift shop items are priced too high, better dresses and coats, for example. For coats, you shouldn't pay more than ¼ of the new price of the coat.

Buying clothes from mill and factory outlets

Mill and factory outlets are especially common in the South. Unless the store is an actual outlet run by the factory or mill, it cannot really be considered an outlet. Many stores imply that they have lower prices because they buy directly from the mill. But few of them live up to this promise.

In many outlets, the quality of the merchandise is poor , irregular, and you usually cannot return defective items.

Towel and linen outlets may have some real bargains, but usually they charge by the pound rather than by the single item. This may sound like you are getting a bargain, but check to see how much each item is actually costing you. Check carefully to see if the towels are irregulars, if the selvage has pulled threads that will cause the towel not to wear as long. Also compare the price of the irregular to the ordinary price on sale.

Many stores, even discount stores,

have their own private brand or label of clothes. The quality of the clothes is not as good and the price is not always competitive, so check the quality very carefully and compare it with brand names. Poor workmanship and poor materials are more common among private brands. If the seams are terribly small (even if the edge is overcase or zigzagged) or if the size is very skimpy, these are signs of poor quality. Many inferior clothes are foreign made (this excludes the fine European knits and fine foreign woolens).

When buying clothes through a mail order house be very careful unless you have the opportunity to check the quality of the clothing before buying it.

You should also avoid buying clothes in dime stores. Clothes here are usually inferior private brands, and the quality is poor compared to what you are paying. The clothes are not even necessarily cheaper than what you would pay in a department store. Compare the prices carefully, don't assume the clothes will be cheaper. Avoid buying from budget stores in department stores. The merchandise can be inferior in quality and made from poor materials. For the quality of merchandise you are getting the clothing is expensive. You will find better quality products in the regular departments at sale prices that are better buys.

CHILDREN'S CLOTHING

Baby's clothing is sized by weight and height while toddlers' and pre-schoolers' are sized by weight, height, chest, and waist measurement.

Baby clothes

Baby clothes must be soft, lightweight and comfortable, with no stiff fabrics or rough trim. They should be warm, easy to care for, and well made. Clothes that open down the front are preferred to those that pull over the head. Knit fabrics are used for underclothes and sleeping clothes because they allow for ventilation and yet are warm. Woven fabrics are used for dressy and outerwear. Avoid any clothes that need ironing. Any fastener that does not scratch or irritate the baby can be used. A drawstring fastener should be used only at the bottom of clothing, never at the neck opening.

Since a baby grows so quickly, buy only the minimum of clothes, and avoid buying clothes during a growth spurt. (There is a growth spurt at 2-3 weeks and one at 2-3 months of age). Dresses and slacks should only be bought as you feel the baby can use them. Buying too far ahead may also mean that the clothing will never fit the baby.

A basic layette for a newborn baby includes,
  4-6 nightgowns, wrappers or kimonos
  4-6 shirts
  3-5 dozen diapers (the flannel are more absorbent and the stains will wash out better, the ones with the double seat and the single sides are preferred. Disposable diapers are expensive to use and some babies are allergic to the chemicals used on them.)
  2 pairs plastic waterproof pants
  2 cards diaper pins
  2-5 bibs if baby is bottle nursing
  1-2 lap pads
  2-3 receiving blankets
  1 outdoor blanket
  1-2 crib blankets
  1-2 mattress pads
  3-6 crib sheets
  1-3 towels
  2-3 washcloths
  1-2 dresses, 1-2 slips, and 1-2 sweater and bootee sets are optional.

Toddlers

Clothes for toddlers are cut full enough to fit the child while in diaper stage as well as the toddler who still has short legs and baby fat. Whey buying pants and shirts use the child's weight measurement, but for other clothes use the height measurement.

When children begin to grow taller and slimmer, their clothes are designed differently, using the height measurement, except for shirts which are measured by weight. When girls reach size 7 they then are classified into four categories: (1) regular, (2) slim, (3) chubby, (4) junior. Regular is for the straight undeveloped figure. Slim is for those more slender than the regular. Chubby is for a heavy undeveloped figure. Junior is for above 5' to about 5' ½" and the figure begins to develop.

Boys sizes 4-20 come in slim, regular, and husky. To find the size measure the height, but in determining the group, use the follgwing measurements;

slim - under 76 lbs.
regular - 76-82 lbs.
husky - 83-90 lbs.

Taking measurements

Height-Measure without shoes.

Weight-Weigh without shoes, in underwear.

Chest or bust -Measure under the arms around the fullest part of the chest or bust with the tape straight across the back.

Waist-For underwear and swimwear, measure without clothes around the body at the natural waistline. For pants measure over a shirt. The natural waistline is at the point where the body indents when the child bends the upper part of the body to the side.

Hip and seat measurement-Measure around the fullest part of the hips.

Inseam-Take a pair of pants that fit properly. Place the pants on a flat surface, and measure from the crotch seam to the bottom of the pants.

Sleeve length-Begin at the base of the prominent bone in the back of the neck. Measure along the shoulder, dowf the sleeve to the wrist.

Length-For the length measure from underneath the arm to the point desired as the length.

Waist length-Measure from the top bone at the back of the neck at the base to the natural waistline, then add ¼ inch.

Ease allowance

The ease is the extra room allowed for movement and comfort. Use the following guide to determine the ease allowance needed.

When buying a dress—add 3 inches to the bust or chest measurement, 1 inch to the waist measurement, add 2 inches to the hip measurement.

When buying a skirt—add 1 inch to the waist measurement, 2 inches to the hip measurement. For the length, measure from the waistline to the desired length.

When buying slacks—measure at the point where the child wears the top of his slacks and add 1 inch. For the length, measure where the top of the slacks will be at the side of the body down to the length desired. For the inseam measure a pair of slacks that fit well.

When buying a girls coat—add 6 inches to the chest measurement. For the length, measure from the base of the prominent bone at the center back of the neck to the length desired.

When buying a blouse—add 3 inches to the chest measurement. When buying a shirt for a boy add 4 inches to the chest measurement.

When buying a jacket for a boy or girl—add 6 inches to the chest measurement.

Checking for proper fit and comfort

Before buying clothes have the child

try them on. Check these points for fit and comfort.

The collar should be low enough to be comfortable. It should not gape or bend.

The shoulders should be roomy enough so that the arms can move without being tight across the back or chest, and the shoulder seam should remain in place rather than move around.

Sleeves should be roomy enough to allow for movement. When the arms are bent the sleeves should not be tight or bind at the upper arm. Cuffs should be slightly loose to allow for comfort. The cuffs or hems should be large enough to let out. Raglan sleeves are good because they are larger and allow more room for movement.

The waistline should be loose enough to allow for movement, and growth. Elastic in part of the waist will serve this purpose. But elastic should not make red marks on the skin.

Check the length to make sure that there are hems that can be let out if necessary. Remember when buying permanent press that the old hems and seams will show. Pants should not be so long that they go over the shoes and cause the child to trip. Shirts and blouses should be long enough that they tuck in at the waist and do not ride up, and yet allow a little extra length for growth.

When buying a garment that will be worn over other clothing have the child try it on with clothing, or allow for enough room for the bulk of the clothing.

Body suits are not recommended for small children. The extra bulk at the closure can be uncomfortable, and the binding in the leg openings can also be uncomfortable, especially if it becomes wadded up or folder over, and can be too tight and cause marks on the skin.

For children from 6 to 12 who are very active, clothing and fabric must be very strongly constructed and sturdy to withstand wear and tear. The points that receive the greatest wear should be reinforced, as well as buttons, buttonholes, edges of pockets and closures, sleeve and crotch seams. Trimming and fasteners must be securely fastened.

Simple uncluttered lines and firm evenly woven fabrics do not soil as easily and take more wear. Flat and soft seams prevent irritation.

Rainwear

The front should overlap enough at the opening to keep out drafts. There should be a fastener at the bottom of the front to keep the coat from blowing open.

Socks

Socks with nylon heel and toe takes more wear. Stretch socks allow for growth, but are not as absorbent. When buying stretch socks for children, be sure you buy the correct size. If you are buying for a size 7 foot, and the stretch socks fits sizes 5-7, buy the next size larger.

Knit underwear

Check the seams to be sure they are overcast and flat. The areas with elastic should not be so tight that it binds.

Sleepwear

Sturdy soft fabrics are best. Ribbing on the edges of the sleeves and legs helps keep out the cold. A double thickness at the crotch is preferred and should be cut deep enoough to prevent chafing.

Snowsuits

It must be roomy enough to fit over other clothing comfortably. The neck, or wrists and ankles all need ribbing which fits well to keep out drafts. A tightly woven fabric that has a water repellent finish will resist stain and soil. Check buttonholes and pockets to see if they are reinforced. The zipper must work easily and smoothly.

Shirts

Shirts for boys are sold by size based on chest and neck measurement or on height and chest measurement. They come in husky as well as regular.

Boys' size regular

size	6	8	10	12	14	16	18
neck	11	11½	12	12½	13	13½	14
chest	25	26½	28	29½	31½	33	34½
height	46	50	54	58	61	64	66

Choosing children's clothing

Clothes with let-out tucks are good because they allow room for growth. Avoid clothes that need ironing, or reserve them for dress-up events.

If you are buying used clothing take your tape measure along. Close the zipper or opening, place the garment on a flat surface and measure, allowing for the ease allowance.

Children's clothing must be comfortable and roomy enough to allow for activity. The color, design, and cut must be suitable for children. The pattern of the fabric should be in scale, such as small checks, plaids, prints, and dainty animal prints and floral designs. A printed fabric is less likely to show soil and wrinkles.

Clothes should be lightweight, never heavy and bulky. Avoid heavy stiff pockets, flaps, cuffs, and collars.

The underarm and leg seams should be large enough to allow for movement and to take strain better. Raglan sleeves will take more strain than set-in sleeves. Sleeve cuffs should be deep enough to allow them to be let out if necessary. Shoulder straps should be built up and adjustable. Tucks and pleats in the shoulder of shirts and blouses allow room for growth, and movement. A two piece set lasts longer than a one piece garment.

Buttons will take more strain if a thread shank is used because it is less likely to rip the material underneath.

To encourage a child to dress himself look for these features that make dressing easier—neck openings, clothes that are large, simple, easy to handle, front openings or deep plackets that slip over the head easily. Fasteners should be few in number and easily reached.

Large buttonholes are easier to manage as are slightly grooved, flat, smooth buttons, medium size is best. It should be easy to tell the front from the back of a garment. Slide fasteners should be easily opened and closed.

Clothes that can be worn year-round are more suitable. Spend more for the clothes that are worn the most, and spend less for the dressy clothes that are worn infrequently.

Clothes should not be bought too large to fit properly but should be bought with features that can allow hems and seams to be let out.

Cotton knits do shrink a little during the washing, so buy one size larger than needed. The weave of a cotton knit should have loops that are round and plump, not stretched into long thin loops because it will not wear as well.

Jeans and pants often come with double knees that will take wear a little better. A mixture of cotton with nylon or polyester is easy to launder and does not shrink as much.

If buying low cut western style jeans, measure for the waist measurement 1½ inches below the natural waistline.

Dresses that have no definite waistline allow more room for growth than ones with a regular waistline. Elastic insets at the waist of dresses, skirts, and pants will also allow a little room for growth.

Clothes that are nonflammable are preferred, especially for sleepwear. Hoods should not be fastened to coats or jackets because they cause injury if the hood becomes caught on a door knot or other object. A separate hood that buttons at the neck is better.

Infants' sizes

size	newborn	small	medium	large	extra large
months	0-3	6-9	12-18	24-30	36
height (in inches)	up to 25½	25½-27½	28-32	32½-36½	37
weight (in lbs.)	up to 14	15-19	20-26	27-32	33-36

Toddlers' sizes*

size	1	2	3	4
height (in inches)	29½-32	32½-35	35½-38	38½-41
weight (in lbs.)	23-27	28-31	32-36	37-40

* Toddlers 2, 3, and 4 are the same as childrens 2, 3 and 4.

Children's sizes

size	height	weight	chest	waist	hip
2	34	29	21	21½	
3	37	34	22	21	22½
4	40	39	23	21½	23½
5	43	44	24	22	24½
6	46	49	25	22½	25½
6x	48	54	25½	23	26½

Girls' sizes

size	7	8	10	12	14
chest	26	27	28½	30	32
waist	23	23½	24½	25½	26½
hips	27	28	30	32	34
height	50	52	56	58½	61
weight	60	67	83	95	107

Boys' sizes

size	height	weight
7	48	54
8	50	59
9	52	65
10	54	73
11	56	80
12	58	87
13	59	93-100
14	61	100
15	63½	107
16	64	115
17	65	121
18	66	126
19	67	132
20	68	138

Teen boys' sizes

size	16	18	20
chest	33½	35	36½
waist	28	29	30
hip	34	35½	37
height	64	66	68

SHOES-SELECTION AND CARE

Buying children's shoes

Buying shoes for children requires much care. Children's feet grow irregularly and in spurts. The chart listed below gives the average rate of change for shoes. But don't go absolutely by the chart. Check periodically to see if the shoes fit properly.

Average rate of foot growth for children

age	rate of size change
2-6 years	1-2 months
6-10 years	2-3 months
10-12 years	3-4 months

Poor fitting shoes can cause permanent injury to children's feet because the bones are still quite soft and can be squeezed into shoes that don't fit sometimes without the child being uncomfortable.

The shape of children's shoes should be straight. Check the sole to see if it is straight, or if it flares in or out.

Since children usually outgrow a shoe before it has a chance to wear out, it makes good sense to buy a well made, good fitting shoe in the medium price range. The most expensive shoes are not necessarily the best.

Buying shoes for babies

A baby's shoes gives it a feeling of security when standing, and provide a firm base to stand on.

Children who are not walking yet need a shoe with no heel, that has a flat, flexible sole with some stiffness. However babies need shoes that have a stiffer sole and a well made upper part.

Once a child begins walking he needs a shoe with a firmer sole and firmer heel base than the previous pair of shoes. A shoe with no arch is used because the fat pad in a baby's foot gradually disappears by 3-4 years of age.

Check the shoes to make sure that they are smooth inside, flexible enough to be comfortable, and large enough to allow the feet room to grow and move. A sole with a rough texture is better because it discourages slipping and falling.

Buying shoes

A shoe serves these purposes: allows room to grow, protects the foot, holds foot steady. The foot should not slip around in the shoe, yet it should allow for wiggle room and breathing room for the foot.

Poor fitting shoes can cause poor posture and difficulty in walking.

Measuring for proper fit and size

Have both feet measured every time you buy shoes, especially for children. The number of the shoe size does not mean much because the size varies from one manufacturer to another, but it does give you a point of reference to start from.

A shoe must fit on the sides, at the heels, toes, and the instep.

Be sure to wear the same type of sock trying on the shoes that you will wear with the shoes. The thickness of the sock makes a difference in whether the shoe fits or not.

The shoe should be ½-¾ inch larger than the longest toe. You can judge this by pressing on the toe and seeing if it is ½-¾ inch to the toe. Check the shape of the shoe to be sure it matches that of your feet.

The shape and thickness of the foot is involved as well as the length. Check to see if the width of the shoe is correct. The widest part of the foot is the ball. If you can pinch up the shoe at this widest point of the foot while standing up the shoe is wide enough. The shoe should be snug enough at this point but it should not bulge.

When a shoe fits correctly, the widest part of the shoe will be where the ball of the foot and the arch base of the foot meet. This means that the arch of the foot will fit that of the shoe. If the shoe and foot arch don't correspond the foot is not getting support and the shoe will be uncomfortable.

The upper part of the shoe should not gape open when the foot is bent. The sides of the shoe must not slip, or be loose and should not rub the ankle bone or heel. The heel must fit firmly and tightly so that the foot does not slip around. There should not be extra room between the back of the shoe and of the foot. There should not be enough room to insert your finger in the back of the shoe at the heel.

The toe space of the shoe should be wide and high enough to allow all toes to move. They should fit at the instep so that the shoe is not pulled or strained out of shape at the laces. The instep should allow for adequate circulation and complete freedom of movement.

When a shoe fits correctly, the widest part of the shoe will be where the ball of the foot and the arch base of the foot meet. This means that the arch of the foot will fit that of the shoe. If the shoe and foot arch don't correspond the foot is not getting support and the shoe will be uncomfortable.

The upper part of the shoe should not gape open when the foot is bent. The sides of the shoe must not slip, or be loose and should not rub the ankle bone or heel. The heel must fit firmly and tightly so that the foot does not slip around. There should not be extra room between the back of the shoe and of the foot. There should not be enough room to insert your finger in the back of the shoe at the heel.

The toe space of the shoe should be wide and high enough to allow all toes to move. They should fit at the instep so that the shoe is not pulled or strained out of shape at the laces. The instep should allow for adequate circulation and complete freedom of movement.

Checking the quality of shoes

Don't buy a certain style just because it is the fashion. The shoe must fit properly and be comfortable as well as look good. So check all these points in looking for good quality shoes.

A firm, flexible leather or synthetic sole that bends as the foot bends is important. If the sole is of a man-made material that is not flexible, then it will be uncomfortable. The upper part of the shoe should be pliable, comfortable to wear, and allow for some air circulation. A smooth lining that covers all the inside seams of the shoe and absorbes per-

spiration is important. A reinforced, well-molded rubber tipped heel to give proper support to the ankle is important, since the rubber tip absorbs shock and noise. The shoe should have no bulky stitching, and seams, raw edges, or exposed tacks. The inside of the shoe should be smooth with no wrinkles or ridges, and should be smooth all the way to the toes.

Check the shape of the foot to be sure it matches that of the shoes.

If shoes are so stiff and harsh or uncomfortable that they have to be broken in don't buy them. They will never truly be comfortable and well fitting.

Check to be sure that the upper part of the shoe is in line with the sole. Look at the back of the shoe, and see if the upper part is straight or twisted, with the sole.

Check to see if the heel counter is adequate. This is the stiff reinforcement on the sides and back of the shoe at the heel. This is made of different materials, including leather, man-made materials, and paper, depending on the price and quality of the shoe. The heel counter is important because it holds the foot securely in place. Soft shoes may not have heel counters.

Checking old shoes for fit and wear

Check periodically to see that shoes still fit properly. There should be ½ to ¾ inch of room beyond the tip of the longest toe to allow for comfort and growth. Check the feet for rough spots, red and rubbed places on the heels and toes, blisters, hardened or calloused spots. All these signs that the shoe does not fit properly.

Check to be sure the shoe is not too small. If a shoe is too short it will show more wear near the toe end. Check the heel and heel counter to see if they are worn unevenly or misshapen. Check for nails wearing through on the inside of the shoe. Other signs that are indications that the shoes are too short are: (1) the end of the shoe at the toe curls up, (2) the heel is pushed under, (3) if pink or red spots are on the toes just after removing the shoes, (4) if the toenail has made a crease in the upper lining of the toe. The sole should show more wear at the center.

The arch support may not be providing proper support if the heel or sole wears along the inside edges. This means the arch is weak. Shoes should show more wear at the back or outside line. The shoes may be too tight if the inside lining has formed pockets for the toes. If the shoe is too narrow it will show in several ways: (1) red spots appear on edges of feet, (2) the upper part of the shoe bulges out over the soles, (3) the sole shows wear on the outer edge.

If the shoe is too short from the heel to the balljoint, the shoe puckers or wrinkles near the ball of the foot. If a shoe is misshapen it means the size is incorrect. If the upper part of the shoe bulges over the sole this means the shoe is too narrow.

You should buy the best shoe that you can afford. Buying on sale will save you some money only if the style is suitable and the shoe is comfortable and fits properly.

Sneakers and soft shoes

Check the quality of sneakers by looking for the following points. The sole should be thick and spring back into shape after being bent. The heels should have a reinforced heel counter and the toe should have a toe bumper. These reduce wear on the toe and heel areas because usually these are the first places to wear out.

The insides should be cushioned with a built-in arch. Ventilation eyelets are good because they allow air circulation.

Soft shoes are frequently made with little depth in the toe area. The shoe then puts extra pressure against the toes which in turn causes the toe to wear out first. Deck shoes have thicker soles and more depth then sneakers.

Sneakers and soft shoes are subject to all the same rules of fitting as other shoes. A common mistake is to buy sneakers and soft shoes too small.

Sneakers should be washed and dried at a cool or medium temperature, but avoid using hot water and dryers because high temperatures cause the sneakers to shrink.

For children under 10 years old, don't invest a lot of money in expensive house shoes because they will outgrow them too quickly.

Chapter 4
Furnishings

Drapes

To measure for your drapes first decide where you want your drapes to end on the window. There are four lengths commonly used: to the sill, to the apron or where the window frame ends, to the baseboard, or to the floor. You should put your rod up before measuring and measure from the top of the rod. Measure from the bottom of the rod if you are using a valance, cornice, or if the drapes will be hung on rings.

Choosing a drapery material

Choose a fabric that will fall into graceful folds. If choosing a design be sure that the design will not be distorted or appear unattractive when the pleats are formed. A fabric that is colorfast to fading from sunlight may last longer.

Lined or unlined

Lined drapes hang better and also last longer because the lining protects the drapes from damage by sunlight.

Sateen, polished cotton, and muslin are all suitable as linings. Unlined drapes let more light in and reflect the texture of the material.

Measuring for your drapes

For the width, measure the width of the area to be covered and add 2 inches at each side for a hem. Decide how much fullness you want the drapes to have.

Drapes should be wide enough to hang in graceful folds. A full draw drape is wider than a side drape. The side drape should have a full width for each panel. If a traverse rod is used the draw drapes are 2 to 2½ times the width of the window. For very sheer fabrics it is better to have 2½ to 4 times the width.

So for the side drape you will have each panel the full width of the window plus your 2 inch hem on each side, or 4 inches for each panel. A side panel usually has 5 to 7 pleats.

For the draw drape you will want one half the width measurement of the space to be covered, plus a 2 inch hem on each side or 4 inches in all, plus the distance from rod to the wall, and the overlap at the center (usually 1½ inches for each panel). Add 4 to 6 inches for each pleat you plan to have.

For the length measure from where the drapes will begin at the top of the rod to where they will end. Add enough for a 3½ inch hem at both the top and the bottom.

If your drapes are unlined add 17 inches to the length measurement because unlined drapes have a double hem totaling 8 inches at both the top and the bottom plus a 1 inch heading at the top of the rod. In some materials you may prefer a double bottom hem in a lined drape.

The length of the drape must be in one strip, but the width can be made up of more than one strip if necessary. Allow several inches extra on each strip if the material is not pre-shrunk.

Figure how much fabric you will need of different widths so that you have this information on hand when you shop. In figuring, remember the drapes are cut length-wise. You will need the same amount of lining as fabric. When determining the amount of material you need, remember that selvages are trimmed off before the drapes are cut out.

Measuring for the crinoline

Crinoline, also called drapery Pelon, or buckram, is a strip of stiff interfacing 3-4 inches wide used at the top edge of the drape to help it keep its shape and hang better. You will need a strip for the top of each panel, which will be the width of the panel.

Cutting your drapes out

If your fabric is not preshrunk, do this at home, or if the fabric is not washable have it dry cleaned before cutting the drapes out.

Straighten the end of the material by pulling a thread to make the end straight. Then cut along the thread. Trim the selvages. Cut each length according to your measurement. Cut the lining the same size.

Constructing your drapes

Most of the stitching on drapes is done by hand because there is less chance of pulling the threads and puckering. Drapes look more professional when sewn by hand.

Stitch any strips of material together needed to make the width of each panel

Place the crinoline (a strip of stiff interfacing 3-4 inches wide) on the wrong side of the drape ½ inch below the top of the fabric. Fold the end of the crinoline over 2 inches in towards the center so the fold reinforces the edge of the drape(Figure 7). Baste the crinoline in place with long diagonal stitches, using a heavy duty thread that matches the drape. The stitches should be 2 to 2½ inches long and 2 inches apart, leaving the raw edges of the crinoline free (Figure 7). Turn the top edge of the drape down 3½ inches to form the hem. If you are using a

double hem turn it down twice. Baste ¼ inch above the raw edge of the hem and 2 inches in from each side of the hem. Trim the surplus fabric away from the corner of the hem, cutting to where the crinoline begins and to within ½ inch of the top. Turn the raw edge on the hem under and blind stitch. Press the clipped corners down to form a diagonal line even with the top of the hem and trim leaving ¼ inch (Figure 7). Press the ¼ inch seam allowance in at the trimmed corner. Turn the side hem in 2 inches and baste the mitered corner in place (Figure 7). Baste the side hems in place. Turn the raw edge under on the side hems and hem. Turn the 3½ inch hem up on the bottom of the panel. If you are using a double hem make two turns or thicknesses. Fold the corners in to form a diagonal line but do not trim. Stitch the hem and corners in place neatly.

Lining

Seam the widths of fabric together to form the panels for the lining. The seams in the lining must be in the same place as the seams in the drape. Press the top and side edges of the lining in ½ inch. Turn the bottom hem up and press. Then turn up again if you are making a double hem. Press and baste in place. Then stitch the hem on the sewing machine.

Putting the lining and drape together

Place the lining over the drape with the wrong sides together. Center the lining over the drape so that the spaces on the two sides are equal (about 1 inch each) and so the top of the lining fits very neatly at the bottom of the mitered top corner of the drape.

Before you do any stitching, smooth the lining down and make sure it fits well, allowing for the seams turned in on the edges.

The next step is to stitch the lining and drape together loosely down the center

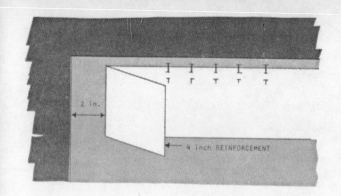

2 in.

◄— 4 inch REINFORCEMENT

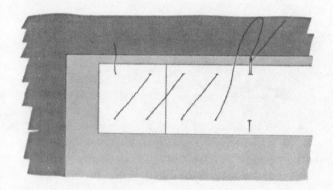

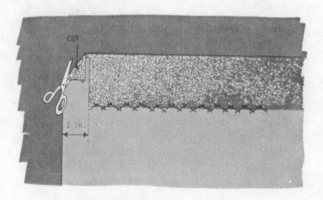

CUT

2 in.

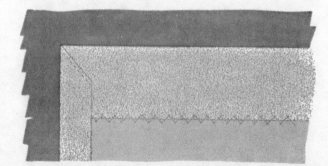

Fig. 7

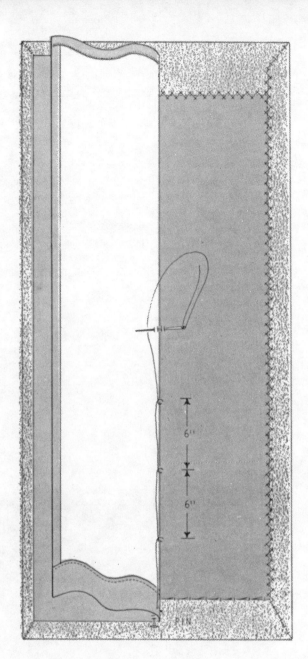

Fig. 8

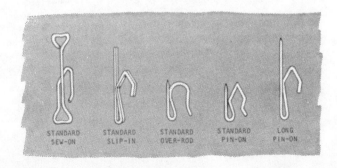

Fig. 9

STANDARD SEW-ON   STANDARD SLIP-IN   STANDARD OVER-ROD   STANDARD PIN-ON   LONG PIN-ON

lengthwise. Do this by folding the lining in half lengthwise with the right sides together *(Figure 8)*. Pin the lining to the drape along this line. Using a very loose stitch, stitch at 6 inch intervals using the buttonhole stitch. If the drapes are very heavy or very wide use 3 or more rows of this stitching instead of just one.

This attaches the lining to the drape so the pieces do not separate as the drape hangs.

Pin the lining all around the edges of the drape and stitch the lining to the edges of the drape using a slip stitch. Do the bottom hem first, then work up the sides. The drape should be flat on a table or flat surface while you do this stitching. If you are sewing weights between the two layers do this before sewing the two layers together.

Pleats

The box pleat and the French pleat (also called the pinch pleat) are the most commonly used pleats for drapes.

There is a commercial pleating tape sold that is sewn along the width of the drape and a special hook is attached which draws the drape up into pleats similar to the French pleat. If you use this tape, just stitch this tape to the wrong side of the drape at the top edge. Insert the hooks which have 3 sections, with a section going in each pleat. This does not look as professional as pleats made by hand.

Measuring for your pleats

The pleats begin 3 inches in from each end of the panel.

Each pleat of the draw drape covers one half of the width of the window, plus 3 inches for the return from the rod to the wall, and 3 inches for the overlap at the center, plus ½-1 inch for ease on each side of the panel. The total of this distance is what your pleated panel should measure. Subtract this width from the width of the unpleated panel, and the difference is the amount that you should take into pleats. 5 to 6 inches is enough for each pleat, so divide the distance to be pleated by 5 or 6. That will give you the number of pleats you will make.

Usually pleats are about 3-4 inches apart; the drapes will hang better if the pleats are not too far apart. You need to find the exact space between each pleat. The number of spaces between pleats will be one number less than the number of pleats because you start and end with a pleat. So divide the number of inches to be pleated by the number of spaces. The result will be the distance between pleats. Use a yardstick or ruler and place a pin where the pleats will begin and with the proper spacing between. Mark 3 inches in from the edges of the drape at each end of the panel for the return. Your first and last pleat will be at these points. Measure the space that the pleat will take up and place a pin at the beginning and the end of the pleat with the proper space between. Continue until you have indicated the placing of the pleats on the entire width of the panel. If the distance doesn't work out exactly move the pins very slightly so all the distance is taken up.

Making your pleats

Fold the edges of the drape so the pins for the pleat come together on the wrong side of the drape. Pin the pleat in place, and continue until all pleats are pinned in place. After pinning the pleats, measure to be sure your pleated drape is the correct width.

Machine stitch each pleat from the top to the bottom of the heading. For the French pleat stitch the pleat then divide the pleat into three smaller equal pleats. Stitch each of the three small pleats with two small stitches. Then pull the small pleats together and make several stitches at the bottom of the pleat to hold them together.

Choosing the correct hook

In Figure 9 are the five types of drapery hooks. The three larger hooks hold the drape on the rod as well as giving support to the head of the drapes. The two smaller hooks only hold the drape on the rod. The standard pin-on hook is used on a traverse rod, while the standard over-rod hook is for a stationery drape. The sew-on hook is not removed for cleaning while the others are.

Hanging your drapes

Press the drapes before you hang them. To help the drape form graceful permanent pleats form the pleats into the entire length of the drape and tie in several places. Beginning at the top of the drape, form the pleats with your fingers down the drape for about 12 inches. Then tie the pleats in place with an old strip of sheet or tape. Continue down the length of the drapes, tying the pleats in several places to hold them. Leave the drapes tied for several days. Then untie or remove the tape.

Using weights

Weights are used in the lower edge to help the fabric drape more gracefully. The number of weights and type used will vary with different fabrics. Some weights are used just at the corners or in line with each pleat. A yardage weight extends through the entire width of the panel and is tacked by hand at the fold of the hem. Weights can either be placed inside the hem or tacked on top of the hem so that the lining hides it.

MAKING QUILTS, COMFORTERS, AND SLEEPING BAGS

A quilt or comforter should be large enough to allow it to cover the sides and foot of the bed with enough length to tuck under the pillow or the foot of the bed.

They consist of three layers, the front and back pieces, and the interlining, which may be batting or layers of old blankets or sheets. In making a quilt, more emphasis is placed on the construction of the top piece, which is decorated by the use of patchwork, applique or embroidery to create the desired pattern. The top of the comforter is usually all one piece and may be pieced if necessary. It may be made from either solid or patterned fabric, but emphasis is not placed on the beauty of the comforter. Since the comforter is reversible the back should be as attractive as the front and possibly be made of similar material not necessarily the same color.

Down is too expensive to use for a comforter but you can salvage the down from older worn out comforters and use it for making another comforter if enough down is left.

Depending on the type of material you use for the top and back, a comforter can cost you as little as $12.00. If you are using old blankets or sheets rather than batting it will cost you about $5.00 less.

Batting

Both cotton and polyester batting are now available. Many people prefer polyester because it doesn't bunch up and get lumpy with wear as the cotton does.

Cotton batting comes in separate pieces or strips which are put side by side and not overlapped. Polyester batting is one large piece that can be trimmed to size with no seams. Polyester batting is also nonallergic. It comes in three thicknesses. The ½ inch thickness is sold for use in quilts, and the 1 and 1¼ inch thicknesses are usually used for comforters and sleeping bags. The ½ inch thickness comes in a variety of sizes and price ranges . The 1 and 1¼ inch thicknesses of batting for comforters are perhaps twice as expensive as the ½ inch thickness.

The fabric for the top and back of a comforter is made of a lightweight tightly woven fabric such as sateen, cotton or cotton blends.

All fabric that is used in making quilts and comforters should be preshrunk and colorfast. If the label on the fabric doesn't say the fabric is preshrunk, then preshrink it before beginning your quilt or comforter.

The top and bottom of a quilt seldom wears out. The quilting stitches may begin to come loose or the batting may become worn and lumpy with age. When this happens new batting is needed. Take the quilt apart and discard the old batting. Place batting between the top and bottom and then quilt the three layers back together.

Old blankets or old sheets can be used for the interlining rather than batting. If the interlining is pieced, machine stitch them together using a ⅜ inch seam, then press the seam open.

The top and bottom of a comforter wears out, and is likely to rip along the lines of machine stitching that holds the three layers together. When this happens the rips can be patched for some time but the comforter cannot be remade as the quilt is done.

The advantage of using cotton or polyester batting is that the quilt or comforter will be light in weight yet will provide adequate warmth, as well as providing a prettier quilted effect. Old sheets or blankets may provide more weight than is really needed. The thinner the lining is the closer the rows of quilting stitches can be together.

The top and bottom of a comforter can be pieced. When you measure for the comforter add ⅜ inch for each seam that will be needed.

When measuring for the quilt or comforter add about 5 inches to each end and side because the quilt stitching can take up a little of the fabric. Allow ½ inch on each of the four sides if you will be using seam binding on the edges.

Quilt patterns

There are several inexpensive sources of patterns for quilt making. Quilt patterns are now listed in many of the pattern catalogues located in fabric stores.

Quilting kits are sold in some needlecraft shops or through needlecraft catalogues, but the price of the kit is usually very high compared to using one of the patterns available or making your own. A quilt kit usually includes the top printed or stamped with the design to be appliqued or embroidered or pieced, as well as the guidelines for the quilting stitches. The contrasting material for the applique is included and you just cut out the pieces along the stamped lines. Thread for embroidery or the applique is usually not included. There are also kits sold for patchwork or crazy quilts but they are not really any more convenient to use than if you cut your own blocks of material. The patchwork quilt is a good way to use up scraps of material left over from sewing. Pieces of clothing may also be used as long as the fabric is not worn thin. When sewing patchwork pieces together by hand use No. 50 or 60 thread, when sewing by machine use No. 70.

Choosing your fabric

The best quality of material that you can afford should be used because a quilt or comforter can be expected to last for many years. A fabric with a firm close weave and soft texture is better, such as fine percale or broadcloth.

The backing should be a soft unstarched fabric that is similar in texture to the fabric for the top.

The directions given here are for quilts and comforters. The only difference is that the comforter can be sewn by machine rather than by hand. If you do not wish to make the quilting stitches, use tacking threads to hold the three layers together.

Preparing the backing

The backing is made up of several widths of material sewn together. It is usually made up of one width of material as the center with a smaller strip on each side of the center strip. The two side strips must be equal in size. Remove the selvages before sewing the strips together. The backing is usually made a little larger than the top. If you do not plan on sewing binding on the edges, you can bring the edges of the backing over the top for a binding. The backing should be cut 3 inches larger on all edges than the top if it is to be used as a binding.

Marking the quilting pattern

The quilting pattern sets the guidelines that are drawn for the quilting lines. The quilting pattern can range from very simple to very intricate and complicated. Usually the quilting pattern corresponds to the pattern of the quilt top. If the quilt top contains flowers, leaves, circles, or other patterns, these designs are repeated in the quilting pattern. Usually the quilting pattern for a crazy or a hit-and-miss patchwork quilt is very simple. The quilt stitching is done about ⅛ inch in from each seam of each square, and in the center of each square. If the quilt consists of both plain and pieced blocks the plain blocks can be quilted more elaborately than the pieced ones.

A plain over-all pattern such as diamonds or diagonal lines is very attractive. The directions of the lines can be changed for variation. Perforated quilting patterns are available to draw the quilting lines onto your quilt.

You can mark the quilting lines on the top either before or after it is put on the frame. If the marking is done in the frame mark all the space you can reach, then quilt it before rolling and marking any more area.

Simple patterns such as evenly spaced diagonal lines can be drawn using a pencil and ruler. Mark lightly with a pencil. As a pattern for drawing curves and circles use a cup or plate as a guide.

Mark two straight lines centered on the quilt top lengthwise and crosswise, then run a colored basting thread down these lines. This must be done before the quilt top is combined with the batting and backing. These two centered lines divide the quilt top into four quarters so you can make sure the quilting pattern is identical or matches as it should.

Placing the layers together

The top of the quilt needs to be ironed before assembling. The comforter top needs to be pressed only at the seam.

Spread the quilt or comforter backing flat on the floor with the wrong side up and smooth wrinkles out. Place the batting on top of the backing, centering it so the batting covers the backing uniformly. The batting must be an even thickness with no wrinkles. Place the top over the batting with the right side up so that it is centered over the batting and backing.

Now baste the three layers together. Baste down the center lengthwise and then crosswise. Begin each line at the center and baste toward the raw edge. Then baste a diagonal line running from one corner to the other end of the top until all corners are basted. Begin the diagonal lines at the center and work out toward the corners. After you baste the layers together then baste the four raw edges together. Do not trim any edges that seem uneven, wait until the quilting is done.

Assembling the quilt or comforter is the most difficult part because it is difficult to baste the layers togegher, making sure that you have no tucks or pleats in the layers. So do this step carefully because you are dealing with a lot of bulk. The layers must be flat and even as possible between the rows of basting in order for the back of the quilt or comforter to look as neat as the front.

Finishing the comforter

Now sew the comforter in the machine on the stitching lines. After completing the rows of stitching, remove the basting stitches. Turn the raw edge under ½ inch and press. Then stitch very close to the fold to form a seam.

Quilting frame or hoop?

If the quilting is done by hand a quilting frame or hoop is needed.

A quilting hoop is smaller, takes less room, and costs about $4-$5 less than a quilting frame. It can be used for needlework projects as well as quilts, and costs a little over $10. When using a quilting hoop begin at the center of the quilt and work out, loosening the hoop and moving the quilt as you quilt an area.

A quilting frame may be made at home or may be bought. It should be large enough to accomodate all size quilts from crib size to double size. A quilting frame that will hold crib size to double size should cost under $15.00. They usually come unassembled, but are easy to assemble, consisting of strips of wood, nuts, bolts, and screws.

Most quilting frames are not large enough to accomodate king and queen size quilts. Sears has a quilting frame with an extension that may be bought for about $5 extra to convert it to a size to hold king and queen size. This extension is good only on the Sears brand of frame, and is not transferable to other quilting frames.

The purpose of the quilting frame or hoop is to hold the quilt perfectly flat and taut in order to have good even hight quilting stitches.

To place the quilt on the quilting frame first use thumb tacks to tack a strip of muslin, twill, or other material to each of the lengthwise bars on the front and back of the quilting frame. The strip of material should be wide enough to hang down from the bar for several inches. The strip of material will be the same length as the width of your quilt. Baste one of the widths of the quilt to the edge of the material that hangs down from the bar. Basting on the inside rather than the outside of the bar. Now roll the quilt up on the bar leaving only the width of the short bars unrolled. Baste the other end of the quilt to the front bar, basting on the inside of the bar. Sew the quilt over the frame very tightly at the corners. This stitching will have to be removed and replaced as you move the quilt in the frame.

The quilting stitch

Use No. 7 or No. 8 quilting needle with heavy duty or quilting thread. Thread the needle with a short length of thread, double it over and tie a knot in the end. Bring the needle from the back to the front and pull it so the knot pops through into the back layer so it doesn't show. The knot will be between the top and back layer. When you come to the end of the thread do not tie a knot. Push the needle between the layers so it doesn't show tracking through about 12 stitches. Clip the thread close to the fabric so that it will not show.

Hold one hand under the quilt against the backing to guide the needle when it comes through to the back. Work the stitching towards you. When you are using a quilting frame and have quilted all the area you can reach, cut the thread holding the quilt tight at the corners and roll the quilt so a new area is exposed.

Finishing the quilt

After the quilting is done, art gum eraser will erase any pencil marks. Cut any surplus batting and backing even with the edge of the quilt top unless you are folding the backing over as a self binding. If the backing forms the binding then cut the surplus batting off even with the edge of the quilt top. Remove all basting stitches from the layers and edges. When using the edge of the backing as a binding first fold the backing to the front so that the raw edge is covered, allowing ⅜ inch of the raw edge to turn under. Pin or press the backing in place. Turn the raw edge under, mitering the corners very neatly. Stitch the backing in place by hand using matching thread so it won't show.

When using seam binding sew the binding to the front of the quilt using a ¼ inch seam, then turn the binding to the back. Turn the raw edge of the binding under to cover the raw edge of the quilt and baste in place. Then stitch.

Making a pieced quilt

Regardless of the pattern that you are using for your pieced quilt there are basic methods used to determine the size of each block and how they are put together.

Measure accurately the quilt size needed to cover the bed. Then plan how the blocks are to be set together, whether there will be plain blocks or borders around the blocks.

After choosing the block design, plan the number of blocks that will be required to make up the needed width and length.

For a crazy quilt made with plain blocks use an odd number of blocks lengthwise and crosswise so that the corners will be alike. The quilt may be designed so that the pieced blocks are on top of the bed and the drop all around the bed is a border.

Trace or draw each unit of your design on tracing paper, allowing ¼ inch seam for all pieces. Then trace each unit onto a piece of medium weight cardboard or fine sandpaper. Cut out the traced design, adding ¼ inch all around for a seam.

Lay the pattern for each unit cut from the cardboard onto the fabric. Use chalk or pencil to trace around each piece, drawing the needed number of each piece. Straight edges of each piece should be cut so that they follow the crosswise and lengthwise grain of the material exactly. Cutting out the fabric pieces requires care and accuracy in cutting. Each unit must be cut exactly true with any corners or straight edges perfectly straight. After the cutting has been done group all the pieces together that are alike.

Sewing the pieces together

Each block is made by sewing the pieces for that block together, beginning at the center of the block and working out. Place the first two pieces together and stitch together using a ¼ inch seam, either by hand or machine. Start and stop exactly at the seam line at the corners or curves leaving the seam allowance free so the next piece can be joined in place. Do not stretch the pieces too much, especially bias edges. The seams should be pressed as you work.

Sewing the blocks together

After all the pieces are sewn together to form the blocks, the blocks are sewn together in strips, then the strips are sewn together to form the finished top. The border is sewn on last. The corners of the blocks and strips must match perfectly. Then press the top carefully after the strips are sewn together.

Quilting tacks

A quilt can be made using quilting tacks rather than quilting stitches. The tacks are made at intervals and hold the three layers together securely. If quilting tacks are used, you still need to baste the three layers together. Quilting tacks are a lot quicker to do than quilting stitches; a quilt made with tacks can often be finished in a week end.

Decide where you want to locate your quilting tacks. They can become part of the pattern of the quilt, but should be no farther apart than 8-12 inches. Mark the location for the quilting tacks. Use heavy duty thread. Thread the needle with a boulbed thread. Begin at the top of the quilt and make a stitch through the layers of the quilt. Cut the thread leaving about a 1½ inch long thread to tie the quilting tack. Take the ends of the threads and tie a square knot securely so it won't slip out. The threads may be cut shorter after the knot is tied.

Sleeping bags

Sleeping bags are made just like comforters. A zipper is inserted down one side, and the top is left open. If the sleeping bag is to be used outdoors or for camping then you should either use a fabric that is treated to be water repellent or buy a can of water repellent spray and treat the cloth before sewing the sleeping bag together.

SELECTING UPHOLSTERY FABRICS

Upholstery fabric should last a long time so check the quality and wearability of the fabric using the guidelines that follow. Special finishes such as soil and strain resistance usually cost more, but they cut down on the amount of cleaning necessary. The guidelines given here can be applied when buying upholstery fabrics as well as upholstered furniture. Plastic and leather are hard for a beginner to sew with because the seams and cording require great skill. Plastic must be cut and fitted properly to keep it from ripping or tearing.

Checking the quality of the fabric

The firmer the weave, the better it will resist abrasion and wear. Hold it up to the light so you can see if the weave is compact and clearly woven.

Check to see if the fabric ravels by looking at the raw edges. If the edge ravels easily the yarn will shift and pull away at the seams, particularly on cushions, and where the fabric is attached to the frame of the chair or sofa.

To see if it resists wrinkling stretch the fabric diagonally. It it stretches and recovers completely then it will hold its shape without wrinkling.

Check the weave to see if the threads are the same count or size in both directions because this means better wear. One with a heavy yarn in one direction and a thin yarn in the other will not take wear and abrasion as well. A twill weave will wear better and resist soiling than one with a plain weave of the same or similar fiber.

A fabric with a flat surface (satin, damask, brocade) does not wear ws well as one that is nubby. The nubby one resists abrasion better than the flat surfaced ones with long threads.

Pile fabrics, including velvet, plush, and frieze, should have firm yarns making up a close deep pile and be firmly woven to the ground cloth. This causes the fabric to take abrasion better than one where the yarns are sparse. A pile fabric with uncut loops is less likely to mat than one that has loops that are cut.

Upholstery fabrics that have a foam backing as a finish, including rubber and synthetic rubber, are good because the backing helps keep the upholstery smooth and firm despite continued use. Fabrics without backing will be more likely to form permanent wrinkles.

There is no way to judge the expected life span of an upholstery material because too many factors are involved other than ordinary wear and tear. Abrasion, soil, heat, humidity, mildew, moths, gas fumes, exposure to sunlight, and perspiration all affect the life of the fabric.

Checking the labels on fabrics

The labels on fabric and upholstered furniture list certain facts you should know in order to care for it. The label should specify whether the fabric is colorfast to light, laundry, dry cleaning, cracking and gas fumes.

The label may also give either a number or a letter that indicates classification. The less expensive fabrics have a low number or one of the first letters of the alphabet. For example a label with K is a more expensive fabric than D, and one labeled with 11 is more expensive than 4.

Some manufacturers are using symbols that list the recommended method of cleaning for upholstered furniture. The label may have either a W, S, W-S, or X. *W* means that water based cleaners or foam may be used. *S* means that only mild water-free dry cleaning can be used. *W-S* means both water based cleaners, foam, and mild water-free cleaners may be used. *X* means that it should be cleaned by vacuuming or dusting lightly. Foam and liquid cleaners of any type cannot be used on this.

Fabric finishes

Upholstery fabrics are often treated with stain resistant, mothproof, abrasion-resistent, and anti-slip finishes.

Silicone finishes, fluorochemical finishes (including Scotchgard and Zyrel) are spot and stain resistant finishes which shield the fabric from both oil and water based stains.

These finishes are not miracles and will not eliminate the need for cleaning to avoid excess soil build-up. A finish that is factory applied is more effective than one you can buy in a can and apply as a spray. But frequent dry cleaning does decrease the effectiveness of the finish whether it is factory applied or done at home.

Checking the yarn of the fiber

There are two factors about yarns that should be considered, the degree of twist and the size of the yarn.

Degree of twist-A low twist yarn has a lower resistance because it has more exposed surface area to attract moisture and dirt. Yarns with loose, curling threads, low twist, and heavy slubs snag and catch more easily than a fabric with a compact, smooth tightly twisted yarn.

Yarn size-The size of the yarn is not always involved in the strength of a fabric because a fabric made of a heavier single yarn with a low twist can be as strong as a fine yarn made of several strands that are tightly twisted. But a smooth lustrous fabric made of fine yarns will become soiled and show stains and spots more quickly than fabrics with thick heavy yarns.

Evaluating the texture of the fabric

When evaluating the texture check the closeness of the weave and the length of the yarn float.

Closeness of the weave-The more threads per inch the better the fabric can resist abrasion raveling, wrinkling, and stretching. But if a loosely woven fabric made of heavy yarns has a laminated foam backing it will wear as well as the tightly woven fabric.

Length of the yarn float-This refers to how much yarn floats on the surface, including nubby texture and raised designs. Long yarns on the surface of a material cause the fabric to be less durable because they cause surface snags, show stain, and soil more quickly. Fabrics that are hard-surfaced with evenly balanced weaves wear better than those with nubby textures, raised designs and long yarn floating on the surface.

Blends of fibers

When the fabric is a blend the label may give you what percentage each fiber makes up but it does not tell you whether the blend occurs within the yarn or between yarns of different fibers. Avoid fabrics whose labels emphasize 100% nylon warp or lengthwise yarns and ignore the rayon filling or crosswise yarns.

Choosing your fiber

Upholstery fabrics are usually blends of fibers, rather than 100% of any fiber.

All the natural fibers, including cotton, silk, wool, and linen, are used in upholstery fabrics because they wear well and are rather easy to care for.

The more inexpensive fibers are cotton, rayon, and acetate but the price depends on the finishing added to the fabric.

Cotton

This is one of the most widely used fibers in upholstery. It is used as 100% cotton as well as in blends; the most popular blend is rayon and cotton. Special finishes can be added to make it resistant to mildew, flame, wrinkles, soil, spot, stain, as well as water repellent.

Wool

Wool wears well and is long lasting. It is rather easy to care for. It is more expensive than other fabrics and can be uncomfortably warm in the summer.

Man-made fibers

Man-made fibers have certain qualities that natural fibers do not have. Synthetic ones are not affected by mildew, are crease resistant, naturally stain resistant, and are usually stable and easy to care for.

Glass

This promises a long life because it is high strength, stain resistant and colorfast. A polymer-coating keeps the fiber from breaking as easily under abrasion and from irritating sensitive skins.

Olefin and polyproplyene

It is strong yet light in weight. It resists stains and is easy to clean because it has low moisture absorbency. Some fabrics made with this fiber have a hand-woven appearance with an interesting texture. This has a low melting point and is easily damaged by cigarettes and sparks from cigarettes and cigars.

Rayon

It is colorfast, fairly durable and is the least expensive of the fibers. It can be bought with various finishes needed for good wearability, and can be either dull or lustrous.

Acetate

It is relatively low-cost and reasonably durable. It has good resistence to soiling. The solution dyed or spun dyed is colorfast to sunlight and air contaminants. It is also naturally resistant to moisture, moths, perspiration, mildew, and molds. It is lustrous and supple.

Triacetate

It is resistant to wrinkling, shrinking and stretching. It is easy to care for and is resistant to high temperature.

Acrylic

It is durable and strong, and resistant to wrinkling, sagging, stretching, and shrinking.

Modoacrylic

It is heavier than acrylic and is more flame resistant. It is colorfast against sunlight.

Nylon

It is long wearing and is used for its strength. It resists abrasion and mildew. It is easily cleaned. Sun is harmful to nylon, especially nylon with a high sheen. It is resistant to water-borne stains. It does pick up oil and grease stains but these stains can be washed out.

Polyester

It has high strength and is resistant to abrasion. It does tend to pill. It has a low resistance to oily stains.

Vinyl plastics

It is popular because it is durable and easy to clean. There are many grades and weights of vinyl, with and without backing. The better grades have a woven or knitted back to add strength and stretch. The knitted back stretches in both directions and is easier to tailor than those with a woven back. The expanded vinyls are quite luxurious and have air-cells that give a cushiony softness like a fine leather. It has a high resistance to abrasion though it can be scratched. Those with heavy backing can be used for areas that take the largest amount of wear. One with a fabric backing is less likely to tear or puncture. Vinyls should be sponged clean with mild soap and water. Strong detergents and cleaning solvents are not used because they cause the vinyl to stiffen and will eventually crack.

Vinyl is nonabsorbent but will sometimes absorb color. It has good resistance to sunlight. Some vinyls will not be comfortable to the touch; the smooth surfaced ones will be hot in the summer and cold in the winter.

Vinyl is difficult to use because it often cannot be sewn on the home sewing machine. The heavy weight is usually only used in public places, the medium weight is used over springs and deep cushioned padding. The light weight is used only in areas that are flat and where high tear strength is not needed.

Leather

It is very expensive and luxurious. But is exceptionally long wearing and highly durable. It is naturally soft and pliable. It is scuff resistant even though it does have a tendency to water spot. It can be finished to resist alcohol, cracking, and perspiration stains.

Urethane coated or polyurethane

These fabrics are available with a synthetic foam applied to a woven or a knit backing. These may resemble vinyl but they do not have the same characteristics as vinyl. They are slightly less durable than vinyl. They are poromeric, or breathable, and have the same natural stretch that leather does. It also has the softness and appearance of vinyl. They have high strength and are resistant to scuffs and tears and will not weaken or crack due to aging or changes in the temperature.

Knits

Knits fit smoothly without unneeded bulk and are wrinkle resistant. They will snag and run under hard treatment. Since knits do lose their shape after long periods of sitting the ones with the laminated backs are suggested.

MAKING SLIP COVERS

Slip covers are a good way to cover a chair or sofa with a worn-out soiled cover. Patterns for slip covers are available in pattern books; the most common style is the daybed type.

You need upholstery straight pins, tailor's chalk, tape measure, a curved upholstery needle 1½-2 inches long, and 15 yards of cotton upholstery cord for a chair, zippers or gripper tape for cushion and chair openings.

The following list gives you an idea of approximately how much material you will need, so you will get an idea of the cost involved. Allow extra for patterns, designs, or plaids that require matching.

Piece to be covered	36 inch material	48 inch material
lounge chair, no cushion	8½ yards	6½ yards
lounge chair, one cushion	9 yards	7½ yards
lounge chair, two cushions	11 yards	8½ yards
wing chair, one cushion	12 yards	8 yards
open arm chair, seat only	3 yards	2½ yards
open arm chair, seat and back	6 yards	4 yards
dining chair, slip seat	1½ yards	1¾ yards
side chair, seat only	1½ yards	1¼ yards
sofa with 3 separate cushions	21 yards	15 yards
sofa with no cushions	15 yards	11 yards
love seat, 1-2 cushions	15 yards	10 yards
studio couch, tailored	6½ yards	4 yards
studiocouch, with 3 pillows	4½ yards	2½ yards
ottoman, top only	1½ yards	1 yard
ottoman with skirt	3½ yards	2¾ yards

Determining how much material you will need

You need to measure each part of the chair or sofa, using the sketches provided here. Draw the pieces on graph paper with a scale of 1 inch representing 1 foot, following the general outline of the piece. Cut the pieces out, labeling each piece with its name and measurement. Place the pieces of strips on graph paper on the lengthwise of the grain as you would place the pieces on fabric. For 36 inch material use 3 inch wide graph paper, for 48 inch fabric use 4 inch wide graph paper.

The instructions here are for one style of chair, but the rules of measuring and making the slip cover are the same, although some chairs may have extra or fewer pieces than the chair used here. Instructions are given for other chairs at the end of the section on slip covers.

Measuring the chair

Back piece-Allow a 1 inch seam allowance on all sides and measure as indicated by the arrows

Inside back and seat cover-These should be measured as one piece with a 1 inch seam on all sides plus 6 inches for the tuckin

Outside arm piece-

Measure allowing 1 inch seams on all sides. Cut one for the right arm and one for the left arm.

Inside arm -piece-Begin measuring at the outside arm curve, going over the top to the inside of the arm
Add a 3 inch tuck-in as indicated plus a 1 inch seam on all sides. You will need two of these pieces.

Top band-Measure beginning at the back of the arm, measuring over the top and down to the end of the other arm
Allow a 1 inch seam on all sides.

Front arm pieces-Measure at the longest point and the widest point
Allow for 1 inch seams on all sides. Cut one for the right arm and one for the left arm.

Cushion-Measure the width and length
Allow for a 1 inch seam on all sides. Then cut two pieces, one for the top and one for the bottom.

Measure all around the outer edges of the cushion for the length of the boxing. Then for the width measure the thickness of the cushion and add a 1 inch seam on all four sides. For a zipper placket allow a 1 inch seam on both ends and 4 inches for the width of the zipper insert.

Cutting out your pattern

If your material is not preshrunk do it before you do any cutting.

Using your graph paper cutting chart as a guide, cut each piece to the nearest rectangle or square.

Covering cording

Take a 30-inch square of material and fold it into a triangle. Then cut along the center fold as indicated in Figure 10 . Place the right sides of the two triangles together and sew as shown in Figure 10 , allowing a ½ inch seam and a 1½ inch extension at each end as shown. Beginning at the extension, cut the entire cylinder into a 1½ inch wide strip.

Use preshrunk cotton cording and cover the cording with the bias strip.

Construction of the slip cover

Arm section-Take the piece of material you have cut for the arm section and pin to the chair. Using your chalk, mark the material where the cording or seam of the chair is. Cut 1 inch outside the line you just drew (Figure 10). Sew your cording on the seam line except at the bottom edge. Clip the curves to within ½ inch of the seam so the piece will lie flat and smooth.

Take the piece of material you cut for the inside arm and lay over the arm, allowing a 1 inch seam below the outside of the arm and a 1 inch seam at the end of the arm. Pin the material in place, smooth down over the inside of the arm, folding the fabric back where the chair arm and the inside back join. Draw a chalk line where the seams will be, allowing the 3 inch tuck in on the lower edge at the seat. If necessary darts can be folded in to take up any fullness over the arm.

Trim any extra material away after allowing for the seam and the tuck-in.

Fold and press a 1 inch seam on the top edge of the outside arm piece. Pin the pressed edge to the inside arm piece at the seam line as indicated in Figure 10. Then smooth and pin the outside arm piece to the chair.

Pin the corded arm front piece into place along the seam line of the inside arm. Then remove the whole arm section from the chair. First topstitch the seam below the outside of the arm, then topstitch the arm front to the side pieces. Repeat for the other arm.

Inside section-Pin the top band to the chair and use chalk to mark the seamline. Then trim away any excess material, allowing for a 1 inch seam on all sides. Cord the seams. Mark the center of the inside section and pin down the center of the inside back. Make a chalk mark along the end and the inside arm curve, allowing for a 2 inch tuck in along the arm curve. Repeat for the other arm.

Pin the corded top band to the top edge of the inside back. Then remove the complete inside unit from the chair and topstitch along the seam of the corded top band.

Pin the inside arm section onto the chair, allowing a 1 inch seam at the front edge of the chair, and a 3 inch tuck in at the back of the seat. Cut any excess material away. Make a 6 inch tuck in at the back of the seat. Pin the material in the center of the bottom of the seat and tuck in the edges of the corner. Then slip

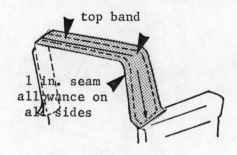

top band

1 in. seam
allowance on
all sides

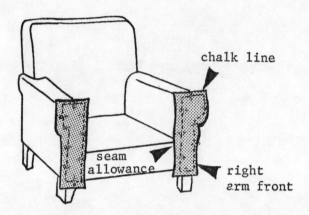

chalk line

seam
allowance

right
arm front

Fig. 10

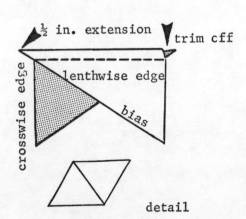

½ in. extension   trim off

crosswise edge

lenthwise edge

bias

detail

Inside Arm Piece

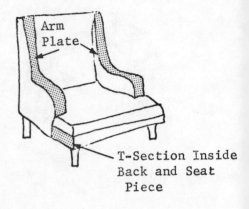

Arm Plate

T-Section Inside Back and Seat Piece

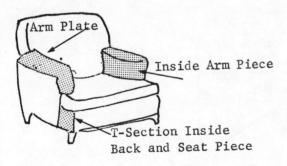

Arm Plate

Inside Arm Piece

T-Section Inside Back and Seat Piece

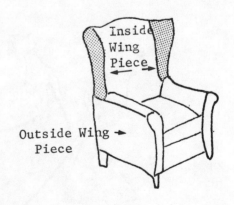

Inside Wing Piece

Outside Wing Piece

Fig. 11

the arm sections you have completed over the arms and pin to the material, slipping the triangular laps at the front under the corded arm front to form the seam, all the way to the bottom of the chair.

Tuck the seam in place along the arm section to the top band. Cord the seams of the back section and pin to the top band and side pieces along the seams. Then unpin the back seam where the zipper will go.

Pin and sew the zipper in place so that one side meets the corded edge and the side of the back forms a ½ inch fold to cover the opening. Leave a 1 inch seam allowance below the zipper.

Then using an ordinary or hidden seam, sew the right sides of the material together along the bottom of the seat, sewing from A to B on each side, then from the top of the arm curve towards the seat.

Flounce

You can make gathers or pleats in the flounce. Allow for a 1 inch seam and a 1 inch hem in the flounce.

Make the pleats or gathers at the top, then sew on the cording. Pin the flounce onto the cover, turning the seam under as you go. Then remove the slip cover from the chair and topstitch. Close the opening with a hook and eye. Turn the hem under 1 inch.

Cushions

Mark the seam line on the cushion top and bottom, and trim any excess material away, allowing a 1 inch seam.

For the zipper, cut the placket strip of boxing in half lengthwise. Then sew the zipper to one strip of the placket boxing, turning ¼ inch under for the seam. Sew the other half of the placket boxing to the other side of the zipper. Then sew the zipper placket to the rest of the boxing.

If you are using gripper tape rather than a zipper, stitch gripper tape on each of the strips of placket boxing, one to the wrong side of the material and one to the right side, turning ½ inch seam under so the raw edge is covered when the gripper tape is stitched down. Then place the gripper tape face down and stitch. Snap together and sew the placket strip to the boxing strip to form a long strip. Apply cording to both sides of the boxing.

Place the right sides of the boxing to the right side of the cushion top together, centering the zipper in the back. Then stitch, using a 1 inch seam. Turn and place the cover on the cushion and pin the cushion bottom to the boxing. Turn the seam under 1 inch as you go. Remove the cover from the cushion by opening the closure. Topstitch, then put the cover back on the cushion.

If you are not using a flounce, you need to finish the bottom raw edge of the slip cover. Allow a 1 inch seam to hang below the end of the chair. Sew cording in place around the legs. You can then pull the bottom edge under and fasten with slide fasteners or snap tape. Sew cord on the bottom edge of the slip cover either at the legs or all around the bottom.

You can also use upholstery tacks to tack the bottom edge in place under the chair where it doesn't show.

Instructions for fitting other types of chairs

For a chair with a wooden arm fit the cover around the arm by folding and cutting the section for the seat bottom in a V form as shown in *Figure 108,* ending ½ inch from post. The edge is then faced with or without a welt. A round wooden arm is handled by cutting a space for the area after making the slit and is then turned under and faced with a round facing or bias strip.

Figure 11 shows a chair with the plate section covering both the top and sides of the arm. This piece is welted. The inside arm piece curves around the arm front and is welted only at the front of the arm.

This pillow back chair shown in Figure 11 has an inside arm piece that covers the top of the arm and around the front. The separate outer front arm piece is welted.

Figure 11 shows a wing chair with an arm plate that continues from the top of the wing to the front of the arm. The wing has a tuck in at the inside arm and back.

Figure 11 shows a traditional wing chair with two wing pieces. A tuck in is allowed on the inside of the wing pieces.

SEAT CUSHIONS

When the cover of a sofa or chair begins to rip and become lumpy it needs to be upholstered. If your chair is basically sound but the cover is worn in spots or ripped then perhaps it doesn't really need to be upholstered, but can be salvaged by patching and making a slip cover. By patching the worn areas carefully and making slip covers you can save yourself time and money since slip covers are cheaper to make than upholstery. Patches should be sturdy and durable. Be sure that you patch all worn areas to avoid extra wear in these spots. If the cushion has become lumpy or too small as a result of age and wear so that it doesn't fill the seat properly you can also redo the cushion without redoing the whole chair or sofa, and the original cover on the cushion can be used again.

Usually if the cushion is too small, it needs new padding over the springs, or the springs may be loose or misshapen. Most of the materials in the cushion can be reused, including the upholstery cotton and springs. So by making slip covers and rebuilding the cushion you can have a chair or sofa that looks like new.

Repairing cushions

Cushions can be made of several different materials. Many newer cushions are now made of a single thickness of foam and are covered with upholstery fabric. Cushions of older chairs and sofas may be stuffed with down, cotton or other loose material that is packed very tightly into the cushion.

Solid foam cushions-A molded cushion begins to wrinkle with age and may even sag at the point of wear. Once they begin sagging, they are worn out and should be replaced. You may be able to cut a piece of foam to the contour and size of the worn area and place it on tip of the worn area to bring it to its original height. But this is only a temporary measure and will not look as good as replacing the foam. The old foam does not need to be discarded, but can be saved to be shredded up. The areas that aren't worn can be salvaged and used to make smaller pillows and cushions.

Molded cushions are sold in many sizes and shapes. It is sold by dime stores as well as fabric centers that have separate upholstery and drapery departments. When you are replacing a foam cushion measure the old cushion and buy a new one that is ¾-1 inch wider than the cord to cord cushion measurements. This is because the old cushion has contracted and dhrunken slightly with age, so allowance is made when cutting the new cushion.

If you are repairing a cushion filled with loose material such as foam pieces, cotton, or down, you can reuse the stuffing material but you need a little extra stuffing to place in the worn areas where the stuffing has become compressed.

If the cushion has become lumpy in spots where the stuffing has been compressed or worn thin, replace the stuffing in these areas. You can sometimes do this by opening the cover at the back seam enough to redistribute stuffing at the lumpy spots and add any extra stuffing needed. But if there is extensive wear you should empty the cushion of its stuffing to refill the lumpy and worn areas. After emptying out the stuffing, break up any lumps. Pack the stuffing back in, adding any necessary stuffing to keep the cushion filled out and fluffy yet solid. Then sew the opening back up with an upholstery needle so that the stitches don't show.

Overstuffed or innerspring cushions

For repairing an innerspring cushion you need the following items:

about 2 yards of some lightweight sturdy material such as muslin, broadcloth, or feed sacks
one 3 or 4 inch curved upholstery needle
2 spools of heavy-duty white thread
new upholstery cotton if the old cotton is not reusable
sturdy strong cord or mattress twine that is small enough to thread through the curved needle

Clip the seams at the lower back of the cushion cover so you can remove the springs. Open the cotton surrounding the springs and pull the springs out of the cushion, leaving the cotton in the cover until it is needed. Be careful that you don't tear or break the cotton because it is in one solid piece several layers thick around the springs.

Clip all the string that is holding the rows of springs together, and remove the springs from their burlap pockets or covering.

Look at the imprint that the springs have left on the burlap case and count the number of rows and the number of springs in each row.

Straighten any bent springs so that all springs are a uniform height.

You now need one strip of muslin for each row of springs the length of the row plus ½ inch seam at each end. Each strip should be 3½ times as wide as the boxing in the cover; this will usually be about 11 to 12 inches wide. For a 3 inch wide boxing 10 inches is sufficient.

The length of the strip is the total of the number of pockets of the row plus ½ inch seam allowance at each end.

Fold each strip in half lengthwise, pulling the material if necessary in order to make the fold on the lengthwise thread and matching the corners. Mark a ½ inch seam on each end of the strip. Then mark the stitching line for each pocket measuring from the seam line at each end. Each pocket should measure 1½ times the diameter of the spring plus ¼ inch. Then stitch the two seams at the ends, backstitching to secure the ends. After all the strips are sewn, the springs can be placed inside the pocket and sewn up. The springs are placed in the pockets one at a time and are sewn on the machine before the next spring is inserted. Compress the spring and slip it sideways into the pocket and push it to the bottom of the pocket. Turn the spring to the upright position and check to make sure the spring is compressed the desired amount and that the pocket holds the spring firmly without binding.

Close the pocket by pinning across the opening about 1 inch down from the top. These pins may have to be moved up or down to make sure the spring is compressed the correct amount. For a 3 inch wide boxing on the cushion, the spring should be compressed to be 2 to 2¼ inches tall. The extra space is necessary to leave room for the padding. The stitching line can be ½ to 1½ inches from the top edge depending on the amount the spring is compressed. Mark this stitching line across the length of the strip. Then insert the springs one by one and sew before inserting the next one.

In some cushions, large interlapping springs are used with strips of burlap brought up through the interlapping sections. If this burlap is being used then make each pocket slightly larger.

Stitching the pockets

After drawing the stitching line, turn the first spring sideways so the strip can be placed under the presser foot of the sewing machine on the stitching line of the first pocket. Remove the pins and hold the spring flat with your left hand so that you can stitch across the pocket. Stop the needle on the line at the beginning of the second pocket. Insert a spring in the second pocket and stitch following the same procedure. When all the springs are stitched in place turn each spring so that it stands upright in the pocket. The fold at the back of the pocket should cross the spring at the center bottom and the stitched edge of the pocket should cross the spring at the center front. Continue until all strips are done.

Making the unit

The rows of springs sewn in the strips are now sewn together to make the unit. Use curved needle threaded with mattress twine or strong cord. Place the rows of springs side by side as they were in the original unit. You can use one of two methods to sew the strips together. You can sew the back and front edges together and carry the cord across the center as illustrated in Figure 12. Or you can sew the edges together at the sides of each spring and carry the cord along the edges of each row, which gives more support to the

padding than the other method does. The springs must be sewn together both crosswise and lengthwise, on the bottom and top of the unit as well. Be sure to keep the springs in correct position in the pockets as you sew.

A slipknot is used when sewing the rows together because it can be made in places where your hands will not reach. Begin by making a slipknot at the end of the row farthest from you, and sew toward you. Use several stitches at the side of each spring and make a blanket stitch before going on to the next spring.

To make a slipknot pull the threaded needle through the fabric under the top wires of two adjacent springs leaving a 6 inch end. Hold the thread from the needle straight and tight, carry the thread end over and then under the straight thread in the needle to form a figure 8 as illustrated in Figure 12. Then with the left hand hold the thread between the thumb and forefinger; with the right hand put the short end through the upper circle of the figure 8 and up through the lower circle as shown in Figure 12. Pull gently on the straight thread in the needle and the knot will slip to the end closing tightly.

Padding the spring unit

Most spring units are padded with upholstery cotton but a layer of moss or hair can also be used in addition. If hair or moss is used it is placed on the top and bottom of the unit before the cotton is put on. Spread a thin layer of the moss or hair to make an even layer. Repeat for the bottom of the unit. The moss or hair is now sewn to the unit, using mattress twine in a straight double pointed needle long enough to go through the unit. The long basting stitches begin at the outside edge and work towards the center. The springs are then wrapped in two or three thicknesses of upholstery cotton. The old cotton can be removed from the cushion cover

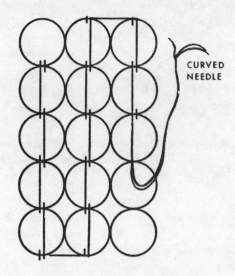

CURVED
NEEDLE

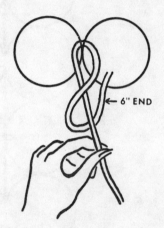

← 6" END

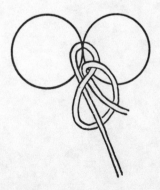

Fig. 12

CURVED
NEEDLE

Fig. 13

and reused. Wrap the unit in the cotton so that the cotton covers the top and bottom overlapping at the sides. Pull the cotton gently on the two open sides so the cotton overlaps, and baste together using long basting stitches.

The unit can now be placed in a muslin cover if desired. This cover can be made using the old muslin cover or the upholstery cotton as a pattern. Slip the muslin cover over the unit. Next you must get the unit back into the upholstery cover. To do this first surround the unit with cardboard. The cardboard acts like a shoe horn. Place a piece of cardboard on the top and one on the bottom. Tie the cardboard in place with heavy string, drawing up the unit tightly so that is is smaller than the cover. All the knots should be made at one end of the unit. Draw the cover over the cardboard so that the end with the knots of string will be at the open end of the cover. When the cover is on the unit untie and remove the strings. Slip the pieces of cardboard out one piece at a time. Draw the open edges of the cover and pin together. Sew, using a matching carpet thread with a jab stitch.

BED, BATH, AND TABLE LINENS

Buy from a department store, chain or local stores that you can trust. Avoid buying linens from small stores that cater to the tourist trade, such as stores in Washington, New York, and Philadelphia. Good linens are usually either wrapped in packages or have labels pasted on them listing the fabric content, manufacturer, and care requirements.

Sheets and pillowcases

The size listed on the package or label is the size before hemming.

Sheets and pillowcases are made of muslin and percale. Muslin is less expensive than percale. It is strong, durable, sturdy, smooth, and firm. Percale is smoother and more lustrous, and lighter weight than muslin. Percale is more expensive because it is usually made from a longer fiber than muslin, and is of a finer and more even weave. Many people prefer percale because it is softer and smoother than the muslin. Usually the muslin wears better and lasts longer than percale, and is usually a $1 or more less in price than the percale.

Some brands of sheets do not state whether the sheet is percale or muslin. Dan River is one example that uses a registered name only on the front of the package. But on the back of the package it lists in fine print whether the sheet is percale or muslin.

Most manufacturers no longer list the thread count on sheets and pillowcases. The higher the thread count the higher the quality, and the higher the price. One with a higher thread count will usually wear better.

Be sure you buy the correct size of pillowcases because they come in standard size as well as king and queen size. The pillow case should measure 2 inches larger than the distance around the pillow, and should be 6 inches longer after being hemmed.

Pillowcases are quite expensive considering the small amount of fabric they are made of. You can usually make your own cheaper out of a matching sheet. But compare the price of a package of pillowcases and the sheet before you buy to make sure it will be cheaper at the price you are paying. The cheapest way to handle the problem is not to insist on every pair of sheets having a matching pair of pillowcases. If most of your sheets are prints, pillow cases in solid colors can go with several sets of sheets.

Follow the instructions for washing your sheets and pillowcases. Since practically all sheets are now permanent press, don't leave them in the dryer after they are dry because this will set wrinkles and is bad for the fiber.

Mattress pads

The flat pads with elastic anchor bands at the corners are available but the fitted pads that have an elasticized skirt give a smooth, neat fit and stay in place better.

Filling can be either cotton or man-made fiberfill such as polyester, nylon, or acetate. The cotton filled costs less but the man-made fillings last longer because they shrink less, do not mat, dry quickly, and look better longer.

Pads are also available with a moisture proof plastic backing. There are also foam latex pads available as well as foam mattress toppers. A foam mattress topper gives more resilience than a quilted fabric pad. It is available in densities from soft to firm and from 1-3 inches thick.

Buying bedspreads

The fabric should be a firm close weave because it wears better than a loose weave. It should be easily washed and resist wrinkling. Heavier fabrics are usually more durable but they are also harder to wash and to handle.

Check the label to see if it preshrunk, colorfast to sun and frequent washings. If it is a tufted bedspread the foundation fabric should be firm and strong.

Measure the bed for the length and width but also the distance from the mattress to the floor.

The ends should be cut straight and the edges should be finished neatly. Any seams should be bound. Hems should be stitched close to the edge with back stitching at the ends.

Quilts and comforters

The same quality standards for bedspreads also apply to quilts and comforters. They must be resilient in order to provide warmth. Press the quilt or comforter between your hands and notice how well it springs back when released. If it doesn't spring back it will get lumpy and flat and lose its insulating quality.

The size listed on the label is usually the size before it is filled and sewed. There can be as much as 4 inches difference between the cut size and the finished size so take this into account when choosing the size.

The price of the quilt or comforter usually depends on the quality of the filling as well as the quality of the top. Usually man-made fiber fills are used now. Down is also used but the price is too high for most people to afford. Down is soft, warm, extremely lightweight and resilient.

Man-made fiber fills include polyester, nylon or acrylic fibers, but polyester is the most commonly used. These can be machine washed and dried and are easy to care for. Cotton and wool are used infrequently in fillings. Long staple cotton is more resilient than short staple cotton which tends to bunch. Better grade wool is scoured and carded; low grades are coarse and may contain other substances. Lamb's wool is warm and lightweight. Polyester may be called Dacron, Kodel, or Fortrel. It is favored above cotton because it does not mat or felt so badly and washes and dries easily. Cotton takes a long time to dry.

Some comforters have a foam backing that is designed to add to the warmth. But foam is certainly less attractive than ordinary fabric and is not as durable as a closely woven fabric.

Comforters and quilts should be closely stitched through the thicknesses. The edges should be neatly finished and stitched to the fabric with no loose or broken threads. The quilting threads should not have any loose threads or broken threads.

Blankets

The kinds of fiber, the nap, the construction, the thickness and the care you give the blanket are all factors that determine the warmth a blanket can provide, as well as its durability. The heaviest blanket is not necessarily the warmest. A lightweight fluffy blanket is usually warmer than a heavy, felted, tight woven one.

Be sure to buy a blanket that is large enough because a blanket that is too short wears from constant strain of being stretched.

Checking the quality

The resilience and bulking of the fiber is what provides the warmth. The weave of the fiber should be close and even. A blanket with a nap can have a looser weave without affecting the quality. But the fibers should be long rather than short, otherwise the loose fibers will form little balls of lint on the surface of the blanket. Hold the blanket up to the light to see if the nap is distributed evenly over the surface and if the yarns are close together. Pull the fibers gently to see if the nap pulls out.

Bindings

The binding is a good indication of the quality of a blanket. Bindings are usually made of nylon or rayon. Good bindings are firmly woven. Nylon wears and washes better because it is resistant to abrasion and should last the life of the blanket. Acetate bindings are subject to gas fading. They may be zigzag or plain stitched, but several rows of stitching will hold better than chain stitching. The end of the binding should be folded enough to prevent ravelling and the thread ends should be secured.

Check the blanket to be sure it is cut and stitched on the crosswise grain line. Strips and patterns usually add to the cost of a blanket.

Fabric finishes

Blankets are available with special finishes to add to the durability. A wool blanket wears better if it has been treated to reduce felting shrinkage. The label may list it as 'Dylanized' or 'Carefree.' In addition wool blankets need a permanent moth control. Blankets made of man-made fibers need a finish to keep the nap from shedding and pulling. These finishes may be called Fiber Fast, Fiber Seal, or Nap-Guard.

There are several types of blankets to choose from, including woven, thermal, non-woven, and tufted.

Cotton thermals tend to stretch with use, acrylic and polyester thermals shrink and stretch the least. Nonwoven blankets require care in use as well as cleaning.

Cheaper blankets made of rayon blends can distort badly in the laundry and should be avoided.

Man-made fibers tend to generate electricity.

Be sure to follow the washing instructions on the label because improper care can shorten the life of a blanket seriously.

Evaluation of different blankets

Wool-These are outnumbered now by blankets made of synthetic fibers, but they outlast other blankets when given proper care and finishes to keep them from shrinking, matting, and moth proofing. Tests show that 100% wool ranks highest in warmth and retains its thickness better than other fibers after repeated washings. They have a high nap, as well as softness and fluffiness, all of which are retained after washing.

It can be ruined and damaged by improper washing or by the use of chlorine bleach. Improper washing can result in shrinking, matting, felting, and loss of fluffiness.

Blankets with 15% nylon and 85% wool are less likely to shrink than a 100% wool blanket.

Cotton-These are most popularly used for cribs, childrens, and summer blankets. They are easily washed and will withstand high temperature. They lose their nap more easily since cotton crushes more readily. It is weakened by mildew and provides less warmth than wool or acrylic blankets.

Cotton thermal blankets are popular because they can be used year-round and provide additional warmth when covered with a sheet on the top.

Nylon-Nylon is used in small amounts as blends with other fibers. Nylon gives extra strength to the blanket. Nylon is used on the surface of polyurethane foam blankets that feel like velour, but these blankets are not as durable.

Acrylic-These have a high degree of resilience. It provides warmth but is lightweight, is naturally mildewproof and mothproof. It is highly resistant to shrinking during washing and retains a good appearance after proper washing. It has low flammability.

Rayon-These cost less than other blankets. They are resistant to moths. There are both good and poor rayon blankets but you cannot judge by just looking at the blanket. A good one is made of crimped new staple fiber; the poor one is made of reworked rayon which wears out quicker and doesn't wash well.

Rayon blankets look fluffy and attractive when new but they lose most of their good appearance after being washed. They stretch crosswise and shrink lengthwise. The nap is easily removed by crushing and during the cleaning and then aren't as warm. They are highly flammable.

Choosing towels

A towel with a tight, firm close weave and dense loops wears well. A towel with close thick loops is preferred for quick drying.

The twist of the yarn influences absorbency because loosely twisted pile yarns soak up more moisture and feel soft to the touch. But velour surfaced towels do not dry as well as other towels because the loops are trimmed off and this sacrifices absorbency.

The texture of the towel, whether soft, medium, or rough is personal preference and doesn't have anything to do with quality.

The side edges of a towel can be finished in several ways. It can be hemmed or have a woven selvate. The hem should be sewed with an overcast stitch with small firm stitches and should be backstitched at the corner. There should be no loose thread ends showing at the hem.

Choose a towel that will not pucker up at either end or at the border after being washed.

Seconds and irregulars are usually good quality; they usually have minor defects that will not affect the durability of the towel. But examine the edges closely to make sure that no loose threads will ravel loose.

Selecting tablecloths

A tablecloth should be large enough to extend 6 to 8 inches beyond the edge of the table so add 20 inches to both the length and width to get the size of the cloth you need. Check to see that square and rectangular cloths and napkins are cut on the grain and have straight corners. Check the hem to make sure it is finished well because this is one of the first places to ravel out in the laundry. Finishes and decorative details should be able to withstand wear and laundering. The label should specify the maximum shrinkage and if the fabric is colorfast.

Choosing tablecloths that are permanent press with either soil release or soil resistant finishes will make your work easier. A soil release finish means that if the soil doesn't come out in hhe first wash it will during the following ones. Solid colors and white colors with this finish show wrinkles more than in printed patterns. Spot and stain resistant finishes cause water borne and oily stains to roll off rather than soak in.

Tea or luncheon napkins are either 12x12 or 15x15; dinner napkins are usually 18x18, 22x22, or 24x24, although other sizes are available. Poor quality napkins are often skimpy in size.

Selecting pillows, mattresses, and springs

The quality can affect the comfort and the durability of the pillow, since a good pillow can be expected to last for 5-10 years.

Pillow fillings

Fillings are of three types, synthetic fiberfill, foam rubber, and feather-down. Synthetic fibers are lightweight, firm, nonallergic. Down is the softest and lightest weight and the most expensive. Foam rubber can either be molded in one piece or shredded; shredded foam lasts longer.

Feathers can be combined with down to make the pillow springier and firmer. Goose feathers are springy and resilient which makes the pillow more bouyant and slightly firmer than one with down. Duck feathers are not as fluffy, strong, or resilient. Chicken and turkey feathers lose their curl and resilience because they are artificially curled.

Latex or foam rubber is bouyant, firmer and more resilient than down.

Comparing pillows

Check the resilience by placing the pillow on a flat surface and compressing it to half its thickness. It should spring back into shape immediately after being released. Firmness is not the same thing as resilience. Knead the filling to determine if it has a uniform consistency.

It should be well filled but light in weight. Balance the pillow over your arm. In a good pillow the ends will not droop down. Shake the pillow vigorously from one end. The filling shouldn't settle down more than 1-2 inches. If two pillows are the same size and plumpness with the same filling, the lighter pillow will usually be the better one. Check molded rubber to make sure it is in one piece.

Pillows should be fluffed and aired daily. Avoid direct sunlight for all pillows. Feather pillows should be cleaned by a professional laundry.

When pillows wear out you can sometimes add more filling from another similar pillow. Add enough of the extra filling so that it is full to within an inch or two of each end of the ticking. But since the filling has lost much of its resilience and bouyance this newly filled pillow will not last much longer.

Mattresses and springs

Although mattresses and springs come in matched pairs, you must examine the quality of each one separately.

The quality of the bed spring does influence the comfort and wearing quality of the mattress. For this reason you should buy the best mattress and springs that you can afford. If your mattress wears out and your springs are still good, buy a mattress that is designed to go with the type of springs that you have.

The springs supply $\frac{2}{3}$ of the total resilience when used with a solid bed mattress but only $\frac{1}{3}$ with an innerspring mattress.

The firmness of the mattress is one of personal preference. If a mattress is not firm enough for you, put plywood or bedboard under the mattress.

Mattresses

Each individual should have a space 39 inches wide and 6-10 inches longer than his height. A firm comfortable bed is worth the investment because it will provide you with comfort as well as lasting service.

A good mattress supports all parts of the body equally well. It is resilient, bouyant, free from noise, and durable. You can determine if the mattress meets these requirements by checking certain features that determine the quality. You can check the materials used, the type of construction, and the quality of the workmanship.

Most stores have miniature copies of the mattress and box springs enclosed in plastic so you can examine the construction, material and workmanship.

Innerspring mattress-The comfort of an innerspring mattress depends on the springs inside. This has greater bouyancy than a foam mattress and maximum amount of adjustment to the body. It can be made up of open coil springs tied together or of pocketed coils. The coil count, coil arrangment, amount and type of padding are all factors in the quality of the mattress. The spring should be a heavy gauge, high carbon wire. The open coil should be well tempered and have the correct space between the coils. It should have at least 160 coils but a better quality has up to 220. The pocket coil type may be more expensive than the open coil. This eliminates noise between the springs and allows more independence among the springs for coil action. A full-size mattress with pocket coils can have 800 or more coils.

The upholstery fabric is important because it adds resilience and it should not lump or pack easily.

Padding is placed directly over the springs before the cover is put on. This padding may be layers of cotton felt, sisal, latex, curled hair, or latex curled hair.

Foam mattresses-These can never have the firmness of an innerspring mattress. They can be made of latex (rubber) or man-made polyurethane foam. Latex usually costs more than polyurethane. A good foam mattress if made of high density foam. Both types of foam are non allergic, dust and lint-free, flexible and lightweight. A 4-6 inch thick foam mattress can adequately support weight up to 100 pounds.

Checking the quality of a mattress

Some types of pre-built edging or border (such as foam or cotton felt) helps the mattress keep its shape by protecing the edges against sagging.

A firm, closely woven colorfast fabric cover is necessary. Special finishes are desirable, such as finishes to make the mattress resistant to water mildew, fire, insects, and germs. Flat handles on the sides that are securely attached, are helpful when moving the mattress. Side wall ventilators four or more in number, will keep the mattress cleaner and fresher by allowing for air movement.

The fabric cover should be smooth and sewn neatly in place, and any tufts should be firm. If the top is quilted, check the sample for broken threads along the quilting lines.

The borders should be strong and reinforced to keep the edges erect and neat.

Springs

There are three types of bed springs: box springs, which are upholstered, open-coil, and the flat spring.

The open coil or flat springs should be used for foam mattresses; the box springs are used for innerspring and latex mattresses.

Box springs-This has spiral or coil type springs mounted on a foundation, enclosed in a box-like frame, insulated, padded and covered in fabric to match the mattress. In better box springs the springs are hand tied to each other, the frame, and the border. The number of coils are equal to the number in the mattress, or if fewer in number, then the coils are made of heavier gauge wire.

Open coil springs-These are similar to boxsprings, but less expensive. They have coils mounted within a frame resting on metal slats. They are padded, and can be single or double deck. The springs are difficult to clean because the dust collects on the inside.

Check to see if there is a baked-on enamel finish to prevent rust, a helical coil tied top which increases resilience and independent spring action, and crossed slats dropped below the frame for greater spring resilience.

Flat springs-These are also called fabric springs. They are located on the bed frame. These are usually used on cribs, cots, rollaway beds, and bunk beds. The springs should be strong and firm. The type with link-type springs is likely to sag. The slat or band type with helical coils is more durable than a band-end type. A high carbon tempered wire outlasts other kinds. The thickness and diameter of the wire determines the firmness

of the spring. Each coil should have at least 7 turns; better quality coils can have up to 12 turns. The tests for quality are the same as for open coil springs.

DECORATING YOUR FLOORS AND WALLS

Choosing a carpet

A top grade carpet should be used in heavy traffic areas, such as the living room, family room, stairs, and hallways. Middle grades are suitable for a dining room or a much-used bedroom, and economy grades can be used in less used bedrooms. For a kitchen or bathroom it is desirable to have a carpet that has a water resistant backing.

The backing of the carpet is important because it holds the fabric together and keeps it from sretching or shrinking. A good quality backing is closely woven. The backing is made of yarns, such as jute, and can be coated with a latex to hold the surface yarns.

A second backing is desirable because it provides more stability and improves the feel or hand of the carpet. If the foam cushion backing is thick, it eliminates the need for any other padding. Synthetic secondary backings that are water resistant are desirable for kitchen and bathrooms.

Denseness or closeness of weave

This is the most important factor involved in the wearing quality of the carpet. The closer the tufts or loops of fiber are together, the more fiber there is in the carpet and the better it will wear. Bend the carpet and push down the pile with your finger. In a dense pile it is hard to feel the foundation of the yarns. For heavy traffic areas a low-loop, tightly twisted, densely packed pile wears better than a carpet with higher pile that is less

CARPET EVALUATION CHART

Fiber	Wool	Rayon	Cotton	Nylon	Acrylic	Modoacrylic (Dynel, Verel)	Polyester	Polypropylene (Olefin)
ABRASION RESISTANCE	Excellent	Poor to fair	Good	Excellent	Excellent	Excellent	Excellent	Good to excellent
RESILIENCE	Excellent	Fair to poor except in newer types; improves with density.	Low, fibers can be raised with vacuum cleaner.	Excellent	Excellent	Excellent	Fair	Fair
SOIL RESISTANCE	Easy to clean. Not as easily spot cleaned as synthetics.	Poor. Soil resistant finishes available.	Fair. Tends to show soil. Soil fibers. Easily finishes available	Good; Slightly in delustered clean. spot cleaned.	Good harder to spot		Medium	Good to excellent. Is stain resistant.
CLEANING SPECIFICATIONS	Can be cleaned easily. Avoid ine detergents.	Clean with special precautions, jnkot all dry cleaners can be used.	Clean with special precautions. Not all dry cleaners can be used. See rayon.	Cleaned very easily.	Easily cleaned by standard methods.	Easily cleaned	Easily cleaned	Very easily cleaned
EFFECT OF COMMON HOUSEHOLD ACIDS, SOLVENTS, ETC.	Destroyed by strong alkalies, and attacked by weak alkalies. Resits weak acids.	Unaffected by normal household acids and solvents. Lye and bleach destroy fiber and color		Resistant to most acids and solvents.	Good resistance to most acids solventsolvents.	Good resistance to most acids and solvents	-----	-----

dense. Naturally a shag carpet will be less dense but it should have yarns long enough to cover the space between the rows of yarns.

The height and style of the pile may be less important. But a textured surface does not show heavy traffic as much as a smooth plush pile does. A sculptured design shows less soil in heavily used areas but is slightly harder to clean. A velvet carpet with a plush pile shows traffic more than the other styles.

The fiber may be important but it is not always possible to judge the quality of the fiber itself. The following chart lists fibers and their characteristics.

Carpet padding

A good dense padding is useful because it makes your carpet last longer by absorbing most of the shock, wear and tear from the carpet. Even if the carpet is inexpensive or is used in light traffic areas, the padding is still important. The less dense the pile of the carpet the less able it is to stand up under wear. All paddings are insect and moth-resistant, and some are mildew resistant for use in bathrooms and kitchens. For use in light and medium traffic areas use a 40-48 ounce pad, for heavy traffic areas use a 48-50 ounce pad. There are three types of padding, felt, rubber and foam, and pneumatic cellular type.

Felt padding is dense yet firm. It may have a rubberized coating to make it more resilient and stable. A 40 ounce pad is recommended for most home use, and 48 ounce for heavy use.

Rubber and foam are sold as flat sponge rubber, foam rubber, or waffled sponge rubber. These are bouyant, and more resilient than the felt types. A high density foam rubber is considered better because it compresses more than the sponge rubber, but both are good for absorbing noise. A 50 ounce pad

of a ¼ inch thickness is recommended. Polyurethane of foam paddings come in a variety of densities, so choose the one that gives the support and firmness you need. It is considered best for below-grade installations to guard against dampness. A ⅜ inch thickness is recommended.

Pneumatic cellular pad is newer than the other types. It is made of polyester and is such a good insulation that it cannot be used on radiant heated rooms.

Selecting a wallpaper

Wallpaper is sometimes a better choice than paint if your walls are in bad condition. Because wallpaper can be washed off easily it is easier to maintain than painted walls and is cheaper in the long run since a wall covered with wallpaper will last longer and look better than a painted wall. A nonwashable wallpaper can be treated to be washable either before or after it is put up. Some wallpapers with plastic coatings can even be scrubbed. Roller prints are cheaper than screen prints, but both can be plastic coated for durability. The price of the roller printed wallpaper is determined by the quality and weight of the paper used.

Vinyl wallpapers are heavier than other wallpapers and come with two different types of backing—paper and fabric. On a vinyl wallpaper the pattern is printed on the vinyl surface. Because vinyl can be scrubbed clean it is ideal for kitchens, bathrooms, and utility rooms. Vinyl wallpaper can be pulled off the wall when you wish to replace it.

Be sure to prepare the wall surface properly before putting the paper on. If the wall is not prepared the wallpaper can not be stripped off the walls very easily and may leave the wall surface uneven as it pulls layers of paint off.

Fabric can be applied to walls instead

of wallpaper. There are several ways of attaching the fabric to the wall. The quickest and easiest method is to use a staple gun, but staples cannot be used on solid plaster. Other methods of attaching fabric to the wall include double-stitch pressure sensitive tape or spray-on adhesive, which are put on the back of the fabric. Velcro (available in sewing or notions departments) can be attached to the back edge of the fabric and to the wall. If this is used, the fabric can be removed to be washed. Whatever you do, be sure to preshrink your fabric.

Fabrics may be sprayed with fabric finishes to make them resist soil, and water.

Matting and framing pictures

You can save a lot of money by matting and framing your own pictures and paintings. You can buy frames that are already assembled, or you can buy pre-finished parts and assemble the frame yourself. Old pictures or paintings with good frames may be bought at thrift shops, garage and rummage sales—discard the painting and use the frame. Student art shows are also a good source of frames. Examine the frame carefully to see if it is in good condition and will fit.

There are several steps involved in framing a picture. If matting is used, that comes first, then the picture is put in the frame, backing is added, and then the wire is added for hanging.

Using a mat

A mat is used to provide a suitable background or to increase the size of a small picture so it will fit a larger frame.

Mats may be made of mat board sold at art supply stores, good quality colored art paper (cheaper paper may fade), and Bristol board with a dull finish. Mats can also be made by covering medium weight cardboard with wallpaper or fabrics such as burlap, denim, monk's cloth, shantung or broadcloth.

When cutting your mat be sure the width of the bottom margin is greater than the side and the top margin, although the side and top margins can be made the same.

The window cut for the picture must be slightly smaller than the picture so the cut edge of the mat is hidden behind the picture.

Cut the mat to fit the frame. Then place the picture on the mat and mark the window that you want to cut for the picture. A sharp straight edged razor is satisfactory for cutting the mat. Hold a piece of metal, such as a metal-edged or a t-square against the cutting line, and cut the mat, holding the razor against the metal as you cut. Keep the corners clean and neat. If the first cut fails to go all the way through the mat board cut all the way around a second time.

Covering the cardboard with fabric or paper

Cut the window out of your mat first. Then cut the fabric or paper an inch wider and longer on all the outside edges than the mat. Be sure the fabric is cut on the grain. Place the fabric or paper on a flat surface with the right side down, and center the mat on it. Cut the corners at an angle as shown to avoid too much thickness on the back of the mat

First fold the top edge down and glue in place, then do the lower edge, then the sides one at a time. Cut out the fabric or paper in the window of the mat but leave 1 inch on all sides to turn to the back of the mat. Clip the fabric or paper diagonally at the corners Fold back the sides, one at a time and glue in place. Do not pull the fabric too tightly, but just enough so that it isn't loose on the right side of the mat. If the fabric is pulled too tight the mat will warp. Allow the glue to dry before putting the picture in the mat. The picture is taped or glued at the top edge only to a piece of cardboard cut to fit the frame. The picture should be centered on the cardboard so it will fit the mat perfectly.

Mounting a picture on a backing

Watercolors and other paintings and drawings on papers are mounted to prevent them from buckling after being framed. It is also a method of preserving maps and pictures on perishable papers. Good cardboard, pressed board, beaverboard, and special mounting boards are all used for mounting. Cut the mounting board slightly larger to allow for adjustment.

Use adhesive such as rubber cement, library paste, or flour paste. Rubber cement is the easiest to use but because it discolors it is used only on charts and pictures of no value. Library paste must be spread very smoothly and is placed under heavy pressure until it is dry. Flour paste is economical and convenient but it is subject to mold, mildew, and insect damage. Be very careful that the adhesive does not squeeze from under the picture. After the picture is placed over the adhesive, use a heavy roller, such as a rolling pin, dark room print roller, or one used for linoleum to smooth the picture down. Usually the mounted picture is finished with a coat of varnish or was. Pour the varnish or wax on to keep brush marks to a minimum. Be careful to not get dust on the picture until the varnish dries.

Place the picture in the frame. Make sure the glass is clean on both sides before putting into the frame. Place a piece of cardboard or other backing paper over the back of the picture, or glue the paper on after the picture is in the frame. Drive a nail in on each side temporarily and adjust the frame as needed to fit the picture. Check a matted picture to be sure that all edges are the correct size before driving any more nails in. Then drive brads about 2 or 3 inches apart on all four sides of the frame.

If backing paper is used, put it on now after the picture is in the frame. Dark brown wrapping paper is fine. Cut the paper 1 inch larger on all edges than the frame. The glue is applied hot to form a perfect seal. Brush the hot glue to the back of the frame ½ inch from the outside edge. Dampen the backing paper and lay the dampened side down on the back of the frame. Smooth the paper out, beginning at the center, then press the edges down with a clean cloth. The paper will be wrinkly but as it dries it will be smooth and taut. After it dries the excess paper can be cut away from the frame with a straight edged razor. To attach heavy cardboard backing rather than paper, use gummed tape (not masking tape) cut in strips and mitered at the corners.

A screw eye is placed on each side of the frame in the upper fourth of the frame. Cut a piece of picture wire twice the length of the frame. Run the wire through each eye twice to prevent slippage. Then pull the wire tight so it will not droop, and wrap the end of the wire over the wire stretching across the frame.

Making your own rugs

Rugs can be made of scraps of wool as well as old wool clothing and blankets. They can be braided, crocheted, or hooked. They can be made of polyester scraps which are bought at fabric outlet stores or saved from scraps at home. They can also be made of old nylon hose. The hose are first bleached or washed several times until they are all the same color, then they can be dyed if desired. If you buy old wool items at rummage sales and thrift shops to make into rugs be sure to treat them to kill any clothing moths that might be present.

Chapter 5
Furniture

BUYING NEW AND USED FUR-NITURE

Checking The Quality Of Upholstered Furniture

You can't look at the inside construction of an upholstered piece of furniture to judge the quality. But by looking at certain details on the outside you can determine the quality.

The upholstery fabric has a lot to do with the durability and life of the furniture (See Chapter 4).

Feel around the edges of the frame to see if it is well padded so that wood or metal is not noticeable. Feel around the outside arm to see if it is well padded. Cheaper pieces may be hollow here. Examine any welt seaming to see that it is straight and neatly sewn. The smaller the welt seam the better the quality. Does the grain patterns or ribs of the material run straight lengthwise and crosswise. Count the number of seams in the back of a sofa, the less there are the better the quality. Look at an exposed seam to count the number of stitches per inch. There should be 7-11 depending on the fabric and the type of seam used. If the upholstery on the sides is pieced it should be neat looking with the pattern well matched. If the cushions have zippers, they should be neatly concealed. Is the cushion reversible or is the underside a different material? Sit down and see if it feels comfortable, especially around the arms. Is the front edge under the cushion soft and well padded? Is spring con-struction used in the front under the cushion? Spring construction, which is more expensive, wears better. Is the back too short or uncomfortable? Look at the piece as a whole to see if all the sides, back, front, are all finished well. Are the legs and other exposed wood finished well?

Choosing Wood Furniture

Furniture can be made of solid wood or it can be made of wood or plastic veneer. A properly made wood veneer panel is 80% stronger than a solid piece of wood of the same thickness. The danger of solid wood is that it is likely to warp or split. Veneers may also be made of laminated plastic resembling wood grain. These plastic laminates are resistant to staining and scarring. The disadvantage is that other wood will show through underneath if it does chip or dent or needs refinishing.

If a furniture label lists that it is "solid," this means that all parts are made of one type of solid wood. "Genuine" and "combination" mean that several woods may be used, including plywood.

Poor quality wood furniture has several coats of cheap varnish sprayed on and appears too glossy. Good quality wood furniture has a smooth, durable finish. The finish should feel very smooth with no rough areas, which look clear and satiny. A thin brittle finish can chip and wear off easily, just as the thick painted-look finish.

Painted furniture should have a soft rubbed-on look. A painted finish damages easier than natural wood and needs to be guarded from abuse.

Checking Wood Furniture Construction

It should be well constructed and substantial. Chair legs should be doweled or mortised-and-tenoned. Corner blocks glued and screwed in place should be used to reinforce legs. Signs of poorly constructed wood furniture include parts that are fitted together with lots of glue and glued reinforcements, and noticeable nails.

Doors should fit well and close easily. They should not sag.

Carved details should be carved, not glued on the surface to make it appear to be carved. All parts of the furniture should be smooth and evenly finished. The backs of chests and drawers should be sanded and should have at least a coat of finish to serve as protection against moisture or insect damage. Otherwise the wood will shrink and swell as moisture fluctuates. This can damage the wood.

Check the grain of the wood. Furniture made on the slope or the cross grain of wood will not last long and isn't as strong.

The back panel of furniture should be recessed into the upright posts rather than stapled or nailed flush with the sides.

The frame The corner bracing at the legs must be screwed and glued into place for rigidity. The joints should be smooth, flush, and tight. In well-made furniture a mortise-and-tenon or double-doweled joints are used. The back panel should be sanded and stained.

Hardware The drawer and door handles should be firmly attached and should allow you to open them easily. The surface of poor quality metal handles may be coated thinly with metal so that it will peel off easily. Metal handles should be resistant to tarnish.

Drawers Drawers should be close fitting at the front and sides, and the joints should be well glued. A dove-tailed joint at the back of the drawer is used in better quality furniture while in poor quality furniture it may be set in a groove. Oozing glue on the pieces indicates poor fitting pieces and careless construction.

The drawer bottoms should be firm and set tightly into grooves in the sides. Drawer bottoms that are only nailed will come loose, and thin bottoms may warp. Corner blocks on the underside give the bottom needed strength.

The drawer should have easy sliding glides of metal or wood under the drawer or at the sides.

Whether the drawer is smoothly finished is not as important as good construction. You can finish the drawer yourself if the furniture is well made otherwise.

Chests A chest should stand firm, straight and rigid on the floor. It should not twist back and forth. A frame made from kiln-dried hardwood is essential for non-warping and sturdiness.

Unfinished Furniture

The construction and quality of unfinished furniture can be judged in the same way as other furniture. If the furniture comes unassembled, be sure that assembling directions are included. Examine the sample assembled piece in the display to check the quality carefully before buying. Be sure you are getting the same quality as you would be getting in finished and assembled furniture. Unfinished pine furniture is not considered one of the best buys because the quality is often poor. You can sometimes get used furniture of much higher quality at the same price.

When buying unfinished furniture look for smoothly sanded surfaces and even grain.

Buying Used Furniture

When buying used furniture add to the price any materials and supplies that you will use for finishing, upholstering, or slip covering the piece.

Check very carefully to see that it is sturdy, strong, and not wobbly. If it is damaged, unglued, or broken, determine whether you have the skill necessary to fix it. If the finish is marred or damaged, can you fix up the spots or will you have to refinish the whole piece? If the wood is dirty can it be satisfactorily cleaned? Loose or missing handles on drawers or doors can be easily tightened or replaced as needed.

Drawers that sag or fit improperly can sometimes be sanded on the edges to fit better. If the poor fit is due to swelling caused by moisture, one coat of finish can be put on the outside of the frame as well as the inside, outside, and bottom of drawers to protect them from moisture.

If used tables or desks have marred, stripped, or chipped tops that seem to be beyond repair, you can fill the damaged areas with plastic wood and make the surface even, and cover the top with contac paper to hide the defects.

SIMPLE-TO-MAKE FURNITURE

Wooden boxes such as orange crates can be bought from produce stores very cheaply and used as tables. The heavier the wood the sturdier the table. It is preferable that the slats of wood be nailed together rather than wired, because the boxes are usually too flimsy to support much weight. But they can be used as storage chests, toy chests, or sewing boxes. The ends of the wires must be wrapped or cut very neatly so there is no danger of injury. Use sand paper to sand by hand all surfaces of the boxes. This is an important step because all splinters must be removed. Then a coat of shellac or varnish or penetrating sealer can be applied if desired. Wood packing crates can also be finished using the same method.

These wooden boxes or crates can also serve as the foundation for other pieces of furniture. A wooden box can serve as a foundation for a table if a piece of plywood or a solid door is nailed to the bottom of a sturdy box. A box can be placed at each end of the table top to serve as a desk. Set the boxes on the short end to make them taller. If desired, slats of wood can be inserted into the upright wooden boxes to make storage drawers for the desk.

Tables can be made of plywood or flush doors, but to keep the cost down the legs can be made of pieces of sturdy wood or sawed off pipes. Ready-made legs, whether folding or banquet style, are very expensive and add to the cost considerably. Old barrels can also serve as the legs of a table.

Old barrels can be finished neatly to serve as coffee tables or as serving areas. If the barrel doesn't have a top, nail slats of wood across the top to close it up. Old trunks can be refurbished by applying a coat of paint.

Old wooden baskets with handles can be picked up or bought cheaply at produce stands. These baskets can be used as magazine holders, trash cans, laundry hampers, sewing baskets, toy chests, and more. Use sand paper and sand the basket by hand to remove all splinters that might come out easily. You may wish to paint or finish the wood, but usually the top and bottom ring are already painted.

For wall shelves that are put on brackets and tracks, you can use either pine shelving or plywood. There are different qualities of brackets and rails; the heavier ones are better quality and support more weight. Finished shelves that are sold in the different widths and lengths are very expensive. Pine shelving is sold in building supply and lumber stores by the running foot in different widths. The store will usually cut it to the width and length you need, but they may charge a nominal shop fee for cutting it. Plywood can be cut to shelf size but it is not as strong as pine shelving and the edges can never be finished very neatly. Thin plywood will sag in the center and will not support heavy weight. Sand all the surfaces of the shelves lightly by machine or hand. Then apply a finish as needed.

You can build simple bookcases of plywood or pine shelving but this requires a certain amount of carpenter skill to get the shelves to fit properly. Screws should be used rather than nails because screws will support more weight and will not pull out.

Large cushions placed on the floor as chairs are very expensive to buy and make. The price of foam for padding is really what makes the price of the cushions so high. But if you have a cheaper source of padding, the cushions are easy to make.

Simple storage chests can be made using cardboard boxes. The boxes are covered very neatly with paper and are stacked together. These boxes cannot support a lot of weight but the amount they can support can be increased by placing thin plywood boards between the boxes so they will hold books, and other heavy items.

Plywood or flush doors made into desks can be completed with a set of boxes to serve as desk drawers. The cardboard boxes should be stacked inside each other or on top of each other.

For boxes that will be used without a cover, fold the top flaps to the inside and glue them down to give the box extra strength.

The boxes can be finished on the outside with paint or with paper. Enamel paint can be either high gloss or semi-gloss. Painted boxes are long lasting, don't soil easily, and can take several cleanings.

Leftover newspapers, wallpapers, gift wrapping, or colorful scraps cut from magazines can all be used to cover the boxes. Paper coverings last longer and are easier to clean if you add a coat of lacquer or plastic spray after the box is covered.

FINISHING AND REFINISHING FURNITURE

Refinishing furniture is not difficult, even for beginners. Three essential requirements for refinishing any piece of furniture are time, patience, and care. With these three basics you can turn second hand specials, hand-me-downs, or antiques into pieces of beauty and distinction. When selecting furniture for restoration carefully study the styling and beauty of the wood. You need not be an expert on wood or finishes to select and refinish furniture. Local museums displaying restored and refinished pieces of furniture are good sources of information on finishes, styling, and wood beauty. Furniture showrooms and shops are also valuable sources of information. Good wood furniture is scarce and expensive today and new wood does not have the mellowness, smooth look and color of aged wood. This color and appearance greatly enhances the beauty of any wood furniture. It can not be duplicated with any finish or combination of techniques. Satisfaction may be gained not only from the finished piece but with the new skills you have acquired to complete the task. Before you consider refinishing a piece, ask yourself the following questions to determine if restoration is worthwhile.

Is the piece sturdy? Can loose joints and broken pieces be repaired or reconstructed without remaking the entire piece? Is it designed well? Furniture of good design is always worth refinishing.

Are you willing to take the time and care to do a good job? Can you follow through? Is refinishing necessary? In some cases a thorough cleaning is all that is necessary to renew the life of a piece. Will refinishing replenish its beauty and usefulness?

To understand the process of refinishing, you need to know something about wood—your working material. A general knowledge of wood will help you in selecting and applying the appropriate finish for your particular taste and needs. Wood is broadly classified into two groups, hardwoods and softwoods.

Hardwoods	Softwoods
ash	spruce
beech	fir
birch	pine
cherry	cedar
mahogany	larch
oak	cypress
walnut	

As a finisher, you will be more concerned with whether a wood is open grained or closed grained. Open grained wood has large open pores covering the entire surface. Closed grained wood has smaller tighter pores. To achieve a smooth finish, open grained woods must be treated with a special coat of paste filler to make the surface smooth and ready for the finish.

Open Grained	Closed Grained
ash	fir
elm	cherry
chestnut	basswood
oak	spruce
mahogany	poplar
hickory	maple
teak	cedar
	pine
	birch
	gum

Wood grain is basically the difference between the springwood and summerwood. During the spring, the tree absorbs more water and grows at a faster rate. During the summer, growth is slower due to the scarcity of water. This causes the springwood to become porous and light while the summerwood to be dense and heavy. Springwood is usually a lighter color than summerwood. This color variation is what most people recognize as wood grain.

Some of the most beautiful grain patterns found in furniture were made by peeling large logs of hardwood to form thin layers of wood known as veneer. Veneer is usually 1/24 of an inch thick, but it can be made thinner. Veneer is usually made of hardwood because of the high cost of using solid hardwood. It is glued onto a less expensive material such as plywood or pressedboard. Veneer is used to form beautiful, distinctive surfaces where solid wood can not be used because it will split from shrinking and swelling. For our purposes veneer is just as good as solid wood. Careful treatment of veneer must be taken during the refinishing process due to its thinness. The same finishes applied to solid woods are used on veneered pieces.

Safety Precautions

Furniture refinishing requires the use of many solvents, most of which are highly flammable. Follow all instructions for each finishing material or cleaning solvent used. No solvent should be left open nor should brushes or rags be allowed to remain in the open air. The words 'flammable' or 'keep away from flame' means that these fluids give off vapors at room temperature which can be ignited by a spark. Operating a light switch, striking a match or even a pilot light in a gas range or water heater can ignite these fumes. Follow these rules whenever using flammable materials or solvents:

Work area *must* have good ventilation to carry vapors away to prevent inhaling of toxic fumes.

Read all manufacturer's labels and directions.

No smoking

Cover and replace caps on all flammable liquids immediately after pouring and while you work.

Remove all papers and rags and place in metal cans with tight fitting lids. Do not leave them in open containers under any conditions. They can ignite and cause a fire under certain conditions.

Wear rubber gloves and old work clothes and use goggles when needed.

Learn each step in its proper order and the time it takes for each.

Tools And Equipment

Good quality tools and equipment are necessary to achieve a smooth finish. Expensive equipment is not necessary to finish furniture, and you can buy most equipment as you need it. Almost all tools, equipment and supplies can be bought at hardware and paint stores or through a cabinet maker's supply house.

The most important tool you will use during the refinishing process is the brush. Good quality brushes help you achieve a satin smooth finish. The quality of the brush depends upon the styling and quality of the bristles. When buying brushes look for the following features:

tapered bristles to a fine point
fine springy bristles
varying lengths of bristles
long bristles in place of short ones
chisel shaped edges in place of square ones

New brushes work better after they have been broken in. First twirl the handle of the brush between the palm of the hands with the bristles pointed downwards. This will free any loose bristles that may be in the brush. Next soak enamel and varnish brushes in a solvent made of half varnish and half turpentine; for paint and stain brushes use one part turpentine and two parts linseed oil. Soak shellac brushes in denatured alcohol. Suspend the brushes in the solution for 2 hours. Do not let the brushes lie on the bottom of the can because this will deform the shape of the bristles. After soaking, remove the brush and wipe the excess solvent off on old newspapers. Wrap the brush in foil or brown paper until ready to use, and lay on its side.

Brushes come in a variety of widths. For large projects you probably need at least a 3 inch brush. For small projects you may only need a 2 inch brush. Remember that the less brushing you do the better the chances for a smooth finish.

The three types of brushes for refinishing are the varnish, the enamel, and the sash brushes   Varnish and enamel brushes are sturdy brushes with a chisel edge. They are normally 3-4 inches in width. They should be used on large areas such as table tops. The sash brush is used for fine work around turned legs, carvings and spindles. They have long handles to reach into small areas. They come with oval, round, or flat bristle heads with varying bristle lengths. The edges can be both chisel and straight.

Save your new and best brushes to apply your finish coats of shellac, lacquer, or varnish. Use the older brushes for the stain and sealer coats. Good cleaning of brushes is essential for long usage. It takes only a few minutes using the following steps to clean your brushes properly:

Clean out excess paint or finish on old newspaper.

Pour turpentine, benzine or commercial cleaning solvent into a clean can (coffee cans do nicely).

Work bristles against the sides and bottom while holding the brush.

Pour out dirty solvent and replace with new solvent once or twice more till the solvent remains clean with no paint or finish being given off.

Wash in detergent and warm water and wrap carefully in foil or brown paper to help retain the brush shape.

Spraying on a finish is the alternative method to brushing on a finish. Good spraying equipment is expensive and cheap models do not give you a smooth high quality finish. Most industries and professional finishers use spray guns because they are faster and several coats of quick drying finish can be applied quickly and smoothly in one day. Spray guns do not insure a smooth finish in the hands of a beginner.

Sandpaper And Smoothing

Sanding is the final preparatory step after all repairs and patches have been made. Sanding gives a piece a satin smooth surface which permits stain and finish to penetrate uniformly over the surface. In areas of the country where humidity levels vary or remain high year round, the wood surface should be smoothed just before application of the finish or stain. A delay of 10-20 hours will cause the wood fibers to become raised again requiring 9 gre sanding. The best method of sanding is hand sanding. This prevents damage to veneer and fragile decorations and carvings. Sanding machines are available and are often used to cut down the amount of time spent on hand sanding.

Sandpaper is graded according to grit size and abrasive material. The four most common abrasive materials are flint (off white in color), garnet (red), aluminum oxide (brown), and silicon carbide (black). Silicon carbide paper is the best for refinishing because of its lasting ability and the fine grit sizes available. Grit size is indicated by manufacturers' terms such as very coarse, coarse, medium, fine, and very fine, or by grit number. Both are found on the back of each sheet of paper. The higher the number the finer the sandpaper. For example No. 400 would be used for the final sanding while No. 60 would be used for very coarse sanding at the beginning. A special grade of sandpaper known as wet dry paper is available in very fine grit sizes. It is used in the final sanding stages for rubbing down a polish. It can be used to sand wet surfaces or to rub linseed oil or soap solutions into the finish to obtain a high gloss.

Sanding (whether by hand or machine) should always follow the grain of the wood and never across the grain. Sanding across the grain leaves small scratches which will be difficult to sand out.

When using large sheets of sandpaper, divide the sheet into four equal quarters so that it will be at an easier size to work with. On flat surfaces you will find it much easier to sand if you wrap the sandpaper around a block of wood 2" x 2" x 4" with a piece of felt or rubber glued to the working surface to serve as a pad. Sand with the sandpaper wrapped around the padded block. A small wire brush can be used to brush dust out of the sandpaper to prevent it from clogging and extend the life of the sandpaper.

Moldings, turned pieces, curves, or flutings require special treatment. A dowel stick of appropriate thickness wrapped with emery cloth is used for turnings, curves, and carved areas. Sandpaper wrapped around a sponge works well for sanding curved areas because it will bend to fit the curve. In cases where the area is discolored or pulpy where the remover still remains use a small tapered three cornered file to file the areas clean.

To protect inlaid wood or areas where the grain runs in different directions, mask off the sections with masking tape before sanding to prevent the sandpaper from scratching the other surface. If the surface is veneer use only 000 steel wool to sand because sandpaper will cut into the veneered surface and the scratches will show after the finish is applied.

If the surface is solid wood use No. 240 or 280 silicon carbide paper for the beginning sanding. Apply even pressure while sanding. Next use No. 340 or 400 paper to smooth the surface even more. For the final sanding use 000 steel wool. Steel wool removes all the hair grain and allows the stain to penetrate uniformly. If the hair grain is not removed, the surface will have a coarse cloudy appearance.

To achieve extreme smoothness on *darkwoods only* such as walnut or mahogany,

follow the same procedure for the first two smoothings. Then for the final smoothing use 1000 crocus cloth. Crocus cloth uses iron oxide to smooth the surface. It gives the wood a reddish tint which cannot be removed. Crocus cloth is found at local hardware stores.

After sanding, clean the surface with a vacuum cleaner then wipe the entire area with a tack rag before applying any stain or finish. Powdered abrasives such as pumice and rottenstone are used to polish a finish to a high gloss. Mix it with linseed oil or crude oil and apply in paste form. Rottenstone is the finer of the two for achieving a mirror smooth surface.

You can make your own tack rag or you can purchase one from the local hardware store. To make your own tack rag, wash a closely woven piece of cheesecloth several times. Dip the cloth into warm water and wring slightly. Then wet the cloth with turpentine. Dribble varnish freely over the surface of the cloth until it appears to be yellow. Wring the rag into a tight roll to force out the water and allow the turpentine and varnish to sink into the cloth. The rag should now be able to pick up dust and leave no moisture behind. In case it dries out while being used, just sprinkle a few drops of turpentine and water over it again. To protect it from drying out, store it in a jar with a tight fitting lid.

Miscellaneous Tools

You may find a need for other tools as you progress. There is a list of assorted tools you may find useful at some stage of the finishing process:

palette knives (for patching holes, gouges and cracks)
cabinet scraper or putty knife (to scrape off old finish and remover)
bar clamps and c clamps (to hold pieces firmly together until glue dries when

repairing damaged pieces)
    screwdrivers
    brushes (varnish, sash, and enamel)
    steel wool
    brace and bit
    woodworking vise

Repairing Old Finishes

Many natural wood finishes that are dull, discolored, and scratched may only need to be cleaned. A new coat of varnish, shellac, or lacquer can then be applied. Determine the type of old finish on your particular piece using the following procedures.

Lacquer-Lacquer thinner will soften and remove lacquer finish.
Shellac-Denatured alcohol solvent or shellac thinner will soften a shellac finish.
Varnish-Gum turpentine does not soften it.

Clean the old finish with a mixture made of ¼ gum turpentine and ¾ boiled linseed oil (the linseed oil is purchased boiled; you do not boil it yourself).

If the old finish is shellac, use the cleaner sparingly. To apply the cleaner first heat some water and pour into an old can or cup. Shake the cleaner and pour enough into the cup to cover the surface of the water. Dip a piece of lintless cloth into the layer of cleaner floating on top of the water. Apply to a small area at a time. Dry to keep the excess away from glue joints because it will soften the glue and weaken the joint.

Use a toothbrush or cotton swab in cleaning carvings and grooved areas which will be difficult to clean.

Use 000 steel wool to remove dirt if necessary.

Use a clean cloth soaked in clean warm water to wipe clean the surface.

Wipe the entire surface dry with a clean dry cloth.

After a thorough cleaning with the cleaning mixture, apply a coat of paste wax or greaseless furniture cream that contains beeswax to furniture that is dried out and lacks luster. For furniture that is not dried out, apply a polish made of denatured alcohol, strained fresh lemon juice, olive oil, and gum turpentine in equal parts.

Some finishes can be repaired without refinishing the entire piece. Remember that these remedies are only for the finish and not for the wood surface below. If the wood surface is damaged the piece will need to be refinished.

White Marks Or Rings

These are caused by water and excessive heat. To remove them, dust the surface with FFFF pumice powder using an old salt shaker to distribute the powder. Rub with the grain using 000 steel wool dipped in boiled linseed oil or lightweight mineral oil. Apply the remedy to the entire surface to prevent spotting. After the spots have been removed wipe the entire surface with a soft cloth. Commercially made products are also available to remove white spots on the finish. If the pumice paste fails to remove the white areas try one of the following applications.

Dampen a cloth and place it over the white spot. Hold a warm iron over the cloth allowing the heat to warm the damaged area without resting on the area. Use denatured alcohol and a soft cloth to rub the white area using another cloth. With another clean cloth rub boiled linseed oil onto the area or try using equal parts of linseed oil, turpentine and vinegar.

Mix salt and lightweight mineral oil to form a paste and rub it lightly onto the area with 000 steel wool. Wipe the surface clean with a clean cloth.

For white spots on a lacquer finish, dampen a lintless cloth with lacquer thinner and rub quickly and lightly over the area.

On furniture with a wax finish dampen a cloth lightly with turpentine or paint thinner. Rub the area lightly and quickly. Then rewax the spot or section.

For furniture with a penetrating sealer lightly sand out the spot using No. 320 sandpaper. Reapply sealer or oil using the directions given here for finishes.

Scratched Finishes

A scratched finish can be repaired without refinishing the entire piece. Determine whether the finish on your piece is an oil finish or a natural finish (shellac, varnish or lacquer). Woods with a natural finish should be cleaned with the cleansing mixture listed earlier. This will help blend the color of the scratched area to the color of the finish. Scratches can be masked on woods with a natural finish by rubbing oily nutmeats, such as walnuts, pecans, brazil nuts, and butternuts into the scratch.

On wood surfaces with an oil finish, use a pad of 000 steel wool dipped in lightweight mineral oil, paraffin oil, or boiled linseed oil. Lightly rub the oil into the wood using a cloth dampened with a small amount of oil. Wipe the surface dry with a clean dry cloth.

Several quick remedies for scratches without refinishing the entire piece are as follows. On furniture with a lacquer finish use lacquer thinner to soften the lacquer finish around the scratched area. Apply the lacquer thinner sparingly with a toothpick or small brush. Shellac finishes require the use of denatured alcohol solvent or shellac thinner to soften shellac around the finish. Varnish finishes require the use of gum turpentine to soften the varnish to cover small scratches.

On stained woods with a natural finish, it is easier to color the scratch. To color a scratch apply one of the following stains or solvents to the scratched area using a toothpick or small brush: colored varnish, thinned colors in oil, clear varnish tinted with colors in oil, commercial scratch remover, or varnish stain premixed in wood colors.

After the stain or solvent has dried for 24 hours, rub the surface lightly with a lintless cloth. If the scratch still shows repeat the procedure. Keep applying coats till the color matches the original finish. When dry, rub varnish and shellac finishes with pumice, oil and lacquered surfaces with rottenstone and oil.

Charred Areas

Charred areas on the finish can be repaired if the burn is not too deep. Remove the old wax and polish from the burned area using a cloth dampened with turpentine. Brush and scrape the burned material out with 000 steel wool or with a knife blade. Dampen a cloth with denatured alcohol and sponge the burned area. The alcohol will help bleach the burned area. If the area is shallow, fill it with several coats of colored sealer or varnish stained to the color of your wood. You may also use clear sealer or varnish to fill in the shallow area. For deep holes no larger than a thumbnail fill the area with lacquer stick. For larger holes see the section on repairs to the wood surface.

Use lacquer stick only for natural wood finishes, lacquer varnish, or shellac. Lacquer stick can be applied without removing the old finish or after the second coat of finish has been applied and dried. If lacquer stick is used before applying paint and varnish remover, the remover will soften and smear the patch out of the hole. Lacquer sticks are available in various shades. To achieve the best color, use one clear lacquer stick and one the color of the wood surface and fasten them together with masking tape. To apply lacquer stick, heat an old screwdriver or knife over a flame, preferably from a clean source such as an alcohol lamp or sterno. Wipe any char from the heated screwdriver or knife with an old cloth. Place the hot knife against the lacquer sticks where they are bound together and guide the drop into the hole. Press the warm lacquer stick firmly into place with moist fingers. Heat the knife again, and use it to clean and level the patch. Repeat the process until the hole is well filled and level with the surrounding surface. Take a single edge razor and shave off the raised portion until it is level and smooth with the wood surface. With a soft cloth and denatured alcohol remove the lacquer from around the edges of the patch. Be careful when using the alcohol because it will soften the patch. Smooth the patch with 000 steel wool and wipe the patch clean with a dry lintless cloth.

Refinishing

Before you begin to refinish, review all safety precautions. Arrange a work area where the piece will remain undisturbed till you are finished. Cover all work surfaces and floors with a layer of old paper. When working in an area where the floors are finished, an inexpensive plastic dropcloth spread under the newspaper will prevent any liquid from soaking through. Follow the following basic steps when refinishing any piece of furniture:

Remove all hinges, handles, hardware, wooden knobs, upholstery, caning, table leaves and doors or any part that can be dissembled with screwdriver.
Remove the old finish
Repair and patch any holes, dents, cracks, etc.
Prepare wood for the finish
Sand and smooth
Stain (if desired)
Fill
Apply the finish

If the glue joints are badly loosened, have them redone by a skilled woodworker.

Removing The Old Finish

Determine the type of old finish on your particular piece of furniture. For furniture with a natural finish use a good grade of commercial paint and varnish remover. For furniture with a shellac use only denatured alcohol and 00 steel wool. Paint and varnish removers are available in paste, semi-paste and thin (water-like) consistencies. The paste form is easier to use because it clings to the surface and does not run and drip. Both paste and semi-paste will not drip or run when applied to vertical surfaces. They can be spread on thicker allowing them to stay on longer so they can soften the old finish more thoroughly. Most removers have a wax or paraffin base to retard the evaporation of the remover. Once the finish is removed a waxy film will be left behind because of the waxy paraffin base present in the remover. If this film is not removed it will keep the new finish from drying and adhering properly. This waxy film can be removed by rubbing the surface with benzine, turpentine, or a similar solvent. Use clean cloths frequently to prevent the silicones in the wax base from transferring back from the cloth to the wood surface. Repeat the application of turpentine until the surface does not feel waxy. Allow the surface to dry for 24-26 hours between applications of benzine or turpentine.

Some new removers do not have this waxy base and leave no residue. They are much better to use on surfaces with carvings and surface grooves. Failure to remove the waxy film in only a few places will cause spots in the new finish.

There are several things to consider when buying paint and varnish removers. The best and often the most expensive removers contain methylene chloride. Check the contents of the remover. Removers containing methylene chloride have little or no paraffin base. These removers do not require the use of paint thinners to rinse the waxy base off. Removers containing methylene chloride do not discolor the wood and are nonflammable. Their main disadvantage is that they are very volatile and need very good ventilation while being used.

The least expensive removers contain benzine and methanol. They are undesirable because they contain paraffin. Paraffin based removers require an after rinse of turpentine or benzine.

Alkaline mixture removers are also available. They must be dissolved in water before used. These removers prove very unsatisfactory because they darken the wood surface, raise the grain and loosen glue joints. Check all labels to determine which removers are alkaline.

Remember that some removers are highly flammable and must be handled with caution whether indoors or out. When using remover, work in a well ventilated room. A garage with an open door is ideal. If you decide to work outdoors avoid direct sunlight. It will speed the drying of the remover. Most removers irritate the skin. Take care to avoid skin contact and wear rubber gloves, old shirts with long sleeves and goggles to protect your eyes. Splattering of remover can occur when brushing out intricate curves or when you are working on a piece at eye level.

Always try to apply remover when the piece is in a horizontal position. This minimizes the chance of the remover running and dripping onto other areas of the piece. Drawers and small chests can be laid on their sides or backs so that they lay horizontal.

Apply remover with a minimum of strokes. Allow it to flow on instead of being brushed on. Brush in only one direction. Use the flat side of the brush instead of the tip when applying to give a thicker application. After each stroke dip into the remover again. Do not brush back and forth once you have applied the layer. Brushing only allows air to work its way in and speeds up the evaporation of the solvents.

Apply remover to one section at a time such as a leg or table leaf and not to the entire piece. You may wish to cover other areas with paper to prevent the remover from dripping onto other sections. If the remover does drip onto other sections, clean it off immediately or spots will form and show up on the finished product. Removal time depends on effectiveness of the remover, type of finish being removed, and thickness of the coating. Removers should soak on the surface for 10-30 minutes. Test the section by scraping with a putty knife or cabinet scraper after 10 minutes to determine how fast the old finish is being softened, then at 5 minute intervals thereafter. Do not let remover remain on for more than 30 minutes. As a general rule, removers usually stop working after they have been on 30 minutes.

Unless you are using a remover that can be removed by water, you must scrape off the softened finish and remover with a dulled putty knife, spatula or even a piece of wood tapered into a dull edge. You may need a second coat of remover to soften the residue left from the first coat. To get the surface clean on the final scraping use a pad of 00 steel wool for veneer and 0 steel wool or a brush with stiff bristles instead of a scraper.

To clean away remover in grooves or carvings use an orange stick, toothbrush or cotton swab. For round surfaces such as legs or rungs wrap fine steel wool around twine or burlap raveling, then dip it into the remover and wrap around the area. Take one end of the string in each hand and pull back and forth until the old finish comes loose. Counteract the action of the remover by scrubbing the surface with a denatured alcohol solvent. Use a pad of 00 or 000 steel wool and dip into the denatured alcohol solvent. Wipe again with a coarse cloth such as burlap. Keep cleaning with alcohol until the wood surface does not appear smokey or light or feel slimy. If the remover is not all cleared off with alcohol the new finish will be sticky and will not dry.

Care must be taken when using and applying remover. Remover will soften the paste wood filler used to fill the pores on open grain wood such as walnut, oak and mahogany. If this happens, apply a new coat of filler before you apply a new finish.

After you have finished removing the old finish, dispose of all used rags and paper in an airtight container and leave them outside. A garbage can with a tight fitting lid will do. Do not place used rags or old used cans of solvent in an incinerator. Close the lids on all containers of solvent and place in a well ventilated area. Never leave saturated rags or soiled paper lying around. They are a serious fire hazard.

WARNING: Some people believe that lye is a good remover for old finishes in place of paint and varnish remover. Lye burns the wood surface and in some cases turns the wood into pulp. Lye once applied is hard to remove and often cannot be completely removed. It causes the new finish to become sticky and prevents it from drying. It can cause the new finish to come off completely.

Preparing The Wood For The Finish

Careful preparatory work will pay off especially if you are using a transparent or translucent finish where blemishes and discolored areas can show through unless carefully repaired. Even on opaque finishes, cracks and splits will show unless carefully prepared.

Dents

Dented areas on a wood surface are caused by compressing the wood fibers greatly in one area. Dents can be removed from solid wood pieces but not veneered pieces. The glue holding veneered pieces will soften and loosen the veneer causing it to buckle. To remove dents in solid wood pieces place several damp woolen rags over the dented area. The heat and moisture caused by the iron will cause the wood to swell to its normal height. This process sometimes stains the wood surface and should be done before removing any dark stains from the wood.

Grease

Any grease must be removed from the wood surface so that the new finish will adhere properly. Scrub the grease spot with dry cleaning solvent with a brush, and then with steel wool No. 000. After scrubbing with the brush and steel wool, repeat the procedure two or three times, allowing 24 hours between applications and scrubbings. If the grease spots persist, make a paste of fuller's earth and dry cleaning solvent and apply the paste to the greasy surface. Allow 24 hours to dry, then brush off and repeat if necessary. WARNING: These solvents are highly flammable and toxic. Follow all precautions and manufacturer's warnings. Work in a well ventilated area.

Removing Stains

A mild bleach is often used to lighten gray or faded wood and to remove dark spots and stains. Wear rubber gloves when mixing and applying the bleach solution. Mix 2 ounces of oxalic acid (found in hardware stores and paint stores) with 2 ounces of tartaric acid powder (found in drug stores and chemical supply houses). Place the dry chemicals in a glass container and add 1 quart of hot water to dissolve the crystals. Use the mixture while hot and reheat whenever you wish to use it. This solution is poisonous so label and keep well out of the reach of children.

Apply the solution to the entire surface concentrating on the stained areas. Keep the entire surface wet. Turn the cloths frequently and change cloths as you apply the solution. Leave the solution on for 20 minutes. To counteract the bleach mixture use a solution of 1 tablespoon of clear ammonia (nonsudsing type) with 1 quart of cold water. Use the ammonia solution to wash the bleach off the wood. Wipe the surfaces clean with a clean dry cloth soaked in clean water, then wipe the surfaces dry with a cloth. Allow 24 hours to dry. If the stain persists, repeat the bleaching procedure. After you have bleached a wood surface you should use a facial mask when sanding the surface. The dust can irritate your nose, throat and lungs.

Filling Cracks And Splits

Cracks and small holes can be filled with acrylic modeling paste. The white color of the paste can be tinted with powdered pigment or acrylic paint. When used on larger areas it tends to dry slowly and crack at the top surface. To serve as a filler you should keep the paste the consistency of window putty. If it becomes stiff, thin it with a little acrylic painting medium. Standard wood putty can be used to fill deep cracks with modeling paste on top. To apply paste or putty use a palette knife. The broad edges of these knives will produce a smooth surface. Plastic wood is not used because it doesn't provide a good surface for finishing.

Powdered pigments can be found in yellow ochre, raw and burnt sienna, and raw and burnt umber. Intermixing of these colors will produce the needed color to add to the putty or paste. Burnt sienna and burnt umber resembles red maple, walnut and mahogany. Yellow ochre or raw umber is used for yellowish woods.

Glossy wood surfaces are difficult to match. Polished wood has a quality which

colored filler cannot provide. Cracks should be filled flush with the surface with while acrylic modeling paste. Grain marks can be etched into soft acrylic modeling paste or the soft putty to make the area blend better with the surrounding wood. After the paste or putty dries, polish well. Alcohol soluble dyes of the appropriate color should be mixed to the consistency of water color. Apply this color to the dry paste with a sable brush. After drying, apply a coat of fast drying varnish to deepen the color and produce a high gloss.

Quick Repairs Of Loose Joints

Some loose joints can be repaired without complicated carpentry work.

If possible disassemble the joint completely and remove as much old glue as possible with an old doublecut file. Old glue and broken dowels can be removed from holes by using a brace and bit. Carefully bore into the old hole making sure the new hole is the same or slightly smaller than the old hole. Use a wood vise to hold the piece steady and straight while boring the hole.

Use a plain white glue or hide glue to reglue the joint. Apply pressure with bar clamps, C clamps or a rope tourniquet. Apply enough pressure to pull the joint firmly together and force some of the glue out. Remember that too much pressure will force all of the glue out and create a weak joint.

If the joint cannot be taken apart, work the glue into the joint. Needle-like injectors are also used for forcing glue into loose joints. These are available in hardware stores or by mail order from companies specializing in cabinet makers supplies.

Repairs On Veneers

To repair blistered veneer remove all dirt and dust. Loosen as much old glue as possible with a thin knife blade. Apply white glue or hide glue with a knife blade or an injector and spread as evenly as possible. Apply pressure with C clamps or weights if clamps can't be used. Never wipe off excess glue while the glue is still wet. It causes the glue to penetrate into the wood. Glue that has penetrated the wood will not take any finish and will become dark spots on the wood surface.

If a piece of veneer is missing you can obtain veneer scraps from cabinet makers supply houses or in cabinet makers shops. Cut the veneer using an exacto knife and fit the missing piece into the area. Clean all dirt off and glue the piece into the space using white glue. Place books or other heavy objects on top of the new piece of veneer to apply pressure to insure a good bond. If possible use a scrap block of wood to place on the top and bottom and apply pressure with a C clamp.

Loosened hardware is caused by enlarged screw holes. You can remedy this by filling the holes with wood putty. Let the wood putty dry at least 24 hours. Redrill the holes using a drill bit slightly smaller than the size of the screw, or you can fill enlarged holes with wood splinters so that the screws will grip more firmly.

How To Apply Oil Stain

For an even penetration of oil stain and to prevent mudiness use a wash coat mixture. Clean the entire surface with a dry cloth and a tack rag. Mix your stain and test it on an obscure corner or on a scrap of wood of the same variety for new wood. If the color is too dark thin it with turpentine; if the color is too thin darken it by leaving the stain on longer. Apply the mixture with a lintless cloth or an old brush. Work on one area at a time, such as a table leaf or a leg. Do not let the stain drip onto other areas or this will cause spotting. Wipe off any drips immediately. Leave the stain on long enough to give the desired color. Wipe off all the excess before it sets. Dry 24 hours or longer. Smooth the surface with 000 steel wool.

How To Apply Water Stain

Mix water stains by placing the powdered pigments in a glass jar. Cover the opening with a clean cloth or old hose. Add warm water according to the manufacturer's

MAKING YOUR OWN STAINS FOR HARDWOODS

Hardwood	Raw Sienna	Burnt Sienna	Burnt Umber	Raw Umber	Special Colors
WALNUT					
Dark brown			4 parts		1 part VanDyke Brown
Red brown		½ part	4 parts		
Yellow brown			3 parts	2 parts	
MAHOGANY					
Brown		3 parts			1 part Maroon Lake or Rosepink
Red		3 parts	½ part		2 parts Pink
OAK	4 parts		1 part		
CHERRY					
light	2 parts	3 parts			
dark		only			
MAPLE					
Brown			Only		
Honey		1 part	1 part		

A part is not a specific measurement, only an indication of the right proportion of color to use.
Test all stains on an obscure corner before applying to an entire area.

instructions. You can get the right color by diluting or adding more colored pigment. Test out your stain on an obscure corner or on a scrap piece of the same wood.

Wipe all areas to be stained with a damp sponge just before applying stain to insure even penetration. Apply the stain with a lintless cloth or an old brush. Do not let the stain drip onto other areas or this will cause spotting. Wipe the dripped stain off immediately. Work on one area at a time. Allow the stain to remain on long enough to obtain the desired color then wipe off with a clean cloth. Allow the piece to dry slowly. Fast drying will cause the wood to crack from swelling and shrinking too fast. Smooth the surface with 000 steel wool. Use great care around edges where the stain can be rubbed off.

Finishes And Finishing Methods

The kind of finish coat you apply depends on the condition of the surface (whether the piece is old or new), how the piece is expected to be used and the type of surface coating desired (glossy, nonglossy, or opaque), and sometimes the type of wood you are finishing.

The three basic types of finishes are surface, penetrating, and opaque. Surface finishes include lacquer, polyurethane (plastic), shellac, and varnish. Penetrating finishes include oil and wood sealers. Opaque finishes include paint and glazed or antique finishes.

Most surfaced finishes produce a hard glossy surface which is easily scratched. They must be rubbed with abrasives after each coating to reduce the amount of scratches. All finishes should be applied in dust free rooms on clear dry days. Always allow longer drying times in damp, humid or rainy weather conditions.

Varnish is used more for refinishing than for new furniture. It is highly resistant to stains from water, alcohol and other liquids.

Varnish adds depth and color to most refinished pieces. Varnishes are basically of two varieties—fast drying and slow drying. The difference can be seen in the final finish. Fast drying varnishes tend to become brittle and hard, producing a high gloss when rubbed down and polished. Slow drying varnishes produce a softer layer of finish but tend to become gummy when rubbed and sanded down. A special varnish known as spar varnish should not be used on furniture because it will become sticky and dull after a short period of time.

Varnish can be bought to produce a high gloss, semi-gloss, satin, or a flat finish. Use a good quality varnish brush to apply the varnish. For large surfaces such as table tops use a 2" or 3" brush to apply the varnish. Use a smaller brush for table legs, moldings and carvings. Dip the brush into the varnish to ⅓ of the length of the bristles. Remove the excess by tapping the bristles against the inside of the can rather than across the rim. Dragging the bristles across the rim of the can will cause air bubbles in the brush which transfer to the finish. Air bubbles are difficult to brush out before the varnish begins to dry.

Before applying the varnish vacuum clean the surface. Then wipe the entire surface with a dry lintless cloth and then with a tack rag. Varnish should not be applied if the temperature in your work area is below 70°F. Varnish does not flow on smoothly at low temperatures and tends to become brittle if allowed to dry at low temperatures. Begin applying the varnish to surfaces that show the least such as underneath table leaves, and work into the surfaces that show the most. Apply the varnish while the piece is in a horizontal position if possible. Work towards yourself rather than away. Avoid brushing a surface repeatedly. Brush the varnish on as smoothly and quickly as possible to reduce any brush marks.

Thin the first coat of varnish by adding 1 part turpentine to 4 to 6 parts of varnish. Thinning the first coat will help the varnish to flow on smoothly especially on new wood surfaces. The porosity of new wood makes it difficult to apply unthinned varnish. Varnish any moldings first. Let the varnish dry 48 hours or longer depending on the weather conditions.

For carved and molded areas use 000 steel wool to smooth the surface after each application of varnish. For flat surfaces sprinkle pumice powder (FFFF) over the varnished surface with a salt shaker. Use a blackboard eraser dipped in boiled linseed oil and rub the surface lightly with the grain. Rub around all edges very carefully to prevent rubbing through the varnish. Wipe the surface clean of pumice and oil with a dry lintless cloth. Apply a second coat of varnish from the can (no thinning needed). Let the surface dry 48 hours or longer. Rub the surface again with pumice and oil. Apply the third coat of varnish and let dry 48 hours. Use a gloss coat for a shiny surface or a satin or full coat for a matte or dulled surface. Allow 4 days to dry if gloss is used. Make a creamy paste using lemon oil or crude oil, and pumice. Rub the paste into the surface with a felt pad. Rub with the grain overlapping the strokes by ½ the width of the pad. Avoid bearing down or you will cut through the varnish especially along the edges.

For the final polish use rottenstone and oil after the surface has dried overnight. Rottenstone is a much finer grit than pumice. Rub the rottenstone in with a felt pad following the grain. Inspect by wiping off the paste with a clean rag and examining the surface for a high glossy luster. This cleans off blemishes and brush marks.

Shellac

Shellac is actually a form of varnish known as spirit varnish. Shellac is made from the flakes of resinous material obtained from lac bugs. The flakes are dissolved in denatured alcohol to form a liquid. The natural color of shellac is amber brown, labelled as orange shellac. By bleaching the resin base of shellac you can obtain a clear shellac.

Shellac is usually described and labelled as 3 pound, 4 pound, or 5 pound cut. This means that 1 gallon of alcohol has been used to dissolve 3 pound, 4 pound, or 5 pound of shellac flakes. As a general rule thin shellac with denatured alcohol before using.

Shellac produces a hard clean surface coating. It is a good sealer for porous woods. It dries quickly which helps eliminate some of the dust problems you have while the finish is drying. The major disadvantages of using shellac are: it stains quickly from water, alcohol and other liquids, it must have one coat of paste wax to stand up under use, it deteriorates with age (even in sealed cans), it scratches easily, and it is not good for furniture that is used daily or that undergoes considerable wear and tear.

To apply a shellac finish, thin the first coat of shellac using a mixture of 4 parts shellac to 1 part alcohol. Brush the shellac on evenly and quickly and let dry for 24 hours. Lightly sand the surface with 000 steel wool. Wipe the surface with a dry cloth then with a tack rag to remove any dust. Apply the second coat of shellac using a mixture of 2 parts of shellac to 3 parts of alcohol. Let the surface dry 24 hours. Lightly sand with 000 steel wool. For the third coat, thin the shellac using a mixture of 3 parts shellac to 2 parts of alcohol. Let dry for 24 hours and sand lightly with 000 steel wool. For the 4th, 5th, and 6th coats use a mixture of 4 parts shellac to 4 parts alcohol. Always sand lightly between coats of shellac with 000 steel wool. Rub the final coat of shellac with rottenstone and oil as described for varnish finishes. Apply a coat of paste wax with 000 steel wool, rubbing with the grain. Wipe off any excess with one clean cloth and polish with another clean one.

Hints On Applying Shellac

Apply in thin coats for more durability
Work quickly because it dries quickly
Use soft bristle varnish brushes
Flow the shellac on using as few brush strokes as possible

Brush across the grain using long strokes with the bristle tips stroking with the train.

If shellac is used as a sealer coat for sealing stains or before varnishing use only a 1 or 2 pound cut shellac.

If shellac is used for the finishing coat use a 3 pound cut shellac.

Orange shellac is used primarily on pine or for special effects on woods such as mahogany and walnut. You can lighten the orange shellac by mixing it with clear shellac.

Chapter 6
Shelter

WHERE YOU LIVE

Decide which sort of community is best for what you have in mind as a way oa life.

If you have youngsters, look at the schools. Availability of services in the form of auto repairs, grocery stores, medical care, and religious centers are matters of concern for many people. Check these facilities. If you are buying land in a community check not only the zoning ordinances, but also check with the city engineer or city hall to see what schemes are on the drawing board for new highways, schools, or other government developments nearby.

Buy as much land as will meet your needs that you can afford. It is awfully nice to have a little space between you and your neighbors. In municipalities, taxes and assessments for sewage, water, streets, and sidewalks are based on the width of a lot. A corner lot can be taxed higher than others if it has two street frontages.

If you are thinking of buying a home site in the country remember that you will have to pay for the construction of power and telephone lines if there are none. Water supply has to be checked, and sewage disposal.

For any kind of structure, a flat spot is easiest to build on. Whether you are putting up an A-Frame or something more elaborate, levelling a building site can cost money. So look for some flat spot big enough for what you have in mind.

A view is emotionally soothing. Try to envisualize what you will see from different parts of your proposed plans.

Be sure that the site you are looking at doesn't serve as a catchment basin for rainwater. If it is low it can collect water from any kind of a higher spot, whether a hillside or a nearby road.

Large boulders on the building site are expensive to move, unless you can afford to build a home around a boulder. A friend of ours in Arizona did just that. His living room with a fireplace crouched next to a native boulder, was indeed a conversation piece.

One distressing thing often seen is the conversion of what may have been a cow pasture to a building site. A house without trees is just too bare.

Topsoil is important if you plan on doing any kind of planting on a site. However it can be built up by the use of dried manure in each planting hole. It is expensive to remedy a poor site, but it is possible.

A source of drinking water needs to be available. If you are out of the city limits be sure to check with the county Board of Health on sewage disposal and septic tank construction regulations. Some municipalities are prohibiting the hook-up of new homes onto existing sewer lines. Check on garbage collection, its frequency, its cost.

Lastly you will have to pay a lawyer for a title search. He will check the deed in the appropriate records. However the buyer should demand of the seller that the property corner markers be in place permanently, or be easily found. It is a good idea to walk over the property lines with the seller to spot the property markers. Not having those can be an expensive proposition. You will still be charged for a survey even if the corner markers are in. You will also pay extra if you request that the complete boundary lines be marked.

PAINTING YOUR HOUSE

The most expensive thing about painting is the cost of the labor. Paint and supplies are only a small portion of the cost involved. By learning some basic techniques you can paint as well and effortlessly as the experts. If you sell your home within 6 months of painting it, the cost of labor, paint, and supplies is tax-deductible.

Paints come in flat, gloss and semi-gloss finishes. Flat finishes are recommended for ceilings, bedrooms, and living rooms. Semi-gloss paints or enamels are less shiny than gloss enamels. They are sometimes used for walls, but usually are used for wood trim in rooms other than kitchens and baths. Flat paint is not used for kitchens, baths, and utility rooms. Gloss finishes are recommended for kitchens and bathrooms because they are easily washed and quite resistant to wear.

Walls and ceilings in light, soft colors make the room seem larger, lighter, and cheerful. The same color is used for walls and woodwork because the room will seem larger, less broken up and more restful.

A gallon of paint will usually cover both the ceilings and walls of a 11 x 12 room, using only one coat. If your room is larger than this or if you will need more than one coat, measure the length and width of the room as well as the doors and windows in the room.

Preparation

Move all furniture away from the walls to the center of the room. Remove all curtains, drapes, rods, window shades, blinds, pictures, and picture hooks. Cover the floor and all aurniture with drop cloths, old sheets of cloth or plastic. Remove lights, window shutters, and other fixtures that are not to be painted should be removed. If you are not using a paint guard when painting the windows, cover the edge with masking tape.

Both painted and well-papered walls can be painted. Painted walls should be clean and smooth before you paint. All loose flakes of peeling paint should be scraped off, all cracks and nail holes should be patched with a spackling compound. When using an emulsion paint, combine the spackle compound with some of the paint instead of water so that the patched area will not absorb any more paint than the rest of the wall. Nails in the ceiling that are showing through the paint need to be nailed back in and covered with spackling compound so they will not show when they are painted over. Then the scraped and patched areas should be sanded until smooth.

Brush and wipe the dust off all surfaces to be painted with either a dry mop or a cloth. If the old paint has a glossy shiny finish, sand the surface lightly so that the new paint will take. Or if you prefer you may scrub it with a strong detergent.

Any grease, dirt, and stickiness, must be removed by washing with detergent. Any mild household cleaner can be used. The ceiling is washed first. Then begin at the bottom of the wall, and wash up to prevent streaks from forming, washing the trim as you go along the wall.

All patched areas are painted over and allowed to dry before the whole area is painted.

Rust should be removed from hardware, radiators, or other metal before painting. Any areas around windows or bathtubs where the joints are open need to be caulked before painting. Caulking must dry for 24 hours before being painted.

Preparing A Wallpapered Wall

Only latex paints should be used over wallpaper because other paints will soak into the paper, making it difficult to remove later.

Loose edges of wallpaper should be repasted and sanded when dry until smooth with fine sandpaper.

Dust the wallpaper with a dry mop, clean cloth, or vacuum cleaner. Remove grease spots by using a paste of cornstarch and a non-flammable cleaning fluid. Let the mixture dry and then brush off. The treatment can be repeated if necessary.

Painting Procedure

Do the ceiling first, then the walls containing windows, and finally the interior walls.

The ceiling is completed without stopping. An entire wall or entire window or door should be completed without stopping.

If the woodwork is painted while the walls are papered, paint the woodwork before the wallpaper is put up.

If both the wall and woodwork are done with the same paint, do the woodwork as you proceed down the wall.

For windows, first do the sash, then the frame, and the trim. For doors, begin at the top and paint the molding, then the panels and edges.

Paint baseboards from the center toward the edges, using a paint guard or shield to protect the floor and wall.

To avoid closing off a stairway when painting steps, paint every other step, then when dry paint the alternate steps.

Brushes Or Rollers

You need a 3½ inch or 4 inch nylon brush that is flagged and tipped for walls if you are not going to use a roller. For woodwork and trim and for corners where the roller will not reach you need a 2 inch nylon brush that is flagged and tipped. You also need a roller set with a type of roller made for the paint you are using.

Caring For Brushes And Rollers

Wrap brushes and rollers in aluminum foil or wax paper to keep them in condition, and lie them flat overnight or during the rest period.

Brushes should be cleaned in the recommended thinner for the paint. The brushes are dried and then wrapped in paper or plastic. Lay the brushes flat or store the brush standing in a container with the bristles up.

Using A Brush

Paints, thinners, paint removers, and paint brush cleaners are all toxic so keep all soiled clothes, papers, and supplies out of the way of children.

Some paints and solvents must be used with adequate ventilation.

Do not dip a paint brush in a can of paint, instead pour a small amount of paint in a large wide can, such as coffee can. Then dip the brush into the can. Don't overload the brush or roller with paint because the excess will just drip off. When using a roller, pour a small amount of paint into the roller tray.

Dip the brush into the paint. Begin painting at a corner, whether you are painting the wall or the ceiling.

For a wall, paint a strip of wall beginning at the ceiling 2-3 feet wide. Paint next to the woodwork if necessary. Then paint on down the wall for the 2-3 strip as you begin, brushing freely in all directions. Finish with brush strokes running up and down. Continue painting the wall in strips until the wall is completed before beginning on another wall.

Using A Roller

First use the brush to paint a strip of wall at the edge of the ceiling for 2-3 feet. Then use the roller, painting down the wall a large V or W beginning at the area of the ceiling that you used the brush on. Then roll the roller crosswise to spread the paint evenly. Finish with up and down strokes.

Painting Ceilings

Using the small trim brush, paint a 3-4 inch strip along the four edges of the ceiling. Then use either a wide brush or a roller and finish the ceiling. If using a brush, brush freely in all directions. Then finish with brush strokes that run all in one direction of the ceiling.

Usually the ceiling is painted with the walls. This is because the ceiling is the first part of the paint to darken and discolor and it will look dingy and dirty if not painted when the walls are painted. Ceilings with radiant heating in them are the first to darken. If only the ceiling is painted, or if the walls are painted a different color use masking tape at the edges of the wall so that it doesn't get painted.

Choosing Paints

Bargain Paints

Paints that are reduced or on sale because they are very old are not bargains. Such paint loses much of its quality and is risky to use because it becomes too thick, and the color is uneven because the paint settles while you use it.

Do not buy several paints to mix together because different kinds of paints cannot be combined readily.

Choosing An Exterior Paint

An exterior paint is subjected to much more wear than an interior paint. An exterior paint should have six characteristics: (1) It should be durable and expected to last for 4-6 years. (2) It should have a normal form and rate of wearing, such as the self-cleaning paints have. (3) It should have a clean, highly reflective color. (4) It should be resistant to dirt, moisture, blistering and peeling, resistant to stain by corrosive metals. (5) It should have good covering or hiding qualities. (6) In some localities it should be resistant to hydrogen sulfide fumes.

The exterior of a house is either wood, masonry, or metal and each one has its own painting needs.

The surface must be dry, free of oil, grease, dirt, and dust. The paint may peel, blister or retain moisture if these are not removed. Paint when the temperature is from 50-90°F. Dry air and sunshine are considered best for paint.

Most paint failure is not caused by using poor paint, but is caused by choosing the wrong paint for a surface, or by not preparing the surface properly before painting.

Blistering and peeling is usually caused by moisture beneath the paint or improper cleaning of the surface. If moisture (in a high humidity area, for example) is likely to be a problem, use a paint which is not moisture sensitive. If blistering and peeling occur, correct the cause of the moisture, then remove the peeling paint and blisters and apply a paint which is not moisture sensitive.

Nails, screens, and roofing can rust and cause brown streaks on light colored paint. When aluminum and copper corrode they produce gray or green streaks. These metals should be coated with an anti-corrosive primer before you paint, or if you want the metal to retain its natural color, apply a clear primer such as marine varnish. If metal stains occur on painted wood the spots will have to be sanded and repainted. On natural masonary the stains cannot be removed but they will wear away in time by themselves. The metal should still be treated to prevent corrosion.

Mildew can also be a problem. Some paints are mildew-resistant. Exterior latex paints are especially prone to mildew, so the surface should have a mildew retardant used as a primer coat first. Before repainting with a mildew-resistant paint, wash the surface with a strong detergent in warm water. Trisodium phosphate can be used as a detergent using 1 tablespoon to a gallon of water. Be careful when using this because it can be quite toxic. Wear rubber gloves and be extremely careful that it does not drip on your body or hair. Allow the surface to dry thoroughly before repainting.

Chalking can become a problem with exterior paints because weathering and rain can cause the paint to chalk. This usually only happens when the wrong type of paint is used, such as an interior paint used on an exterior surface. If chalking is undesirable, select a paint with no chalking qualities. Chalking is not desirable on the window shutters of un-painted masonary because the paint will chalk and run on the masonary.

MOBILE HOMES

One of the greatest housing changes on the American scene has been the explosion of mobile homes. Cheaper than conventional homes, they offer an opportunity of owning a home for many people with limited incomes.

Mobile parks have been a problem sometimes with exploitive owners taking advantage of a shortage of space, particularly in large city suburbs. A group of mobile home owners, tired of being exploited, forced the county legislature of Suffolk County, Long

Island, to enact what may well become model legislation. Under the new laws (1) Park owners cannot force mobile home owners in the park to buy services or supplies from him or anyone he selects. (2) The park owner cannot collect a rake-off for the sale of mobile homes in the park unless he made the sale.

Some park owners have insisted that mobile homes using the park must be bought from them; other park owners have added charges for space rental if visitors stayed as guests. The best solution for such problems is an organized effort of mobile home owners to have legislation passed that will protect their interests.

MAJOR APPLIANCES
Televisions

Color tv sets are expensive to buy and run. A color set uses about 600 KWH of electricity a year, a solid state color set about 440 KWH a year. The solid state black and white set uses about 120 KWH per year, while the black and white tube model uses 350 KWH a year.

With 10 years generally considered the life span of a tv set, a recent study showed that a $400 color set will cost another $400 to repair and operate over a 10 year period.

Washing Machines

The greater the number of cycles, the higher the price and the chance of problems. If you wash mostly cotton and have school kids and a worker in the house, a heavy duty washer is practical. Special cycles for lightly soiled clothes and synthetics are probably not needed.

If you are a family without youngsters, a machine with more cycles and temperatures might serve your needs. This will cost more but provides a wider choice of controls.

Cold water use is much recommended for energy conservation. Unfortunately we have found that it doesn't work well with permapress materials, which were made to require higher temperatures to look neat.

Washers range in their water capacities from 9, 10, and 12 pounds of clothes. If you live in a small apartment the small size will be an almost automatic decision. If you have a large apartment and more people dependant on the machine, a larger tank is needed.

Water enters the washer by one of two methods. In cheaper models a time-fill method is used which allows water to run in for a given period of time, and then stops. Water pressure of about 15 pounds per square inch is required. The other method is controlled by a meter that allows water to enter the washer until a certain level is reached. The machine will not begin to wash until water reaches this level.

Most automatic washers require from 22 to 44 gallons of water per complete cycle, and de luxe models use more than economy models. Wash and wear cycles may use more water than regular cycles because of extra cold water brought in before the first spin.

Good and thorough rinsing is needed. If this is inadequate you can wind up itching wildly from the dried detergent in the clothes. Machines will provide anywheres from one to nine rinses. One rinse should be a deep rinse as a minimum, additional ones are better for cleaning soap or detergent out of clothes.

Water extraction is a major concern, because it is difficult as well as messy to move a load of inadequately spun clothes from a washer to the dryer, and places extra demands on the dryer. If the rate of spin is high, more water is removed. However more wrinkles go into the clothes at higher spin rates, so a compromise has been worked out which allows some models to have two spin rates, high and low. The high rate might be used for items that are not ordinarily ironed or that need no ironing.

Clothes Dryers

This appliance is just about indispensable, especially in cold or rainy climates where clotheslines have limited use for outside drying. Louisiana State University estimates that it takes about 12 minutes to hang a 12 pound load of wash on a clothes line and then take it down. Add to that 12 minutes walking time to and from the clothes line and the back strain of moving wet clothes to the line and it is evident that a workable dryer is a necessity and not a luxury!

Four years ago we bought the cheapest electric economy model Sears sells, for $60 on sale. It tumble dries, has one heat level and a timer. A good machine doesn't have to be expensive.

One of the problems in installing a dryer is the need for venting to permit the escape of the moisture-laden air driven off in the drying process. Small portable models are less of a problem because the amount of moisture is comparatively small but since over 95° of all dryers are of the vent type, the moist air from drying must be led out of the house by plastic or metal pipes. The cost of venting depends on how much tubing is needed and the trouble that is involved in getting the end of the tube into the open.

Venting kits are available at hardware and building supply stores. If you are handy you can do the installation 'yourself. The biggest job may be punching a hole in the wall to get the tube into the open.

Gas dryers are readily available and usually cost somewhat more than electric models, although they are less expensive to operate (see table, p. 175). If you decide on a gas dryer, be sure the appliance comes equipped with an automatic lighting arrangement, rath-

Comparison Between Gas And Electric Dryers

	Gas	Electric 120 Volt	240 Volt
Circuit required	Existing 120 volt receptacle	Requires own circuit	Requires own circuit Can be converted to 120 volt
drying rate	long	short	short
purchase price	more than electric	cheapest	medium to high
operation costs	low; ⅓ to ¼ electric dryer costs	higher than gas	higher than gas

er than a match motivated one. The best type, which is slightly more expensive to buy but cheaper to operate, is the electric glow coil lighter which functions only as needed. The automatic pilot burns continuously and is less desirable from the energy conservation viewpoint.

If you decide on a gas dryer be sure it comes equipped with a safety device to guard against gas escape if the pilot light goes out. Gas dryers are readily adapted to any kind of gas locally available.

Refrigerators

When buying a refrigerator you need to make three major decisions.
1. Do you want a combination refrigerator-freezer or a standard model?
2. What size refrigerator do you want?
3. What kind of a defrosting system do you want?

The standard models provide fresh food storage and a limited space for short time holding of frozen food. The freezer section, usually at the top, is part of the refrigerator space. There is usually a movement of air between the two sections making long term storage less than excellent.

In a combination refrigerator-freezer, the top compartments are insulated from one another and no air movement occurs between them. The freezer compartment remains at °F. which allows long term storage of frozen foods.

Both types come in a wide range of sizes. A rule of thumb can provide 6 to 9 cubic feet of refrigerator space for a family of two, with 1 additional cubic foot for each additional

family member. A family of four would want between 8 and 11 cubic feet of refrigerator space. If a combination unit is being considered, 2 cubic feet of freezer space for a family of two is needed, plus 1 cubic foot more for each additional member. A family of four would want about 4 cubic feet of freezer space in a combination unit. These are flexible figures. Frequent entertaining and social activities might require somewhat more space than this formula.

There are three combinations or kinds of defrosting systems available. The simplest and cheapest is the manually controlled system. This requires that the refrigerator be turned off and the accumulated ice be allowed to melt around the coils, caught in a large tray, and then emptied. Defrosting should be done three or four times a year. How often you need to do it depends on the efficiency of the unit as well as how often and how long you have the door open. A wooden or plastic scraper can be used to scrape off the accumulation of frost around the unit, reducing the need for defrosting. However don't use an ice-pick for the job. This allows the gas to escape, and ruins the refrigerator.

The major build-up of frost in a freezer is usually at the top of the unit. Careful use of a wooden or plastic scraper will help reduce frost build-up in the entire unit.

As a refrigerator gets older the rubber gaskets around the door should be checked. Sometimes these crack or peel away, forcing the cold unit to work much harder.

One item sometimes overlooked is the side on which the door of the unit opens, if it has one door. Be sure that the spot you have chosen for the refrigerator leaves room for the door to open up. If you get a combination unit the problem is two fold.

There are many extras available for a refrigerator. An ice-maker is one. Another is a cold water dispenser. Both are nice, but they add to the cost and require more energy.

Vacuum Cleaners

These are a necessary luxury, particularly for carpeting. If your place has small area rugs, it may be cheaper to shake them and dust up than to invest in a vacuum cleaner. But if you feel that a vacuum cleaner will save you time, ask yourself a couple of questions before you go out looking.

What size will store conveniently for you? Closet space is always a premium and a large awkward machine is troublesome to store out of the way. What size can you handle conveniently?

What uses will the machine be put to? For floors, carpeting, and rugs a wide range of machines can serve well. If you have a workshop area, something a little bulkier is needed.

Can you afford it? Is it really necessary?

In addition to the tank models, upright models are available. An upright can weigh as little as 7 pounds and is easy to maneuver because it is one unit; canister and tank models have to be hauled around by their hoses or wands. They are also bulky to take from room to room, particularly up and down stairs.

A used vacuum cleaner is worth considering. They are relatively simple machines and beyond the motor failing, there are few things that can go wrong with them. A rebuilt or little-used model should last as long as 10 years.

Some machines are noisier than others. Keep that in mind when trying out models at the store, and remember that the noise level will be higher in a room at home than in a large showroom.

Kitchen Ranges

If you rent an apartment or buy a home and no kitchen range comes with the house, you must decide whether it is to be built in or free-standing and whether you want gas or electric.

To help you compare we have included a table adapted from the California Agricultural Extension Service. Study it to see what the advantages and disadvantages are for each kind.

A kitchen range should last 15 years or more, with care. It is a major investment of money so look around a bit before buying to see which model meets your needs.

A built-in range has some built-in disadvantages. It can't be moved, so if you move it has to stay. It is usually more expensive to buy and to install, takes up more space than the free-standing models and if not installed properly can be a headache.

Free-standing models have some drawbacks too. If you move it may not fit into the next home also, standard models have low ovens which may call for stooping. However free-standing models are usually cheaper, take up less space and are easy to move.

Your particular situation will influence the choice. If there is a limited kitchen area the free-standing model may be a necessity. If you have a larger kitchen and some extra cash, the built-in model may be what you want.

Although natural gas is the most common kind used in the homes, bottled gas (found in suburban and rural areas) is equally usable with a gas range. Safety devices for gas systems are required on all gas stoves and ovens. These prevent the flow of gas if the pilot light goes off. Either an electric coil lighting system or a flame system may be used.

Your final decision as to gas or electric, built-in or free-standing will be governed by costs and personal preferences.

Comparison Between Gas And Electric Ranges

Factor	Gas Range	Electric Range
Installation needs	Gas line, pressure regulating systems	Wall receptacle; 240 volt wiring in a 240 volt range circuit with individual cut-off by fuse or circuit breaker.
Heat efficiency	50% heat loss	20% heat loss
Hazards	Boilover can extinguish flame.	Electrical shorts can be a problem.
Problems	Pilots heat up kitchen. Pilots can go out due to drafts, boiling over, low gas pressure.	Surface utensils should be flat to fit the unit and make compact. Oven utensils heat up.
Low temperature oven controls	140°F.	150°F.

Dishwashers

A dishwasher is no luxury-it is essential. The percentage of families in the United States who use one is increasing steadily. An automatic dishwasher saves hours of work and eliminates a dreary job.

Studies have shown that dishwashing by hand, including cleanup, takes about 75 minutes a day. With a dishwasher that time is cut to about 35 minutes a day. Washing by hand usually requires more hot water than the machine does.

Automatic dishwashers reduce the bacterial count on dishes from a high of 390 bacteria per dish when hand washed, to 1 bacteria per dish in a machine.

It is cheaper to use a dishwasher only when the machine is full of dishes. For a family of three it may take two meals to fill the machine up.

There are gas dishwashers available, but they are not as commonly sold as are electric units.

The amount of water needed to wash a load of dishes ranges from 7 to 15 gallons, using water directly from the hot water line. In December 1974, the New York City Consumer Affairs Department estimated that washing a load of dishes cost 9ᶜ (with electricity at 9ᶜ a kilowatt hour). Each time a machine is operated, about one kilowatt hour of electricity is used.

There are two major classes of dishwashers, portables which move around on wheels, and built-in models. These can be minus any cabinet work, or under-the-counter models which require cabinet walls.

Portable models are moved into position near the sink, connected to the water supply and turned on. When not in use they move out of the way against some wall of the kitchen. A small table-top dishwasher holds so few items and uses so much water that it is not worthwhile.

Machines can be either top loading or front loading. A front loading machine may be a little easier to get into because it pulls out in two sections, top and bottom. With a top load machine, you have to fold back the top rack to get into the bottom rack.

There are two types of drains. In one a pump moves the water out of the machine into the sink drain. The others have gravity drain, and requires a drain through the floor to an outlet, and is found only on installed models.

We prefer a machine that has two complete cycles of washing, both with fresh detergent and fresh water. One rinse is adequate, but some machines have as high as four rinses which adds to the water bill.

Machines come rated by "place settings." A ten place setting capacity really means the machine will handle dishes, cooking utensils, and flatware for five or six people.

Machines are available with a range of special cycles for cleaning heavily soiled dishes, heating plates, and rinsing dishes that will be washed later on so that the food doesn't dry on the dishes. These add to the cost and energy requirements.

Water Heaters

This item is less likely to be bought than most of the appliances in this section. However a few words and ideas may help you save money if you should need one at some time.

First look at the amount of hot water used daily for various household activities:

dishwashing, hand — 5 gallons
dishwashing, automatic — 10 gallons
automatic clothes washer/load (depends on cycle used) — 25 gallons
standard clothes washer/wringer — 15 gallons
tub bath — 15 gallons
shower — 10 gallons
preparing meals — 5 gallons
odds and ends of cleaning — 3 gallons
personal washing — 3 gallons
hand laundry, load — 10 gallons
baby bath — 3 gallons

A rough rule of thumb to determine the needed tank size is to allow 10 gallons per day per person, 20 gallons for a baby, and then add 10 or 15 gallons onto that. In our home with three people our 52 gallon heater provides more than enough hot water for an automatic dish washer, clothes washer, three bathrooms, and a darkroom

Heaters are available for use with electricity and gas, natural or LP. Electric water heaters have an advantage in that they can be installed in almost any location; underneath a cabinet, in a closet, under the stairs or in an attic. They require no venting, which a gas water heater will require.

They come in all sorts of shapes from round to square, tall, short and in between. The shape you select will depend on the space available for it.

We recommend the quick recovery type of water heater, whether gas or electric. They replace hot water as quickly as it is used, and do not require more electricity than a standard model.

The electric models have two electric heating units to do this job, gas heaters use a burner with a high BTU rating. The models cost about the same in any case.

The quick recovery electric units are rated and plainly marked to indicate the tank capacity, the pressure the tank can withstand, and the location of the pressure safety valve.

USED MAJOR APPLIANCES

Refrigerators

1. Be sure the refrigerator has been running for at least 24 hours before you buy it, if it has been stored.

2. Find out how old the unit is. A refrigerator is expected to last about 15 years. The age will give you some idea of how much you can expect.

3. Check the gasket around the door to see if it is in good shape. This piece of

equipment is indispensable to keeping cold air in.

4. Check the outward and inside appearance of the unit to see if it seems to be intact, with no broken shelves or unusual wear and tear.

5. Smell the inside. Bad odors can get into the material of the refrigerator and cannot be removed.

6. Check the electric wires to see if they are frayed or worn. Check if the unit will fit into the area you have in mind for it. Does the door open on the correct side for the space you have? Do you have the right electrical connections for it, and lastly how does the price compare with a new unit with a guarantee?

Newspaper ads, store sales of floor models or damaged models, repossessed models all offer opportunities for savings.

Electric Stoves

1. Turn each of the surface units to high and see if they turn cherry red. If a coil does not get red it is burned out. Replacing it adds to the cost.

2. Put a ruler across the top of the coils to see if they are reasonably level. Dips mean loss of heat.

3. Check the door to see if it opens easily and stays partway open. Check to see if it closes tightly, an important function in baking.

4. Check the racks and rack supports to see if the racks move in and out easily.

5. Check the age of the stove. They have a life expectancy of about 16 years.

6. Turn the stove on to see if the top heat units of the oven heat up for broiling, and the bottom units for baking.

Then decide if the stove will fit into the space you have in mind for it. Do you have

a 210 volt wiring circuit? Compare the price with a new model with its one year guarantee.

Gas Stoves

Check points 3, 4, 5, and 8 listed under electric stove above.

1. Turn on the burners and see if gas is coming through. If not they may need cleaning with a fine wire.

2. Check the broiler drawer to see if it closes tightly.

3. Turn on the oven. If it is lighted with a match hold the flame near the burner and turn on the gas. If it doesn't catch, turn off the gas and try the same procedure again. If it still fails to light it may require a service call. Automatic pilots take a little time.

Then decide if you have the right connections for the stove, and a suitable place for it. Is it worth the price?

Washing Machines

Opportunities to buy a used washing machine can result in savings if you have some idea of what to look for.

1. Try the agitator to see if it moves easily. If it does, it may be attached too loosely.

2. Remove the agitator lifting straight up. Check the tub to see if it is smooth. If it is cracked or chipped it can damage clothes.

3. Find out how old the machine is. A normal life expectancy is about 10 years.

4. Inquire as to the size of the family owning the machine. If it is a large family the machine will have been used more heavily and its life expectancy shortened.

5. Ask for the machine to be demonstrated to see if there are any leaks or other mechanical difficulties.

6. If you are looking at a wringer type washer see if the rollers are in good shape, and see if they release readily.

7. Move the machine to see if the castors or wheels move easily. They may need replacing, which is not expensive but worth noting.

8. Check the outside of the machine to see if it is in good condition.

Having come this far, the same questions as for other major appliances are useful. Do you have the proper outlets or plumbing connections? Will the machine fit into the spot you have selected for it?

SMALL PORTABLE ELECTRICAL APPLIANCES

These are small easily moved appliances used in a small area of the home. Many of them, like the toaster and coffee pot, have become integral parts of our homes. The following notes may help you in selecting the one best suited for your needs. Buying a used minor appliance is somewhat risky, because repair costs can be high in comparison to original cost. Simple items, like a waffle maker for $5, can have little go wrong with them. Other more complex things, like blenders and mixers can be more troublesome when bought used.

Buy only those you will use often enough to justify your investment. If you don't like waffles, there is no need to buy a waffle iron to be used for guests. It is cheaper to buy frozen waffles.

Irons

Electric irons come in two kinds, steam-dry and spray-steam-dry. The spray-steam-dry, at the touch of a button, will put out a sprinkle oa warm water through an opening at the front of the handle.

The standard steam iron puts out steam through openings in the bottom as you iron. The steaming stops when the iron is placed straight up, in the resting position.

We prefer the spray-steam iron. It converts easily from dry to steam, the tank can be refilled with water, and it heats rapidly.

A second much used type is the spray iron, which throws out a water spray.

When you get ready to buy, there are a few things to look for. The most practical temperature dial will list fabrics, not temperatures; check on how much trouble is involved in filling the tank; check out the iron rests when it is standing up between passes; make sure it converts easily from steam to dry.

Coffee Pots

We have a great many coffee pots, but our favorite is the Mr. Coffee pot, that can make from 2 to 8 cups at a time. A given quantity of home ground coffee gives us more cups in Mr. Coffee than in any other unit we use. We like the glass container, and there is no boiling or bubbling.

We use four cup travel percolators made of metal when we travel to motels and hotels. You can get an automatic percolator which either shuts off when the desired strength is reached, or turns to a lower temperature to keep the coffee warm. The non-automatic percolator keeps perking away until you unplug it.

A few points to keep in mind when shopping for a percolator.

1. Be sure you can pour the coffee out without the cover falling into the cup.

2. Try to have a light of some sort to tell you when the coffee is ready to serve.

3. A dripless spout is heavenly.

4. Get a well balanced, not easily tipped shape.

5. Have a circuit breaker to protect the coffee percolator from damage if the contents boil away.

6. A submersible percolator makes washing easier.

7. Be sure you can see how much water or coffee is in the pot.

Travel models are simple and you sacrifice some of these features for such a unit.

The major choice in the vacuum type coffee maker is whether you want glass or metal. We prefer the glass units, feeling that the coffee tastes better.

Other important points to consider are the need for insulated handles that won't heat up, a cover that can be used with either top or bottom bowl, and a signal light to show when the coffee is brewed and ready to drink.

Espresso makers and simple flared pots for Turkish coffee are other coffee options. We have an electric coffee grinder that roasts, grinds, and blends our own coffee. We think our grinder has long paid for itself; since it grinds very fine we get more cups per pound of coffee. We buy most of our green coffee beans from a fabulous little coffee shop in New York, Empire Coffee and Tea Company, 486 Ninth Avenue, New York 10018. They have bags of just about every kind of coffee around, and that includes excellent French or Vienna roast Columbian beans, caffein free! They also have the best price around on coffee pots and accessories.

Mixers

An electric mixer can save a lot of arm wearying work in the kitchen. It is a mechanical servant that saves your energy and helps turn out a more uniform product. A good mixer can mash, whip, mix, beat, cream, and blend. Some come with attachments that enable them to grind meat, juice citrus, slice, shred, and do a number of other kitchen chores.

Most kitchen mixers have removable heads that allow removal and use as a hand mixer.

Some beaters are off center so that you can add ingredients easily while the machine is in operation. If you have one that has the beaters in the middle of the bowl area it may have to be halted to add things. Whatever you do, don't raise the beaters with the machine in operation. You will get unusual kitchen walls!

In buying a mixer you must decide what your main uses will be, how many speeds you really need, and whether you want metal or glass bowls.

Blenders

If you have a baby around, a blender can make it easy for you to prepare the baby's food at home. Blenders chop, liquify, whip, mix, crumb, grate, and do all sorts of things. Blenders cannot mash potatoes, whip egg whites or knead dough. They cannot extract juice from fruits, but we do put peeled pomengranate fruits in at the lowest speed to separate the juice and the seeds.

Our blender has solid state controls, made of components so small as to be measured in fractions of an inch. These controls last longer with less problems than older large controls. The cost is slightly higher with solid state controls because there are usually a larger number of speeds available.

A feature on some few blenders allows you to use certain jars in place of the container that comes with the machine. This is handy if your container is broken, and a convenience if you are processing quantities of food for storage.

Toasters

This is a luxury that we all like. You can buy a model that turns out two slices, four slices or even six slices of toast. Some models require that you push down the slice, others go down from the weight of the slice placed in the machine. Some models have the heat controlled by the amount of humidity in the bread, with a longer toasting period for bread with a higher moisture content.

Some complex models work as a toaster as well as a small oven, useful for one or two people. These combination units can be used to toast sandwiches, keeping extra slices of toast warm and even for baking.

When buying a toaster be sure there is a darkness control, that the machine is on some sort of insulation to keep your table from burning, and that the handles are well insulated to keep your hands from burning. A removable crumb tray at the bottom makes it possible to clean the machine.

SMALL APPLIANCE MAINTENANCE

Maintenance of small appliances at home is a good way to save money, get something fixed in a reasonable time, and prolong the life and usefulness of a home labor-saving device.

Our table is a handy guide for simple repairs you can often do yourself on small home appliances. Be sure when you are doing this kind of work that the appliance is disconnected, to avoid shocks. The tools needed are simple—a small screwdriver, small adjustable pliers, and some electrical tape.

Replacing a plug is not difficult, and requires parts that are easily available at hardware and discount stores. Fixing a broken heating unit can be relatively simple if the break is near the terminal. Rewiring a lamp is simple.

If you determine you can't do the job and take it in to be repaired, be sure you get a price quote first.

If you have an old appliance that you cannot fix, it may be cheaper to go ahead and buy a new one.

Damaged Plugs And Cords

If you are checking one of the small appliances listed in the table and decide you need a new plug or a replacement cord, check both. If the plug has bent or loose prongs, it should be replaced. If the cord is frayed it needs to be replaced. Replacing a cord other than for a lamp is a bit more complicated, since each item is built differently.

If only the plug needs replacing you will need a screwdriver, a sharp knife and a new plug, with a UL label. A plug with a shank for better grasping is a good idea.

We have provided sketches and step by step guide for this repair job (Figure 14).

A. Cut the damaged plug above the damaged cord section.

B. Remove the damaged plug from the cord, and slip a new one on.

C. Separate the two sections of the cord for an inch and a half.

D. Tie the underwriter's knot in the two sections of the cord.

E. Use a sharp knife, or wire strippers to remove about a half inch of the insulation from the end of the wires. Be careful not to cut any of the small wires inside the insulation.

E. Twist the clusters of wires together, for each of the two sections you have previously separated in a clockwise direction.

G. Pull the underwriter's knot down firmly.

H. Pull each wire around each terminal to the screw.

I. Wrap each wire around its screw, clockwise.

J. With the screwdriver tighten each screw. The insulation should be next to the screw head but not under it.

K. Replace the insulation cover back on the plug.

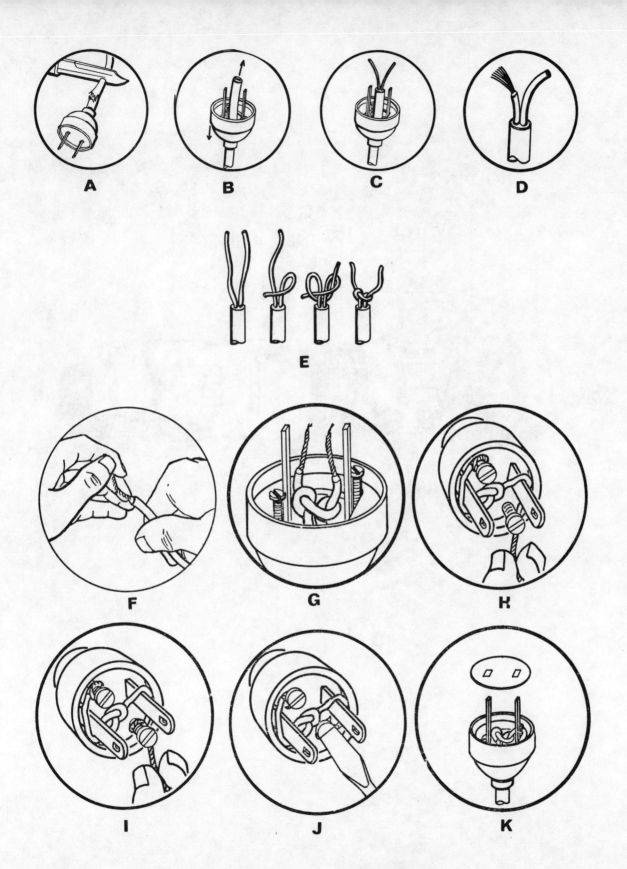

Fig. 14

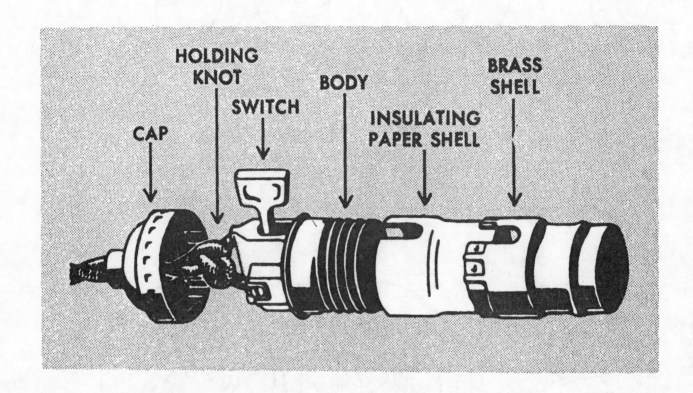

Fig. 15

Simple Repairs For Small Household Appliances

Appliance	Symptoms	Cause	Remedy
Can openers	1. Won't cut 2. Won't cut lids off completely	1. Can be installed incorrectly 2. Dent in can	1. Check position of can in opener 2. Turn can over, or skip dented areas
Fan	1. Noisy vibration	1. Bent blade 2. Motor damaged	1. Turn blades to see where rubbing occurs. Metal blades can be forced back in position. 2. If No. 1 doesn't work, take in for repairs.
Heaters, space or radiant	1. Coils fail to heat	If open coil type, check to see if coil is broken.	If break is near a terminal (screw-like), clean insulation from end of wire cord and fasten around the terminal in the direction screw is tightened. Other breaks require shop repair.
Iron, dry	1. Heats slowly 2. Overheats 3. Fails to heat	1. Connected to extension cord or light socket 2. Thermostat too high, or broken. 3. Blown fuse; cord or plug needs replacing; heating element burned.	1. Plug in to wall outlet 2. Set thermostat lower. If this doesn't work it needs shop repairs. 3. Replace fuses, cord or plug. If these do not work, needs shop repair.
Iron, steam	No steam, or irregular spurts	Water passageways have become clogged with deposits	Use mineral-free water. Special solvents are available.
Electric blanket	Fails to heat	1. Fuse blown 2. Cord or plug need replacing 3. Switch not functioning	1, 2. Repair 3. Replace switch
Hotplate	No heat	1. Fuse blown, cord or plug broken 2. Broken heating elements	1. Replace needed parts 2. Same as heater
Percolator	Won't function	1. Fuse blown, cord or plug broken 2. Percolator fuse blown 3. Clogged hollow stem	1. Replace needed parts 2. Locate fuse on bottom of appliance and replace 3. Clean with water or straightened metal hanger
Toaster	Won't work	1. Fuse blown, cord or plug broken 2. Heating elements burned out	1. Replace needed parts 2. Replace with new one, or take to shop for repair.
Roaster or fry pan	1. Not heating 2. Not hot enough 3. Too hot	1. A-Thermostat off B-Fuse blown, cord or plug broken 2. A-Thermostat too low B-Connected to long extension cord. C-Lid bent out of line 3. A-Thermostat too high B-Thermostat broken	1. A-Return thermostat or replace needed parts B-Replace needed parts 2. A-Set thermostat higher. B-Connect to wall outlet. C-Replace lid 3. A-Turn thermostat down B-Return unit for new thermostat

Appliance	Symptom	Cause	Remedy

Waffle iron	1. Won't heat
	2. Overheats (automatic)
		1. A-Fuse blown, cord or plug broken.
		   B-Connecting cord broken between elements
		   C-Heating coil burned out
		2. Broken thermostat
			1. A-Replace needed parts
			   B-Replace cord.
			   C-Replace
			2. Return for repairs

Mixer	Beaters strike bowl	1. Beaters not in firmly 2. Machine head not adjusted	1. Seat the beaters firmly in sockets 2. Adjust beater height until beaters barely touch bowl.
Blender	1. Leaking 2. Stalls	1. Assembled incorrectly 2. Overloaded	1. Check assembly and tighten 2. Remove some of contents

Pressure cooker	1. Leaks steam
	2. Pressure gauge fails to register 0
		1. Worn gasket
		   Leaky petcock
		2. Gauge damaged
			1. Replace gasket
			   Replace petcock
			2. Replace gauge.

Rewiring A Lamp

This is a simple procedure and can be done in fifteen minutes or less. You will need a pocket knife, screwdriver, pliers, and 6 feet of cord plus the length of wire needed within the lamp, usually 5 to 6 feet.

We use wire size No. 18 AWG, and buy it in a 30 foot roll. We prefer a plastic or rubber covering because it is easiest to work with.

The switch-If the switch is defective, take it to the store and get an exact duplicate for a replacement. There are three kinds of lamp switches in use—push-through, turn-knob and chain. Some switches are 3-circuit for use with low, medium, and high light bulbs.

At one end of the length of the cord you have measured, attach the plug according to the directions we have given before. When this·is finished, follow these steps. Figure 15 shows the parts of the socket and the switch assembly.

1. Remove the shade holder, lamp shade and bulb plus the diffusing bulb if there is one.

2. Separate the cap from the brass shell by pressing on the shell (where it is stamped "press").

3. Pass the free end of the cord through the lamp.

4. Then pass the cord through tie socket cap, tie a knot in the cord, and attach wires to the terminals on the socket just as you did with the plug.

5. Replace the brass shell and push the cap into place. Be certain the fiber insulator is in the shell as the assembly is telescoped into position. The notches on the shell will click into position over the projections in the cap. Then be sure the socket is seated properly.

6. Replace the bulb and plug into an outlet.

7. If you have a lamp with a porcelain socket, simply connect the new wire at the terminals.

ENERGY USE AND SOURCES

To get some idea of appliance cost per month and year, use the following formulas with the information in the following table. The number 1000 is used as a means of converting watts into kilo (which means 1000) watt units, which is how electric bills are sent out.

For annual costs-Estimated KWH consumed annually x cost per KWH equals annual operating cost.

For monthly costs-Average wattage per appliance at estimated hours/use month is divided by 1000. This figure gives the monthly cost of operation.

Annual costs are useful for items used continuously during the year. Monthly costs are best used for seasonal appliances, such as air-conditioners.

Energy Consumption Of Household Appliances Given In Kilowatts Hours (KWH).
(Adapted From Electric Energy Association)

Appliance	Average Wattage	Estimated KWH Consumed Annually
blender	386	15
carving knife	92	8
coffee maker	440-1000	50-125
deep fryer	1,448	83
dishwasher	1,201	363
egg cooker	516	14
frying pan	1,196	186
hot plate	1,257	90
mixer	127	13
oven, microwave (only)	1,450	190
range-with oven	12,200	1,175
with self cleaning oven	12,200	1,205
sandwich grill	1,161	33
toaster	1,150	40
trash compactor	400	50
waste disposer	445	30
freezer (15 cu. feet)	341	1,195
freezer (frostless 15 cu. ft.)	400	1,761
refrigerator (12 cu. ft.)	240	725
refrigerator (frostless 12 cu. ft.)	320	1,215
refrigerator/freezer (14 cu. ft.)	326	1,829
(frostless 14 cu. ft.)	615	1,000
clothes dryer	5,000	1,000
iron (hand)	1,100	150
washing machine (automatic)	500-700	100-150
water heater	2,475	4,219
quick recovery	4,474	4,811
air conditioner (room)	750-1,500	650-1,400
electric blanket	177	147
dehumidifier	257	377
fan (attic)	370	377
fan (circulation)	88	43
fan (rollaway)	171	138
fan (window)	200	170
heater (portable)	1,322	176
heating pad	65	10
humidifier	177	163
hair dryer	381	14
shaver	14	1.8

sun lamp	279	16
tooth brush	7	0.5
radio	70-100	85-110
radio/record player	109	109
television (black & white)		
tube type	160	350
solid state	55	120
(color) tube type	300	660
solid state	200	440
clock	2	17
floor polisher	305	15
sewing machine	75	11
vacuum cleaner	630	46

Natural Gas vs. Electricity

Most of us have no choice between natural gas or electricity. The apartment or home we rent or buy usually has these utilities installed.

It is too expensive to switch from one source of energy to another, but if an existing system wears out or goes out of action then it may be well, if you have a change in mind, to ask for estimates on a change-over of your energy system compared to replacing with a new model of the same kind.

Natural gas as an energy source is in some cases more efficient than electricity. But there are many factors involved which you should know about.

Comparison Of Natural Gas Costs And Electricity Costs For Providing Energy For A 1,800 Square Foot Heated Area On A Yearly Basis.

	Cost
Gas water heating	$ 72.96
Electric water heating	$102.84
Gas cooking	$ 15.00
Electric cooking	$ 35.48
Gas water heating	$ 72.96
Electric water heating	$102.84

Heating And Cooling

Sky-rocketing fuel bills can't be stopped, but there are a few things you can do to help.

With fall, cover over each window that you do not plan to open during the winter with sheet plastic. This serves as a cheap storm window and is available at variety and hardware stores. A hand staple gun is a help in getting the material fastened tightly.

A particularly vulnerable area is around any window air conditioners you may have. You can use weather stripping and plastic sheets to cover the fronts of your air-conditioners, as well as the sides, top and bottom of the window space they occupy. A cover for the outside, either bought, or home made is recommended. Around doors you can staple weather stripping to reduce air movement.

For conserving heat in our house we close the heavy drapes in the living room and draw the curtains over the large glass doors in the kitchen and study at night. All of this helps to keep the warmer air of the house warmer. On sunny days we open the drapes to allow sunshine to help warm the house.

If you live in an apartment there is nothing you can do about insulation. However if you own your own home, adding insulation at strategic points can cut down on fuel costs. The attic, and the walls are two important areas.

If your heat comes through vents from the furnace on the bottom floor, be careful that nothing stands over the vents and interferes with the movement of warm air into the rooms.

You can use ordinary masking tape on the windows where the two parts of the frame come together. Use a caulking gun and apply caulking on the inside and outside of the house closing up cracks in the foundation. We have found that carpeting of any kind cuts down substantially on cold floors.

The location of a "high" temperature thermostat can be a problem. If it is in a draft or cold spot it will turn on sooner than if it is in a protected spot

Some winter insulating measures are helpful during the summer. Storm windows are not, because you will probably want them open to get any breath of fresh air available. However masking tape and other measures will help. The insulation around an air conditioner should be checked.

We use our air conditioners to cool the house to a comfortable temperature and then turn them off. To help keep the cool air in, keep blinds and drapes closed on the sunny side of the house in the summer. Light colored curtains and drapes are useful in reflecting some of the outdoor heat. If you have a home with an attic, a fan can be extremely helpful in drawing in cool air at night, making the use of the higher energy consuming air conditioners unnecessary. If you have a two-story home, you can, if you are not concerned about possible burglary, open the bottom of the windows on the lower floor, and the top of the windows on the second floor, encouraging warm air to float out, and cool air to move in.

If awnings are possible, they can help keep temperatures down, if used on windows with west and south exposures.

Air conditioners are desirable if someone in the family suffers from allergies and reacts from heat. They are most useful in stuffy places such as top floor apartments in cities, and they are almost a necessity in places where high humidity and temperatures above 90°F. are frequent. Remember that before air conditioning homes were built with higher ceilings, thicker walls, and larger windows, all making a comfortable room temperature more possible.

If you decide to buy one or more air conditioners to be used in a room, measure the height of the ceiling, the length and width of each room, note how many windows there are, and the exposures. Some ideas of the thickness of the walls may help. Then consult reputable stores that sell air conditioners.

Compare what several dealers suggest for your particular needs. Be sure that you are talking about approved models. These will have a stamp on them saying Association of Home Appliance Manufacturers. If a window unit is rated over 7.5 amps it will require a separate circuit. An electrician may be needed to do this job.

Remember the amount of energy used by air conditioners will depend on indoor and outdoor temperatures. Use as few heat producing items in your home as are necessary. Turn lights off. Keep your home insulated as much as possible.

Overcooling can be a problem. You should not try to cool your home more than 10° to 12° cooler than the outside temperature. Keep doors closed because cooling the neighborhood is an uphill battle. This is a major problem with kids around. Corner locations are poor, mid-room spots are best.

Major electric utilities suggest that if you are gone all day, set the thermostat 5° higher than you prefer. Then when you return at night it will take a short time to bring the temperature back down to where you want it. Turning the unit off completely may not be a real saving, because when you come home the unit will have to work extra hard to bring the temperature down to where you want it. If you are to be gone for several days, or return after sunset, the unit should be turned off.

Filters are important for efficient operation of the machine. They can be cleaned by using a vacuum cleaner or by washing them in the sink.

During the winter, protect the unit from weathering by covering it. We use the same plastic as we use for our storm windows and masking tape.

Light Bulbs

Light bulbs are sold with two measurements, lumens, a measure of the quantity of light given off, and the expected life span. The lighting industry has not been able to combine long life and high light intensity. For example, let's compare two 100 watt bulbs, standard and long life. The standard bulb will give about 750 hours of use, with 1,750 lumens or light output. A long life bulb will give three times the life span, 2,500 hours of use, but only 1,470 lumens.

You must then decide—more life or more light. We use long life bulbs in the places that are hard to reach and require some extra effort to change bulbs. In most homes, lighting is estimated to make up about 5% of the total electric bill.

There is a difference in the efficiency and energy use of standard incandescent bulbs and fluorescent bulbs. Fluorescent tubes give out about four times the lumens of light per watt that the incandescent bulbs produce. But everytime a fluorescent tube is turned on and off it reduces the life span by two hours.

SIMPLE HOME REPAIRS

Repairing Holes In Screens

For a very small hole, use fine wire or thread a needle with nylon thread and close the hole.

For larger holes trim the hole to make the edges smooth using shears (Figure *178 A*). Cut a rectangular patch an inch larger than the hole to be covered. Remove the three outside wires on each side of the patch (Figure *178 B*). Place the patch over a small block of wood or a ruler and bend the ends of the wire back (Figure *178 C*). Place the patch on the outside of the hole so that the bent ends of the wire goes through the screen. Then on the inside of the screen bend down the ends of the wire toward the outside of the screen (Figure *178 D*).

Replacing Screen In An Old Screen Frame

Use a tack puller or screwdriver to remove the molding along the edges of the screen. Do not rip holes in the wood. Then pull all the old screen and tacks out of the frame. If the frame needs to be repainted or repaired do so before replacing the screen.

Cut the screen wire with ½ inch, then tack loosely at two corners and once in the center. Pull the screening tight and tack the wire in place every 1½ inch, beginning at the opposite end. Pull the screen very tight especially at the corners, so that the screen is square. Then tack the screen in place on the other two sides.

To replace the molding use small nails or brads and nail the molding over the tacked edge of the screen. Molding is optional. If using new molding, cut the corners at 45° angles so they form a right angle when nailed together.

Making Window Screens At Home

You will need 1 inch by 2 inch wood to make the frame. Measure the four sides of the window, and cut your strips. Then trim the edges of the wood at 45° angles to form each corner. Nail the frame together at the corners using two nails. If the screen is large you may want to brace the corners to provide extra support. You can use a corner brace or a corrugated fastener.

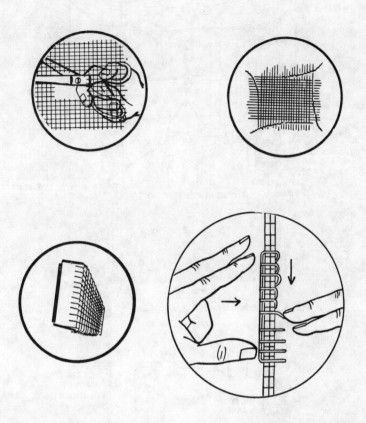

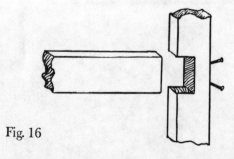

Fig. 16

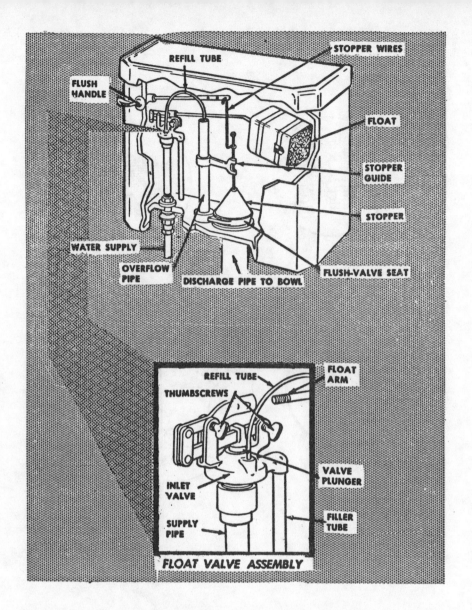

FLOAT VALVE ASSEMBLY

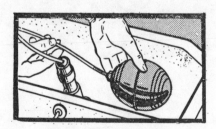

Fig. 17

If the frame is over 4 feet tall, you will need to cut a cross piece to provide extra support for the screen. Saw a notch in the side of the frame that is half the thickness of the wood and as tall as your cross piece (Figure 16). Repeat for the opposite side of the other end of the frame for the cross piece. Measure the distance from one notch to the other notch. Cut your cross piece this length and nail in place, using 2 nails in each end of the frame.

Repairing A Toilet Tank

Check your toilet tank once a year or anytime it appears not to be working properly. If it is not adjusted properly hundreds of gallons of water can be wasted if the float fails to turn the water off at the right time.

When you use the flush handle, the discharge pipe (Figure 17) is opened and the water empties from the tank into the toilet to flush it as the float sinks with the water level. Then the tank begins to fill back up and the float rises again as the water level rises back to normal. If the arm or wire of the float is too high the water level will be too high and will waste water.

The water level mark is usually an inch below the top of the overflow pipe. If the arm is too high, bend it down; if too low bend it up until it trips the water off at the level mark (Figure 17). If the stopper is soft or worn it should be replaced because it will waste water by allowing the water to run through the discharge pipe without the flush handle being operated. The wire of the stopper will be placed through the hole shown in Figure 17 so that the stopper hangs straight down.

Filling A Crack Around The Bathtub Or Shower

There are two types of waterproof filler available: group that comes in a powder form, and plastic sealer that comes in a tube. The plastic sealer is easier to use but is more expensive.

Use a putty knife to scrape the old filler from the crack. Then wash and drythe surface well.

Using grout-Place a small amount of grout (½-¾ cup) in a small bowl. Stir as you slowly add enough water to make a thick paste. Place the grout in the crack with the putty knife using the short end of the knife to press the grout in the crack. Use your finger to smooth the surface of the grout. Pour any leftover grout in the garbage (not down the sink) and wash the bowl and putty knife with water.

Using plastic sealer-Remove the cap on the tube and use a nail or screw driver to make a hole in the metal seal. Squeeze the plastic sealer from the bottom of the tube all along the crack. Do not squeeze so hard that the tube breaks. Use a spatula or putty knife to press the sealer in the crack and smooth the surface. Work quickly, because the plastic sealer dries quickly.

The plastic sealer needs to dry for 24 hours before using while the grout only needs to dry overnight.

Replacing Loose Or Damaged Tiles On Floors Or Walls

Buy the correct adhesive for use with the type of tile you have. If the edge of the tile is covered by molding, you must remove the molding before you can get to the edge of the tile.

To remove the old tile place a towel or cloth doubled over on the tile and place a warm iron over the towel to loosen the adhesive. Then use a putty knife to lift the tile very carefully by the edge. If the tile is not cracked, chipped, or broken it can be used again. Be careful not to damage the tile when lifting it up. Use the putty knife to scrape the old adhesive from the tile and the floor or wall. If your are replacing with a new tile, place the towel on the new tile and warm the tile with the iron so it will be less likely to crack when trimmed to size. Use a knife, saw, or long shears to cut the new tile to fit the space. If you use a saw, saw about halfway through the thickness of the tile. Place the sawed point over a board or table edge and bend along the sawed line. The tile will break evenly along the sawed line.

Spread adhesive on the back of the tile and on the floor or wall. Make sure there is no dirt, gravel or anything on the floor underneath the adhesive because this will cause damage to the back of the tile. Apply the adhesive with a brush or a special wide putty knife. Press the tile in place, smoothing it down.

After ceramic tile has dried, apply grout into the space between the tiles. Smooth the grout in the joint and remove any excess with a wet cloth before it is allowed to dry. Let the grout dry overnight before getting it wet.

Replacing A Window Pane

You will need a new window glass, putty or glazing compound, and glazier points.

Begin working on the outside of the frame and use pliers to remove the cracked or broken glass. Then use the pliers to remove the old putty and glazier points.

When the frame is clear of old putty use the putty knife to place a thin layer of putty in the frame on the outside. Place the glass in the frame pressing firmly against the putty.

Tap the glazier points in place carefully with a hammer placing one every 4 to 6 inches and one near each corner

Then fill in around and between the glazier points with more putty. Smooth the putty so that it forms a smooth seal around the glass.

If the window panes are not broken or cracked the cracked putty can be covered with a new layer of putty. Air can seep through these cracks and raise your heating or cooling bills.

Patching Holes In Plaster Or Wallboard

If there are holes or cracks in your wallboard or plaster, they should be patched to keep the damage from becoming any larger. This must be done before painting.

There are two types of patching compound, spackling compound and patching plaster. Spackling compound is better for infrequent small jobs while the patching plaster is sold in larger packages, costs less and is meant for larger jobs.

Cracks-Using a sharp knife, scrape any loose plaster around the outside and the inside back edge of the crack so that the back of the crack is wider than the front. Use a paint brush or wet cloth and dampen the inside of the crack and around the outside. Mix only a small amount of the patching compound following the directions on the container.

Holes-Fill small holes with the patching compound, pressing the mixture until the hole is completely filled. Smooth the filled hole with the putty knife.

Large holes and cracks-Larger holes and cracks are filled in two steps: fill partially and allow to dry; then finish filling with compound.

For extremely large holes, stuff the hole with wadded newspaper before applying the first coat of compound.

Sanding-After the compound dries then sand the surface until smooth and even with the rest of the wall. A sanding block or sand paper wrapped around a block of wood may be used.

Tools For Simple Repair

Getting service help can be a problem, and a few tools around the house can be real life savers. Our basic tool kit includes the following items.

1. Plumber's helper. Helpful when the sink or toilet gets stopped up.

2. Claw hammer for driving nails and removing nails.

3. Straight bladescrew driver for most wood work.

4. Phillips screwdriver for most appliances, with a cross like blade.

5. Pliers for cutting wires, tightening nuts and bolts, removing nails and tacks.

6. A steel tape measure or folding ruler.

7. An adjustable wrench to adjust to different sizes.

8. A handsaw if you plan on doing any woodwork. A model with about ten to twelve teeth to the inch is fine.

9. A variety of nails, screws, and anchors if you plan on attaching heavy items to the walls like tracks for shelves, towel racks, and such.

In addition we have on hand a ¼ inch electric drill, a power sander, and a small hand planer, for cutting up shelves.

Chapter 7
Notes on Medical Care

MEDICAL CARE

The Consumer's Dilemma

"The medical care business thrives on the passivity of the patient and reinforces the mysticism of medicine. It should be recognized that this atmosphere of benevolence is used primarily for business purposes. The patient should not be distracted from using his critical faculties in dealing with the medical industry. He should try to understand the financial aspects of medical care and then evaluate the quality of the service he has arranged to purchase. At the very least, choosing medical care should be given the same consideration that applies to the process of selecting the man who works on the inside of one's car."

How does one choose the person who works on the inside (and outside of one's body?) Typical traditional selection processes for the family doctor are not very effective.

If you inquire at your local medical society they will often recommend a doctor from their membership list. However, any screening process for membership in local medical societies is usually just a formality rather than being based on competency, and there is never any mention of fees in response to consumer inquiries.

If you call your local hospital and ask them to recommend a doctor, their recommendations are usually restricted to members of their own staff. Once again you are given only partial information.

Many people choose a doctor by asking personal friends to give them the name of their own doctor, but this method of selection also has some serious drawbacks. Friends might recommend a doctor primarily because of that doctor's "bedside manner". Moreover your friends usually do not have any more knowledge in selecting their doctor than you do.

Therefore, what you want is a tool for comparing all or as many as possible of the doctors in your area, a Consumer Guide to Doctors.

A Consumer Guide to Doctors In Your Own Area

Background: As the coordinator of the second Consumer Guide to Doctors project in the nation (in Sangamon County, Illinois, I write from my own personal experience, as well as from the experiences of other individuals and groups which have engaged in similar projects.

In the spring of 1974 I read a newspaper article that spoke of a Consumer Guide to Doctors that had been compiled in Maryland by the Nader-affiliated Health Research Group. Members of the People's Institute of Springfield, Illinois decided to undertake a similar project over the summer of 1974.

Let the researcher beware: If you undertake such a project yourself, remember that it involves much hard work. It also means contending with the local Medical Establishment. Moreover, the vested interests of professionals are often protected by state law. If the past can offer any insight, Consumer Guides to Doctors have been viewed by local medical societies as threatening to their interests, and they may exert a "backlash" against the parties involved in the research.

In Sangamon County, when we began to compile information for our guide, the local Medical Society sent out an ALERT to all of the county's doctors (on pink stationery) which stated, "There is some uncertainty in our thinking as to whether the publication of the full breadth of information obtained may be considered unethical and possibly may be illegal under the Medical Practices Act of the State of Illinois." This act forbids doctors from advertising. It was the contention of the People's Institute that this anti-advertising ban should not apply to the Consumer Guide. The Guide was researched, compiled and published by an independent, non-profit consumer group rather than a self-serving group of doctors. Moreover, it is interesting to note that the listing of doctors in the Yellow Pages of the telephone directory is for some curious reason *not* considered advertising by state law. In addition, only approximately 25% of the doctors practicing in Sangamon County chose to cooperate with the study by agreeing to have themselves listed in the Guide. A similar percentage cooperated with the Maryland project. After all! The State Commission on Medical Discipline can revoke a doctor's license to practice medicine based upon recommendations made by investigatory bodies of local medical societies, and the Commission is composed almost entirely of the leadership of the local medical societies. Therefore, a doctor tends to be very careful about offending the local medical society.*

Moreover, in Sangamon County, the local medical society did everything in its power to discredit the project publically.

If you now (being properly forewarned) would like to know how to go about constructing a Consumer Guide to Doctors for your own locality--- here's how to do it!

*Public Citizen (in conjunction with the Health Research Group and the Mary-

land Public Interest Research Group) has brought federal suit against the Prince George's Medical Society over the proper interpretation of the Maryland "anti-advertising" law. If their suit is successful, the Maryland state law (and by precedent others like it) will offer no protective cover in the future to doctors refusing to cooperate with a consumer survey. The Nader argument is that such laws are unconstitutional since they violate the First Amendment rights of consumers to gather and publish data in non-profit directories that give all the practicing doctors in a community an opportunity to be listed.

How to do it

(1) **A Little Help From Your Friends:** Since you cannot possibly do all the work required to construct a Consumer Guide alone, you need help. If there is no local consumer or public interest group you can plug into, discuss it with friends, relatives, neighbors, and fellow workers. By all means contact the Nader Health Research Group at 2000 P Street, N.W., Washington, D.C., 20036, and they will be glad to supply you with their packet of "how to do it" information (which includes a list of the names and addresses of any other interested groups or parties that are contemplating or engaged in similar research). The Health Research Group will also supply you with legal advice, although of course it is very helpful to have a local attorney as part of, or as consultant to, your own group. (Other relevant sources of information are listed at the end of this chapter.

(2) **Dealing with Your Local Medical Society:** Should your list of friends include your local medical society?In light of traditional medical establishment opposition to Consumer Guides, there is presently some

debate in consumer health research circles as to how to handle the local medical society.

The original Nader approach contends that medical society resistance must be expected as inevitable in any consumer-sponsored survey. Consequently, they recommend against giving advance notice of the project to the local medical society. Instead they propose a one week blitz of unannounced telephone calls to local doctors using uniform questionaires in order to gather information.

Consumer's Union on the other hand cautions against the use of such tactics. It is their opinion that doctors, when caught off guard, become angry and defensive, and that the tacit approval, or at least the neutrality, of the local medical society is very important in legitimizing your project. It is the Consumers' Union position that medical society opposition should no longer be viewed as unwavering, since the idea of a Consumer Guide was even broached at the American Medical association convention in June of 1974, and a recommmendation was made to the body's House of Delegates by the Judicial Council that they adopt the following statement:

"It is not unprofessional for a physician to authorize the listing of his practice in a directory for professional or lay use which is intended to list all physicians in the community on a uniform and non-discriminatory basis; provided that the listing shall not include any self-aggrandizing or qualitative judgement regarding the physician's skills or competence." (Consumer Reports, September, 1974).

Furthermore, the Nader Health Research Group suit against the Prince George County Medical Society, might, in the opinion of Consumers' Union legally break the ice. Therefore, on the basis of such apparent thawing trends, consumers Union contends that consumer groups can now enter cooperative relationships with local medical societies as opposed to the Nader position.

The decision as to which of these paths to follow in relation to your own local medical society is difficult and important one that should receive your careful consideration. It is up to you to choose on the basis of your own project goals and local situation, but here are some personal observations that might be helpful in making that decision.

It might be useful to test the water with your local medical society before you start your research, but in a way that will not tip your hand too much. If the society seems responsive, by all means cooperate with them. However, be wary, for they might be trying to get you to do a watered-down survey as the price for their cooperation. This ploy was attempted in Sangamon County, but our project group refused their offer on the grounds that partial information (i.e., essentially name, speciality, and office hours) from all of the doctors in town was worth less to the public than comprehensive information from one quarter of them. Your group might decide otherwise.

One part of the A.M.A. Judicial Council suggests that information to be published be limited to that presently available in the *American Medical Directory*. A project group choosing this path would be forced to leave out a number of important questions from its questionnaire; among them those relating to fees. Moreover, even this mild statement from the Judicial Council is only *recommended* and has not been officially adopted by the A.M.A. House of Delegates at this writing. Hopefully, the Nader Health Research Group law suit, if successful, will bring about more tangible results both in Maryland and elsewhere.

(3) **Scope:** A Consumer Guide can be neighborhood-wide, city-wide, or county-wide in scope. Moreover, it can attempt to cover *all* doctors(includingchiropracters), or can be limited to personal physicians only (i.e., those who are General Practicioners or who practice family, internal, or pediatric medicine. Consider your needs and your resources, and do not bite off more than you can chew.

(4) **Compiling A List of Practicing Physicians in the Project Area:** The best sources to be used in compiling such a list are: the Directory of Medical Specialists (16th Edition, Marguis Who's Who, Chicago, Illinois), and the *American Medical Directory* (26th edition, A.M.A., Chicago, Illinois). These can be found in medical libraries and in many public libraries as well. Your state or local medical society often will publish a list of practicing physicians. However, these lists are usually not available to the general public. If you have established a cooperative relationship with the local medical society, they can supply such a list for you. If not, you can usually find some individual doctor (or someone else with access to such information) who will give it to you. The Yellow Pages of your telephone directory also list doctors, but it is not a comprehensive listing, and frequently, due to insufficient quality control on the part of the telephone company, not everyone listed under the heading of "Physicians" is actually an M.D.. Finally, if you need more information or want to check on the information that you have, your local health department will occasionally provide you with a list of physicians in your community.

(5) **The Questionnaire:** While the above information sources are helpful, they do not provide *enough* consumer information to be very useful in choosing a doctor. More data (e.g., fees) is needed in order to make an informed choice of a doctor in terms of a health care consumer's particular needs. Therefore, it is necessary to use a questionnaire which can provide more complete information to the consumer. *Consumer Reports* has published (September, 1974) a "Sample Questionnaire For a Directory to Doctors" which is helpful. A sample page from the Sangamon County Guide (based on the Nader questionnaire) can be found as an appendix.

How do you obtain answers to your questions from the doctors in your sample? There are at least two possible courses of action. The original Nader plan calls for a one week blitz of telephone interviewing. The Nader Health Research Group called 560 doctors, with 30 volunteers. It is very important that phone interviewers be trained beforehand in interviewing techniques. Moreover, some questions on the questionaire can be completed in advance by referring to the *Directory of Medical Specialists* and the *American Medical Directory* mentioned earlier. This saves telephone time, and is less taxing to both doctor and interviewer.

The telephone interview phase of the survey is double-checked for accuracy by sending a copy of the questionnaire to the doctor through the mail (a registered letter with a return self-addressed envelope is best) to be corrected, if necessary, and returned with the doctor's signature. This procedure is meant to provide the health care consumer with the most accurate information possible. Since the telephone information often comes to the interviewers second-hand, from receptionists and nurses, it must be verified by the doctors themselves. Moreover, such doublecheck can serve to protect you and your organization from an otherwise unnecessary law suit based on dissemination of possibly false information. Many of the doctors about whom you have received telephone information will not respond in writing. This is often the case because the original source was a secretary or a receptionist, and the doctor would not have consented to give out the information, or because of medical society opposition to the project. Do not be discouraged by this it is typical. In Sangamon County, while initially 60 % of the practicing doctors cooperated over the phone, only 25 % of all doctors cooperated through the mail.

In addition, in order to canvas those doctors with whom telephone interviews only managed to make partial contact or no contact at all, blank questionnaires should be sent out to each of them with appropriate cover letters enclosed to explain the situation.

The original Nader survey instructed both telephone and mail interviewers to notify the doctors interviewed that failure to complete the survey would result in a listing on a separate page under the heading of "No Cooperation" at the end of the Guide. According to Nader, those who cannot be contacted for some legitimate reason (eg., because they are on vacation) should be listed at the end of the Guide on a separate page under the heading, "No Response." According to Bob McGarrah of the Nader Health Research Group this kind of a listing is not meant to coerce doctors into responding, as was the charge of the Prince George's County Medical Society. As he put it, "This was not intended as a threat, but was merely an effort to let each doctor know that we intended to make the most complete directory possible." (McGarrah, *Medical Economics,* March 4, 1974). It is simply providing additional information to the consumer.

The Consumers' Union, on the other hand, contends that the Nader approach, even if not by conscious design, may be too threatening to the respondent. Therefore they do not stress that all doctors who choose not to participate in the survey be listed as un-

cooperative. They suggest a listing of "non-participating" or perhaps no listing at all.

The chances are good that if you seek Medical Society legitimitization of your project one of the designations suggested by Consumers' Union would be considered more appropriate than the Nader listing of "uncooperative.' Once again we have hit upon a touchy subject which your group will have to resolve. How much of the failure of doctors to cooperate is contingent upon issues of *style* (i.e., the dislike of what seem to be implied hreats) as opposed to *content* (i.e., the desire to protect their interests) is, of course, debatable.

In the case of the Sangamon County study, the People's Institute followed the Nader plan and obtained final cooperation from 25 % of the county's practicing doctors, through the mail. We listed uncooperative doctors alphabetically at the end of the Guide. The following explanatory footnoot was placed on the page on which uncooperative doctors were listed: "Once again, let us point out that uncooperative doctors are those doctors who refused, often under pressure from the Sangamon County Medical Society, to cooperate with our consumer survey. Uncooperative does not mean incompetent, and should not be taken in that fashion. It does mean, however, that the above-listed doctors have refused to make public, information which we feel is vital to the consumer in making informed health care decisions". It should also be noted that neither the original Nader study nor the People's Institute study attempt to endorse or rate the doctors, whether they cooperated or not. This task is reserved for the consumer. The Guide is purely informational in that sense.'

Aside from the issue of wording, Consumers' Union deviates from the original Nader strategy in that it recommends the elimination of the phone interview part of the survey (unless such an approach is specifically requested by the doctor). This approach implicitly assumes cooperation from the local medical society, which would not necessitate the one week telephone blitz suggested by the Nader Health Research Group.

Whichever approach you choose, there will, at some point, be a mailing. Here are some tips on how to proceed with this task. If you can, send each doctor a copy of the questionnaire by first class mail in an envelope marked, "Personal". In order to get the doctor's attention, write the words, "Consumer Survey--Please respond by (date)"on the outside of the envelope. Be sure to enclose a stamped, self-addressed return envelope. The cover letter should identify your group clearly and explain that your ultimate goal is the publication of a Consumer Guide to Doctors. Explain the need for such a Guide. as to the questionnaire, invite doctors to elaborate on their responses to the questions where they deem it appropriate. Give them a deadline of 2-4 weeks to return the questionnaire. At the same time inform them that if they do not meet the deadline, you will call them by telephone to make an appointment for a telephone interview. Some doctors find the telephone interview more convenient. Tell them also to feel free to call you before the deadline if they have pertinent questions about the questionnaire or the objectives of the study.

(6) Introducing the Guide: Aside from the raw data, it is also a good idea to prepare an introduction to the Consumer Guide explaining your motivation in preparing it; the way in which you went about it, and how to use it most effectively For more information on this subject see *Consumer Reports,* September, 1974, pp. 689-691. Our guide in Sangamon County also contains a section

entitled, "Explanation of Specialties in Plain English". We believed listing doctors by specialty would not be enough, since many consumers are not aware of what each specialty covers. (A good source of information for this is Stedman's Medical Dictionary.) Then, once we drew up the entire introduction, we checked it over very carefully with a sympathetic doctor in the community before publication. It is important to remember that even if the medical society in your community opposes your project, there will always be some sympathetic doctors to whom you can turn, at least on an anonymous basis, for technical assistance.

(7) Raising Money for Publication Costs: There are basically two ways in which to cover publication costs. One is by obtaining an initial "grub stake" and then selling the Guide to consumers on a non-profit basis. Another way in which to cover publication costs is by soliciting contributions from sympathetic individuals, or groups in the community. In Sangamon County, the first edition of the People's Institute Guide was funded by a local community organization. In addition to some small individual contributions, the second edition (500 copies per edition) was primarily funded by two local collectives near Springfield.

If you have managed to obtain the cooperation of the local medical establishment, your funding source might be the local medical society or the local health planning council. If not, other funding possibilities included Nader-affiliated Public Interest Research Groups (PIRGs), foundations, churches, unions, civic organizations, Planned Parenthood, etc. Do a benefit concert with a loca musical group. Use your imagination!

The following is a sample of our Guide.

Doctor's Name	GENERAL PRACTICE	Doctor's Address
		Doctor's phone number

Office Information: Office hours: 10:00 a.m. to 6:00 p.m. Monday through Saturday
Makes housecalls.
Accepts new patients.
Sees unscheduled walk-in patients.
After hours can be reached at home.

Fees: Initial office visit:
Routine office visit:
Urinalysis:
Complete blood count:
Differential blood count:
Blood sugar:
Pap smear:
Initial office visit includes medical history and check up.
Routine visit varies depending on patient.
Accepts Medicare, Medicaid, private insurance plans and patients without formal health insurance.

Practice Information: Group practice (1 other doctor).
Office personnel: 2 R.Ns; 2 medical assistants; 2 secretaries, 2 insurance workers and 2 general office workers for the group.
Can take samples in office for urinalysis, complete and differential blood counts, blood sugar and pap smear.
Time allotted per patient: 15 minutes.
Secretary handles complaints, then doctor will meet with patient individually.
Languages: English; (one Italian-speaking office worker).
Primarily uses St. John's and Memorial Hospitals.
Primarily uses Rutledge Manor, Illini House, Parks Memorial and Medicenter nursing homes.

Medication and
  Immunization: Prescribes drugs by their generic names.
Prescribes birth control (requires parental consent for patients under 18 years), including voluntary sterilization.
Routinely gives common immunizations to adults and children.

Education and
  Appointments: Northwestern University (1935).
Board certified: American Specialty Board.
Appointments: SIU School of Medicine, supervision.

Here Are Some Further Sources Of Information.

American Mecical Directory, Chicago: A.M.A., 26th edition.

Directory of Medical Specialists, Chicago: Marquis Who's Who, 16th edition.

Ehrenreich, Barbara and John, *The American Health Empire,* N.Y.: Vintage Books, 1970.

Frank, Arthur and Stewart, *The People's Handbook of Medical Care,* N.Y.: Vintage Books, 1972.

Tunley, Roul, *The American Health Scandal,* N.Y.: Dell, 1966.

Consumers Union, "How To Develop A Local Directory of Doctors", *Consumer Reports,* (Sept. 1974), pp. 685-691.

McGarrah, Rob, "It's Time Consumers Knew More About Their Doctors", *Medical conomics,* (Mar. 4, 1974), pp. 1-6.

Nader Health Research Group
Suite 708
200 P. Street, N.W.
Washington, D.C. 20036
202-872-0320

Consumers Union
Box JB
Mt. Vernon, N.Y.   10550

Health/Policy Advisory Center
17 Murray Street
New York, N.Y.   10007

MEDICAL CARE

Moving from one place to another can create a problem of finding a physician and a dentist who are willing to accept your family.

Last time we moved we solved the problem by asking our family doctor and dentist to recommend us to a couple of their colleagues and to send our records. Each of them did this, and we had no problem in our new home. Try that approach next time you have to move.

Public Clinics

Cities and counties run health clinics with a variety of free services available. There is nothing wrong with using these facilities and no stigma attached to their use since they are paid for by our taxes. By using them for routine medical matters you help take the heavy load of work from the overwhelmed private practice physicians who can devote themselves to more serious medical problems.

To find what services are available in your community look in the phone book under the city name, or the county name, for Health Department, Health Center, or Clinic. You can phone to learn what their programs cover.

Most public clinics routinely administer family planning centers, where a gynecologist is usually available to run pap smears and other routine tests, preliminary to prescribing a particular birth control method.

Remember, using the available service provided by tax funds can save you money, and your doctor's time for more pressing medical needs.

Surgery

Sometimes surgery becomes essential. If your family doctor recommends surgery, you are quite free to ask for the opinion of a second doctor, or even a third if you want it and can afford it.

Our own experience suggests that if you want a second opinion, try a specialist, but not necessarily a surgeon. After all a surgeon's profession is surgery and there is a tendency for these specialists to solve medical problems by the means they know best. ˙

The New York Times of December 15, 1974 carried a story headlined "Program Here Finds 28% of Surgery Unnecessary." The article went into some detail and pointed out that of 1,935 persons who asked for a second medical opinion on surgery, recommended by a physician, 28% or 548, were told by the second physician that they did not need surgery.

An example given was of a woman who had been advised to have nose surgery to correct a deviated septum. Her labor union provided an outside consultant who told her she didn't need surgery and recommended nose drops. She followed the consultant's advice and feels fine.

The same article went on to comment that "in 32% of recommended hysterectomies the consultant's said the surgery was not needed."

Self Medication

All of us practice this kind of medical first aid as needed. It seems foolish to bother a doctor with a passing headache or a minor and sporadic heartburn. If any symptoms persist, whether a headache, a sore throat or heartburn, it is time to see a doctor.

Some over the counter drugs can result in health problems if used improperly. The F.D.A. reports that some pain killers have been found to result in serious kidney damage; some drugs taken for the relief of stomach upset can contribute to a worsening of the condition; some stomach remedies used for indigestion may have bromides which may accumulate in the blood stream. Too great a dependence on laxatives can lull a person into a false sense of security when medical attention is needed.

Two drugs taken at the same time may have a markedly different effect on the human body than each taken individually. Patients on anti-coagulants with heart disease, are often warned to avoid too many aspirins.

We rarely use aspirin because we have found that from time to time it will give us heartburn. We use Tylenol at the recommendation of one of our doctors.

F.D.A. reports that experts who evaluated the differences between plain aspirin and Bufferin (essential ingredient is aspirin) were unable to find any difference in speed of action, and "most of the published studies indicate there is little difference in the incidence of stomach upset after ingestion of Bufferin or plain aspirin."

Aspirin has its inherent danger. Children who have eaten too much have been poisoned; allergic reactions can occur; too long use of aspirin can cause kidney damage, and aspirin and ulcers are less than compatable.

Quackery

The F.D.A. recognizes three major kinds of health quackery, all of which cost the consumer large sums of money each year. The F.D.A. magazine, *Consumer,* lists all of these

rip-offs which catch the attention of the federal government by listing charges and dispositions of cases in each issue of the magazine.

Among the kinds practiced on a gullible public are the drugs to melt away fat without the need for dieting; cancer cures that are totally unproven by medicine, and cures for incurable baldness.

Device quackery still has its day for the naive consumer. All sorts of odd machines appear from time to time to perform some miracle. A bracelet or glove may be built up to cure arthritis by radiation; dentures are sold through the mail, a real feat; some machines have been sold to reduce overweight by vibrations. Measuring your own blood pressure may be fun, but only a doctor can interpret the results.

Generic vs. Trade Name Drugs

Generic drugs are those sold by their scientific or given name, rather than a trade or copyrighted name. In almost all cases generic drugs are much cheaper than trade name drugs, and are equally effective.

We prefer to buy generic drugs when we can, because we are reluctant to pay for trade names. Senate investigations have demonstrated that some drug companies have given expensive gifts to medical students, to establish the company's name in their mind in the years of practice and prescribing. These are needless expenses.

How can you try to get generic drugs? When your doctor is prescribing for you, ask him to prescribe a generic drug. Many doctors will agree. Some may argue that they think a trade name drug is more efficaceous.

Remember that every antibiotic sold in the United States has been checked by F.D.A. laboratories and only those generic or trade name that meet government standards can be sold.

More and more public health and hospital users of drugs are suggesting that generic drugs be bought whenever possible, to save money.

Cholesterol And Heart Disease

Like so many things, cholesterol has grabbed the fancy of the public, and many food companies have been quick to take advantage of the confusion that exists.

Cholesterol is a fatty substance that has been found in deposits in the body of people suffering from hardening of the arteries. Doctors and research scientists acknowledge that cholesterol is associated with coronaries, but it far from clear that lowering the cholesterol by diet and medical treatment will reduce heart disease.

Diets are sometimes suggested, that prohibit margarine from safflower or corn oil, ice cream, shell fish, liver or organs, bologna, hot dogs or other foods high in animal fats. A physician friend of ours recommends a less rigid adherence to the diet, but prudence.

Eggs provide an interesting example. There has been a spectacular drop in egg consumption in the United States because of the concern with the high level of cholesterol in eggs, sometimes accused as the number one enemy of the low cholesterol goal. Some scientists claim fervently that there is absolutely no way to place the blame for high blood cholesterol levels on the egg. The same division exists among scientists about whole milk. For most baking and cooking and for cholesterol and economy, use powdered skim milk.

How does one get high cholesterol? One of the major ways is via genetics. Some scientists and doctors place part of the blame for coronaries on the high sugar diet we eat, and look with a feeling of pleasure at the present reduction of sugar in our diets, since the prices have risen so high. Other researchers point a finger at the cigarette as being a contributing factor in coronaries. Overweight has been indicted, lack of exercise, and hypertension.

Your doctor is the best one to advise you. We do suggest that after 40 a cholesterol and triglycerides test be part of your regular check-up.

Chapter 8
Financial

EXTENSION SERVICES

State extenscon services offer workshops and courses as well as bulletins and publications with information that is helpful to us. The courses and workshops vary from state to state but most states offer vegetable gardening workshops in the spring to help you improve your gardening skills. Other courses include furniture refinishing, simple home repairs, quilt making, and mattress making.

To find out what publications your extension service has, write for a current publication list. Publications are usually free to state residents, but you may be charged if you order bulletins from a state other than the one you are living in. Most states urge that you try to obtain the publications that you want through your county agent.

A list of the address of the extension service for every state is given here in alphabetical order.

Cooperative Extension Service
Auburn University
Auburn, Alabama 36830

Cooperative Extension Service
University of Alaska
Fairbanks, Alaska 99701

Cooperative Extension Service
University of Arizona
Tucson, Arizona 85721

Cooperative Extension Service
University of Connecticut
Storrs, Connecticut 06268

Agricultural Extension Service
University of Delaware
Newark, Delaware 19711

Agricultural Extension Service
University of Florida
Gainsville, Florida 32601

College Experiment Station
University of Georgia
Athens, Georgia 30601

Agricultural Extension Service
University of Hawaii
Honolulu, Hawaii 96822

Agricultural Experiment Station
University of Idaho
Moscow, Idaho 83843

Agricultural Extension Service
University of Arkansas
Fayettesville, Arkansas 72801

Agricultural Extension Service
University of California
Berkeley, California

Cooperative Extension Service
Colorado State University
Fort Collins, Colorado 80521

Cooperative Extension Service
Louisiana State University
Baton Rouge, Louisiana 70803

Cooperative Extension Service
University of Maine
Orono, Maine 04473

Cooperative Extension Service
University of Maryland
College Park, Maryland 20742

Agricultural Extension Service
University of Massachusetts
Amherst, Massachusetts 01002

The Cooperative Extension Service
Michigan State University
East Lansing, Michigan 48823

Agricultural Extension Service
University of Minnesota
St. Paul, Minnesota 55101

Cooperative Extension Service
University of Illinois at Urbana
Urbana, Illinois 61801

Cooperative Extension Service
Purdue University
Lafayette, Indiana 47907

Cooperative Extension Service
Iowa State University
Ames, Iowa 50010

Cooperative Extension Service
Kansas State University
Manhattan, Kansas 66506

Cooperative Extension Service
University of Kentucky
Lexington, Kentucky 40506

Cooperative Extension Service
University of New Hampshire
Durham, New Hampshire 03824

New Jersey Agricultural Experiment Station
The State University of New Jersey
New Brunswick, New Jersey 08913

Cooperative Extension Service
The New Mexico State University
Las Cruces, New Mexico 88003

Agricultural Experiment Station
Cornell University
Ithaca, New York 14850

Cooperative Extension Service
North Carolina State University
Raleigh, North Carolina 27607

Cooperative Extension Service
North Dakota State University
Fargo, North Dakota 58102

Cooperative Extension Service
The Ohio State University
Columbus, Ohio 43201

Cooperative Extension Service
Oklahoma State University
Stillwater, Oklahoma 74074

Federal Cooperative Extension Service
Oregon State University
Cornwall, Oregon 97331

Agricultural Experiment Station
Pennsylvania State University
University Park, Pennsylvania 16802

Cooperative Extension Service
University of Puerto Rico
Mayaguez, Puerto Rico 00708

Cooperative Extension Service
Mississippi State University
State College, Mississipp 39762

Cooperative Extension Service
University of Missouri
Columbia, Missouri 65201

Cooperative Extension Service
Montana State University
Bozeman, Montana 59715

Cooperative Extension Service
University of Nebraska
Lincoln, Nebraska 68503

Cooperative Extension Service
University of Nevada
Reno, Nevada 89507

Cooperative Extension Service
Clemson University
Clemson, South Carolina 29631

Cooperative Extension Service
South Dakota State University
Brookings, South Dakota 57006

Agricultural Extension Service
The University of Tennessee
Knoxville, Tennessee 37901

The Agricultural Extension Service
A & M University
College Station, Texas 77843

Cooperative Extension Service
Utah State University
Logan, Utah 84321

The Extension Service
University of Vermont
Burlington, Vermont 05401

Extension Division
Virginia Polytechnic Institute
Blacksburg, Virginia 24061

Virgin Islands Extension Service
College of the Virgin Islands
Kingshill, St. Croix 00850

Cooperative Extension Service
Washington State University
Pullman, Washington 99163

Cooperative Extension Service
West Virginia University
Morgantown, West Virginia 26506

Agricultural Experiment Station
University of Wisconsin
Madison, Wisconsin 53706

Cooperative Extension Service
University of Rhode Island
Kingston, Rhode Island 02881

TYPES OF SALES AND SALE SCHEDULES

By knowing when items can be expected to be on sale you can delay a purchase and save quite a bit of money. Included here is a schedule of the usual sales and the items for sale. A table is also included that defines the different types of sales, such as anniversary and private, and the items on sale as well as the expected savings.

January

This is a big clearance month. Items that are on clearance usually include: Christmas cards, decorations and wrappings, clothing and accessories, stationery, lingerie, cosmetics, furniture, luggage, notions and fabrics, major appliances including televisions and radios, linens, infant needs, furs, beds, floor coverings, decorating accessorites, diamonds, cars, and tires.

February

There are store wide sales for Washington and Lincoln's birthdays. Items usually on sale include: cars, major appliances, men's wear, women's coats and stockings, decorating accessories, floor coverings, fabrics, furs, and furniture.

March

Usually on sale are China, glassware, and housewares.

April

There are usually after-Easter storewide sales. Some of the items usually on sale

Cooperative Extension Service
University of Wyoming
Laramie, Wyoming 82070

include: women's coats, children's clothes, fabrics, sleepwear and lingerie, fashion clearance and diamonds.

May

There are Memorial Day storewide sales. Items usually on sale include clothing for the entire family, infant needs, linens, housewares, luggage decorating accessories, and diamonds.

June

Beginning in midmonth there are clearance sales on summer sportswear. Other items usually include men's clothing, sleepwear and lingerie, stockings, furniture, beds, and floor coverings.

July

There are usually Fourth of July sales. Items on sale usually include summer clothes for everyone, fabrics, linens, jewelry, tires, storm windows, furniture, and beds. Clearance sales at the end of the month include major appliances, garden equipment, and furniture.

August

Items on sale usually include women's accessories, infant needs, linens, rugs, major appliances, garden equipment and garden furniture, furniture, beds, furs and cars.

September

Labor Day sales are usually storewide sales with things in every department on sale. Cars are on sale because it is the end of the year before the new models arrive, as well as tires.

October

There are Columbus Day storewide sales. Items usually on sale include children's clothing, women's coats, infant needs. There may be Veteran's Day sales, depending whether it is in October or November. Cars are on sale to make room for new models.

November

There are Election Day storewide sales. Items on sale usually include women's coats and furs.

December

Infant needs and women's coats are usually on sale. Directly after Christmas there are sales on Christmas decorations, cards, wrappings, and toys.

A SAMPLE SALES CALENDAR

KIND OF SALE	TIME OF YEAR HELD	SALES ITEMS	SAVINGS
inventory	late December, January and July	fall and winter coats, dresses, suits, casual and sports wear	25-50% with average of 25%
seasonal clearance	before and after Christmas, before and after Easter, after Fourth of July	coats, dresses, suits, sportswear and casual-wear, shoes, white goods, furniture	average of 25%, but may be up to 50%
end of month	last of the month, but isn't held every month	stock that has been in the store a long time, soiled items	average of 25% up to 50%
stimulation	August	lingerie, nightclothes, fur, trimmed coats	10-15% on regular stock, 10-15% on special purchase
odd size clearance	August	coats, dresses, shoes	25-50%, average of 25%
dollar days (stimulation)	summer	most items in stock, but may not include coats, dresses, and suits	10-15% on regular stock, 15-20% on special purchases
anniversary sale		storewide with reductions in all departments Check to make sure items are not irregulars or seconds.	10-40%, average of 15%
closeouts	anytime	mostly clothing but housewares, furniture and appliances may be included	25-50%, average of 25%
one day or holiday sales	held on holidays such as Fourth of July or Labor Day.	a few selected items in each department	10-20%
penny sales-For a penny over the regular price you can get two identical items instead of one	any time	a few selected items such as shoes, clothing, kitchen accessories	10-20%

| private sales | any time-These usually occur for charge account customers several days before the sale for the general public begins | clothing, furniture, linens | 10-20% |
| special purchase | anytime. Items bought especially for these sales may be inferior quality compared to regular items. Labels may be cut out so you can't see the brand, or the brand may be a private brand. | clothing, linens | depends on quality of and integrity of store |

Special Types of sales

A good source of furniture, office furniture, and supplies is a state surplus warehouse. In most states you write your offering price or bid on paper an place it in the box with the other sealed bids. Then you are notified if yours was the winning bid. Don't be willing to make the bid any higher than the item is actually worth. Most people make the mistake of paying more than the item is worth which drives the price up artifically. We equipped our complete study in our home with used office furniture from a state surplus warehouse and didn't pay more than $15-$25 for a desk or table. The items are usually in a warehouse for your inspection before making the bid.

Auctions are not usually the places to find real bargains. Unless you have the time and ability to judge the items prior to the items being put on the auction you will be taking a chance when buying. The usual items that are auctioned off are furniture, antiques, real or otherwise, and household items. Most people become so absorbed and excited by the theatrics of an auction that they end up paying more than the item would cost elsewhere or more than the item is worth.

CO-OPERATIVES

Just about every human endeavor can be organized along cooperative lines, but not all are desirable to the same degree. We use the word co-op to mean a group of people joining together to perform a function, in which each member has one vote, and any profits are divided among the members. The primary goal is to save money by buying in quantity to get lower prices, and to reduce some middleman costs, or to share either facilities or services.

The two most common co-ops are food buying and schools. In some rural areas there are also informal co-ops in which neighbors pitch in to help one another in house building and farm operations. A useful type of co-op for the city dweller is the food buying operation. The members elect a manager who is usually a volunteer, but who may be paid. The manager's job includes locating sources of case lots, either through wholesalers or by agreement with a local merchant to sell case lots at cost plus 10%. Some wholesalers do not care to deal with co-ops, preferring institutional customers. The phone can be useful here in checking on who is a source. Then once a week or so, the members make up a list of what they want for the following week. The manager is responsible for distribution.

That brings up the problem of where to store non-perishables. You can use a member's garage for cases. But perishables are a different problem. Fruits and vegetables can be bought the day ahead and kept in a cool place with ease. However this won't work with meats and dairy products. Here, either some agreement for a distributor to deliver is needed, or a large refrigerator.

When we are in a co-op we break up our orders the day before, putting each member's purchases in a box or bag labeled with the buyer's name. The following day members can also pick up the perishables that are in the refrigerator.

This method is neat and easy because there is no inventory to tie up capital. A more expensive and sophisticated method can be used if the co-op is large enough, rich enough, and has adequate storage room. That is to stock standard items on a floor display and let the members pick up what they want on given days. Two days a week is about average for a medium size co-op of 20 or more members. Much more time means that more people need to be available on the floor to help pack and check out. This method requires more capital because of the inventory of supplies that are kept on hand.

Another possibility is a community sponsored canning co-op. We belong to one in North Carolina, and each family pays an annual membership fee of $2, plus a canning fee of 5ᶜ for pint jars, 10ᶜ for quart jars and 15ᶜ for half gallon jars. Only glass is used in the cannery and members provide their own containers.

Each member brings in garden produce or what he may have bought, readies for for processing and then cleans up when the job is finished. The full time supervisor handles the pressure cookers and is directly responsible for the steam equipment.

The operation handles fruits, vegetables, pork and beef. This year over 10,000 jars were processed.

You can also have a cooperative book club. Each member buys one book a year for the club, and at the meetings held twice monthly, these books are changed around. Magazines can work the same way with meetings either being held in some public building available, or in different homes.

The basic requirements for a successful co-op are enough interested members, low costs of activities involved, and dependable leaders and common goals. Large projects are pretty hard to launch and even harder to keep going. Co-ops that succeed tackle a simple necessary job, and have a reserve of willing volunteer labor. The more complex the function, the more diverse the goals, the greater the chance of failure.

We have heard of "land co-ops", not communes, which theoretically allow a number of people to contribute their money towards buying a large tract of land which would then be restricted to environmental activities and used to suit the member's goals. But the problem here is that it requires quite a bit of money, which people willing to pool their resources presumably wouldn't have.

A variety of co-op schools can be established. Tuition can be a set figure, or it can be a sliding figure based on income, decreasing with the number of children from a family who attend the school. In some co-op schools, trained and qualified parents are the teachers; others hire teachers. Some schools require in addition to a modest sum of money per month, that a parent spend one 3 hour school day a week working with the children, and one day a month cleaning up the building. This is theoretically a good arrangement, but it causes problems for parents without partners who work. By agreement, such a parent can hire a substitute to fill in. The drawback to this is that people in the lower socio-economic strata often lack the skills needed for teaching, and generally the cash to hire someone to replace them or to teach. Some co-op schools actively recruit children from such families and subsidize their attendance.

Other services that can be organized as cooperative, include sewing, tailoring, remodeling or home repairs, and hair cuts. In most states it is illegal for an unlicensed person to cut hair for money, but the co-op can be organized so that the services are being exchanged rather than money serving as the exchange.

Baby sitting co-ops

Any small group of people can organize a baby sitting co-op. All that is required is someone in the group to keep a record of who sits how many hours with whose children. At the end of a given period of time, (one to three months) the number of hours you have sat for others should balance out with the number of hours others have sat for you. Refinements as to how to credit sitting with two children in a family can be worked out. It would seem best to provide one credit for each hour per child.

Thus if Family A leaves their two children with Family B for three hours, Family A owes the group 6 hours of exchange sitting, and Family B is owed 6 hours of sitting. Special rates can be arranged for overnight by mutual agreement, and so forth.

Clothes rehabilitation

We have seen a wonderfully effective co-op in Kentucky where members of the community would come in and repair clothes that were used or donated by stores. For each hour of work done, a credit or chit was issued. Then each item of clothing had a fair value, in chits, set on it and the people participating could exchange their chits for clothes. This is one of the best systems of re-cycling we have ever seen. In some towns stores may be persuaded to turn over damaged items to community groups. A persuader would be the use of tax deductible receipts if you have a non-profit group involved.

GETTING YOUR FINANCES IN ORDER

This does not have to a nerve-wracking experience. In fact, it doesn't ever have to be called a budget. What you do need is a general idea of where your money is going. The first thing you need to do is save all cancelled checks and receipts of all kinds. These records will be useful to see where your money is going.

Divide these receipts into categories, putting each group in a large envelope marked with its name, including rent or mortgage payment, utilities, credit cards, insurance, monthly credit payments, car payments, gas or transportation, medical and dental bills, clothing, pet food and vet bills, food, toiletries and beauty aids, and entertainment which includes books, magazines, newspapers, movies, etc.

To get an idea of how much you spend on food, save all your receipts for two months, then take the average. Deduct any unusual items you buy in bulk such as a lot of meat for the freezer or a case of canned food. Non-food items that you purchase at the supermarket should also be deducted from this total, such as paper goods, cleaning supplies, pet food, or kitchen supplies. All these items should be placed in a separate miscellaneous category.

If you eat out often or normally eat lunch out every day, keep a separate category for this.

Make a list of each category and the average monthly cost for each. Some, (such as utilities), will fluctuate slightly from one month to another. Be sure you list any monthly or time payments you are making on major applicances or furniture. Total all these expenses. List your monthly income or your average monthly income beside your expenses. Your take home pay is the key here. Your basic salary or income doesn't mean a thing. Because your salary is $14,000 doesn't mean you have $14,000 to spend.

Certain expenses, such as clothing or medical, may be a little harder to figure because these expenses don't occur on a regular basis. So what you need to do is have a general idea of what you spend in a year for each such category and divide by 12 to arrive at a monthly average.

When your statement for your checking account comes in from the bank, estimate the amount for the checks that are still outstanding. This gives you a good idea of what you actually have without going to the trouble of balancing the checkbook.

Certain expenses are fixed, such as rent or mortage. Utilities may not be fixed but you can count on a certain monthly average. List all of these together and call them fixed expenses. Estimated expenses are all the others that you can only estimate from your receipts, such as food, clothing, etc. The only place you can cut back is in the list of the estimated expenses.

Some expenses may occur on an annual or semi-annual basis, such as insurance payments, but they can be divided into 12 monthly payments in the category of fixed expenses.

Don't buy in anticipation of getting an income tax refund, insurance settlement, or other payment. Wait until you have the money before you spend it. You can really over extend your credit if you spend money before you have it.

Look over your credit card statements carefully because computers can make mistakes. On your telephone bill remember that if your telephone is not working or out of service, you can deduct that portion of the basic charge from your bill. Another thing to notice is that when you move, you receive credit on your telephone bill for the days the phone was not connected.

If you order an item, such as a sofa, appliance, carpet, and delivery takes some time, be sure that the charge does not appear on your bill before you receive the goods. Otherwise you will be charged a finance charge including the time you didn't have the goods. So pay close attention because these errors can cost you money.

Credit cards

The best purpose of a credit card is not to run up a large bill that you intend paying in installments, but is for the convenience of writing one check for all your purchases for that month.

Abusing credit is a common mistake people make, and they seem to feel by using credit they are extending their income. Unfortunately, this is not what happens. What usually occurs is that they overextend themselves to the point where their monthly payments are larger than their monthly income. What people do then is get a consolidation loan, which leaves them with only one monthly payment to make. Actually they are borrowing money to pay off the first loan. Even the consolidation loan is not the best answer, it is also an emergency or relief measure.

The thing to remember when using

credit is not to commit yourself to any more monthly payments than you can realistically make. If you can only afford $75.00 a month as a total for all your monthly installment payments, and are in danger of going over your limit, declare a moratorium on all credit spending until you are in the clear.

If you can realistically afford to pay a larger balance on a credit card off sooner, do so. But don't over-commit yourself or put all your other monthly expenses in jeopardy.

Most credit card agreements as well as monthly statements clearly list the interest rate per month as well as the Annual Percentage Rate. This is usually 1½% a month or 18% a year. A revolving charge account is slightly different than an ordinarily credit card because the revolving charge account can have a higher interest rate. If you have to make a major purchase such as a new furnace or major repairs on your car, you might do better to get a loan from a bank than charge it to the credit card. The interest on most revolving credit card agreements can run up to 5% higher than the same money from a bank. So consider this before you make such a purchase on your credit card.

When you use a credit card and don't pay the balance in full when the bill comes in at the end of the month, you are actually borrowing that money for the period of time that it takes you to pay it off. For example if you buy $75.00 worth of clothing and pay it off in 3 monthly payments, you are borrowing that much money per month. Before running up such bills, ask yourself if you really need to borrow that money every month or if you can delay buying until you have the cash to pay it off.

When you buy an item on sale, take into account how much finance charge you will be paying until the item is paid off. Add the finance charge to the sale price to see how much you are really saving.

Checking Accounts

There are several ways to save money on your checking account.

Some banks offer free checking as long as you keep a minimum balance of $100.00. Other banks have free checking regardless of the balance.

Many have free checks that they provide for you. These free checks can be personalized. The only difference between them and other checks is that they are not numbered. So by writing your own number on the check you can save money.

Borrowing Money

The best place to borrow money is on your life insurance or from a credit union. Your next choice would be the bank.

When borrowing on your life insurance, you are usually not required to pay the loan back, only the interest on the loan on an annual basis. But by paying the loan off you will save the interest. Some life insurance policies lose their value if you borrow too much money on them.

The credit union is a good place to borrow money. A credit union is a share-holding organization, so normally you have to buy a minimum of one share before your application for a loan will be considered. A credit union offers several types of loans, with varying rates of interest.

If you cannot borrow on your life insurance or from a credit union, borrow from a bank. Finance companies are usually not good places to borrow money from. A bank may have loans for different purposes, such as car loans, and home improvement loans, but the interest is the same regardless of the purpose of the loan.

There are two ways to compute interest on a loan, and the procedure the loan institution follows depends on the laws of your state. In a simple interest loan you are charged interest on the remaining balance. In other words when you borrow $1,000 you only have full use of the money the first day you borrow it. So the interest thereafter is figured on the remaining balance. The other way of computing interest is called the lump sum or add-on system. In this system the interest is computed on the basis of the full loan and a proportional amount of the interest is included in the payment every month. You save interest on the simple interest by paying early in the month before your payment is due, and for paying the loan off early. In the add-on type loan you do not save by making your payment early or by paying the loan off earlier than scheduled.

Pre-arranged credit

Some banks have a prearranged credit line or loan system tied in with your checking account so that if you need the money you write a check, knowing that you don't have the money to cover the check. Then the bank transfers the money to your account to cover the check as a loan. You are charged 5% interest a month on the balance of the loan thereafter. Most banks then automatically deduct from your checking account the monthly payment on this loan which appears on your checking statement as such. This system is called different things such as Readi-Reserve or Master Charge Command Checking. In the Master Charge system what happens is that your Master Charge makes up any deficit in your checking account that would normally cause a check to bounce. Master Charge calls it a cash advance and charges you 1% interest a month from the time of the cash advance.

About 50% of the people who sign up for these preapproved credit or loans never use it. It is good for emergencies that may happen while you are traveling.

This preapproved credit is not a method of extending your credit needlessly when you know you don't have the funds to cover a check. It should be reserved for emergency use only and for those unavoidable times when you do not have the money to cover a check.

INSURANCE

Home Insurance

Only the value of the house, not the land it stands on, is insured. Most insurance agents use the standard figure of $22.00 for each square foot of living space, to find the amount that the house should be insured for. $22.00 is supposed to be what it costs to replace or rebuild a square foot now. But as inflation hits the building trade this figure will rise. Don't raise your home insurance in anticipation of inflation, wait until the value goes up and then raise your insurance. Remember that your home insurance has a set value for the contents in the house. So if you have antiques, valuable jewelry, furs, paintings, or anything valued over $300.00 you must have them appraised and insured separately.

Life Insurance

There are five types of life insurance: term, straight life, ordinary or whole life, limited payment life, and endowment. All have premiums that increase with your age except the straight life which remains the same.

Concentrate life insurance on the family breadwinner. You can get from 2-3 times as much straight life insurance as endowment insurance for the same premium. When buying life insurance for protection of the income, use the less expensive types, including term, straight life, or family income plan. Endowment and retirement income policies have higher cash values but give less protection for the same premium cost.

Most young families either buy term or straight life or a combination of the two.

Don't drop one policy to buy another because the newer policy will have a higher premium.

Some life insurance policies have a cost-of-living clause so that the value of the insurance increases with the cost of living. You are sent a bill once a year with the option of purchasing the additional amount of insurance.

Term insurance-Term insurance covers a limited number of years, usually 1, 5, or 10 years. Benefits are collected only if you die during that time. When the policy ends, a new policy must be taken. In addition you can buy term insurance with a convertible clause that allows you to change to another type of policy when the term runs out. This is considered good insurance for the young family.

Straight life insurance-Straight life insurance policy costs do not get higher as you grow older. The rate is more expensive than term, but less than other permanent policies.

This policy builds up a cash value so that its value increases the longer you have it. You can make a loan on this type of policy. If you decide to give up this policy you then can receive the face value of the policy in cash, as a lump sum, over a period of time, or you can save it as a paid-up insurance policy.

Limited payment life insurance-The premium for this is paid for a certain number of years, 10, 20, or 30, or until you are a certain age. Your premium is higher than that of the straight life insurance because you are paying for only a certain number of years and are building up a higher cash value than the straight life. Usually limited payment life insurance is too expensive for the young family.

Endowment policies-This is usually more expensive than other types of insurance. Premiums are paid for a certain number of years with the rates as much as two or four times as expensive as a straight life policy. After the policy is paid up the insured person then receives the face value of the policy. If the insured person dies before receiving part or whole of the face value then his estate will get the face value.

Other types of life insurance-There are combinations of life insurance available. One combination for the young family to consider is the family income policy which combines term insurance and straight life. The term policy part will pay the beneficiary a certain amount for the remaining years the policy has when the insured person dies. For instance if the policy is for 15 years, and the insured person dies in 10 years, then the beneficiary will receive payments for the remaining 5 years of the policy. This insures that there will be enough income when the children are young. But if the insured person lives beyond the term part of the policy the straight life part of the policy continues and the beneficiary will receive the face value of the straight life part of the policy when the insured person dies.

Mortgage insurance   This pays the mortgage in case of the husband's death. This is sometimes sold through your mortgage company. The monthly premium for young men is very low. It is also possible to add the wife to the policy for very little more.

The size of the monthly premium depends on the age of the husband, and increases with age. For a young man it may be as little as a few dollars a month. For a man over 45 it may be as high as $15-$20 a month.

Health Insurance

Most people buy health insurance through the group policy where they work. A group policy is usually cheaper than an individual policy because usually the employer shares the cost with the employee.

Be sure you are informed of the type of policy, its benefits and costs. Check to see whether the coverage is adequate for you.

There are four major types of health insurance: hospital expense, surgical expense, regular medical expense, and major medical expense.

Most people have a policy that includes a combination or supplement of the several policies.

Hospital expense insurance-The questions you should ask about hospitalization insurance are: (1) What is the maximum number of days in the hospital that the policy covers? (2) How much does the policy pay for room and board and how do these rates compare with what the hospitals in your locality are charging? Usually the policy pays for only a semi-private room, and if you choose a private room you pay the extra cost involved. (3) What other related hospital expenses does the insurance pay for, such as drugs, x-rays, anesthetic, laboratory tests, cost of the operating room and recovery room, etc. (4) Is there a deductible that you must pay for only the first hospital visit or for every hospital visit? (5) Can the policy be renewed?

Surgical insurance-This is usually sold as a supplement or in combination with the hospital expense policy. The questions you need to ask about this policy are: (1) Are the allowances for surgery in line with surgeons' fees for your area? (2) What types of services are covered? (3) Is there a deductible? (4) Are doctors visits, including hospital visits, included and if so what is the limit set by the policy? (5) What limitations and exclusions does the policy have?

Regular medical expense insurance-This usually covers doctors' fees, and nonsurgical care in the office, hospital, and home. Some laboratory tests and x-rays may also be included.

Major medical expense insurance-This is a supplement to regular medical insurance or hospital-surgical insurance. It covers the treatment both in and out of the hospital, drugs, medical appliances, nursing homes, special nursing care, psychiatric care, and other benefits.

Usually these policies have a large deductible, $250-$300. The insurance then pays 75-85% of the cost and you pay the remainder. The questions to ask about this policy are: (1) What is the deductible, is it calculated once a year or for each different illness or injury? (2) What percent does the policy pay after the deductible and what percent do you pay? (3) Is the policy renewable? (4) What are the maximum benefits paid, and will the maximum benefits be in effect after your illness? (5) Is there a limit on what the policy pays for hospital room and board, and specialists consultation and treatment.

WHAT IF YOU CAN NO LONGER HANDLE THOSE MONTHLY CREDIT PAYMENTS?

If things get to the point that your debts outweigh your income and you can see no way out, there is a road to follow. It is called Chapter 13, Wage Earner Plan, a federal program for bankruptcy proceedings.

The plan is available for wage earners and provides a bit of federal help in paying debts over a period of time. It is not a way to avoid paying debts. Most of us know of corporations which go into bankruptcy and pay a small percentage of what they owe. This wage earner plan is nothing like the plan for business bankruptcy.

Contact your federal bankruptcy trustee or have an attorney handle the details for you. If your yellow pages has no such listing, phone or write the nearest Federal Clerk of the Court for the correct address which will be in the yellow pages of your phone book under United States government.

The plan can run for 36 months if needed, or for a longer or shorter period of time. The person in debt can keep enough of his pay check to pay the rent, utilities, food, gas, medicines, and such normal expenses. Whatever is left will then be paid to a federal court which will redistribute it to the creditors.

Part of this program involves the co-operation of the creditors who forgive carrying charges and late payment penalties.

During the period of time that the plan is running no new debts can be incurred. If a major medical need comes up or some emergency, the scale of payments can be rewritten. During this period of payments, cars, furniture, and household items cannot be repossessed.

If a private attorney is used, there is naturally a charge for his services. It is strongly suggested that anyone using the plan avoid having an attorney and rely on the trustee. This is just as satisfactory and it is cheaper.

Chapter 9
Miscellaneous Information

HAIR CUTTING AT HOME

Getting Started

Your first home haircut will be difficult, but you can break the ice by trimming your hair very soon after a barber cuts it in a satisfactory manner.Soon you will discover that the top hair is the easiet to cut because the margin for error is greatest there. One must be very precise about the length only where the hair is so short that the scalp is partially visible.

If you are serious about this, invest in a pair of barber's scissors or shears, and then an electric clipper if the venture works out. Complete sets of hair cutting equipment can be bought for under $15, and very good sets can be had for as little as $25.

Confidence and patience are the keys to a good home haircut. Confidence comes in two forms. You must first, of course, believe that if you take your time you can cut hairs to the length you want them. Anyone with reasonable coordination can do this. You must also get rid of the notion that people will think less of you if you do not have your hair exactly as you want it.

The worst that can happen in your first effort is that you will become impatient and cut a few hairs too short in some spot. If you normally wear your hair short, you scalp will be too visible at that spot. Should that happen, take comfort from the fact that the spot will disappear in 3 to 4 days. To take the pressure off in your first try, you can do the work on a Friday night preceding a weekend when you plan to work around the house.

Styles

One of the blessings of our times is that men can wear their hair pretty much as they choose. Do not attempt a new hairstyle on your first try. Rather, you should have your hair cut by a barber in the manner you prefer and then have the person that is going to do the work examine the lengths left on various portions of your head. Examine the contour of the hair ends when the hairs are fully extended. It is a good idea to sketch or take notes, not so much because the cutter will need the notes as because the notes will give the cutter confidence in the first attempt.

Cut the hair in two stages. The first stage is meant to get the approximate length you want all over the head. The second stage is meant to smooth through careful trimming. One should always begin at the sides and back and work toward the top of the head.

The scissors, of course, should be in the right hand, if you are right handed. Use your fingers to extend the hair in the first stage--when you are cutting to approximate length--and a comb for final trimming.

An electric clipper is particularly valuable for smoothing. It is quick and easy to use, but it takes a lot of getting used to. If you are determined to get one, you should probably practice a bit on the ends of hairs that you plan to cut shorter later.

It is important to see well while you are cutting, and to have some room to move around the person's head. The bathroom is usually too small.

Satisfaction

At the beginning you may have to accept something less than perfection. You may make some mistakes, but there are positive aspects in addition to the money you will save.

If you get at all good at cutting hair, you will gain satisfaction from it, just as you do from working in the garden or from carpentry. You will be able to get a haircut when you want it without taking time off from work. You can style my hair as you choose without attaching a name to the particular effect you want. And you can do all this and save between $5 and $10 a month.

SAVING MONEY ON LAUNDRY SUPPLIES

There are several ways to save money, energy, and water on your laundry supplies.

The manufacturers of cold-water detergents as well as the utility companies say that washing in cold water is as satisfactory as using warm and hot water. They also recommend using the delicate cycle because it saves on water as well as energy. But cold water and the delicate cycle are not always satisfactory. They may leave enough detergent residue on the clothes to irritate sensitive skins. The cold water detergents are useful for fine fabrics that would have wrinkles set in when wrung or spun dry while hot. Hanging the clothes on a line to dry also

saves energy but the clothes may feel stiff, especially towels, linens, and have more wrinkles. Permanent press items were designed to be dried in a dryer and will need to be pressed if dried on the line.

Bleach may be needed in items that are discolored or stained and that need disinfecting, such as baby diapers, but it is not needed all the time on all laundry. Some people feel the clothes aren't clean unless they use bleach. But with the use of hot water and detergent, and the heat of the dryer the clothes should be safely disinfected. If soap is used instead of detergent, water softeners may be needed. Special detergent preparations for heavily soiled areas aren't necessary. A paste made up of your detergent with a little water is just as effective.

There are two kinds of detergents, light duty and heavy duty or all purpose. Light duty detergents don't work effectively on heavily soiled clothes. Heavy duty detergents are more effective than light-duty detergents for cleaning moderately or heavily soiled items.

A good layer of suds should be in the water during the wash cycle, unless a low-sudsing detergent is used. Most graying of clothes is caused by not using enough detergent.

Soaps are not very widely used, but they are also available in light duty, heavy duty, as well as low sudsing and high sudsing.

COSMETICS AND TOILETRIES-BUYING AND MAKING YOUR OWN

The cosmetic industry in the United States works hard to convince you that if you select the right hair color, smell or shade of make-up your success in your job as well as social acceptability will be beyond question.

The Food, Drug and Cosmetic Act does not require that a cosmetic fulfill all the hopes and dreams of its all the hopes and dreams of its advertising. The law does require however that a cosmetic be labelled without false or misleading representations, with information about the product, its manufacturer, distributor, or packer and the quantity of its contents. The law requires that a cosmetic be free of injurious substances, be produced in a sanitary plant, and be packaged in a safe and non-deceptive manner.

Records of cosmetic injury complaints are available from the Food Drug Administration by category. Listings include items such as baby preparations, hair cosmetics, lipsticks, and so forth.

One of the biggest problems in buying cosmetics is the lack of ingredient labelling. Rarely can you see what is going into what you have bought. If you make your own cosmetics such as shaving cream, colognes, face creams and such, you know exactly what is going into the final product, and you can easily change your formula if you have an allergy, and best of all you save money.

One of the loopholes in the law that allows commercial cosmetic manufacturers to market a range of cosmetics is the provision that the F.D.A. must prove a lack of safety in the final product, or the toxic or deleterious effect of a cosmetic product before the F.D.A. can act.

The National Product Safety Commission in 1970 estimated that there are 60,000 cosmetic injuries in the United States each year. The role of the schools and colleges of pharmacy in helping the consumer should be strengthened. It seems to us that the Senate Select Committee on Small Business which has been looking into the relationship between medical schools and the drug industry, should now open hearings on the relationship between the schools of pharmacy and the drug and cosmetic industries.

Most people don't have allergies that would require them to use hypo-allergenic preparations. If you know you are allergic to an ingredient, check the brochures of the companies that manufacture hypo-allergenic cosmetics. These manufacturers remove all ingredients that have been known to cause allergies. These are usually natural products, so your hypo-allergenic products are made up mostly of synthetic or man-made ingredients. The hypo-allergenic cosmetics are not any cleaner or healthier for your skin than ordinary cosmetics.

Water is not drying to the skin as some of the cold and cleansing cream advertisers would have you believe. Using water when cleansing your face is not drying or bad for the skin. The basic purpose of any preparation, whether cleansing or moisturing, is to add moisture held in a solution of fat or other oil-type base long enough for the skin to absorb the moisture. If you wet your skin the water evaporates before the skin has time to absorb it, but the moisture in a solution cannot evaporate as fast and more is absorbed by the skin. The oils or other ingredients may soften the skin slightly, but the substance is only the vehicle for the moisture. Now that you understand what cleansers and moisturizers are all about you will realize that they are not magical cure-alls, containing the special answers for your skin. Turtle oil or mink oil is no better for your skin than any other oil. There may be a big difference in the price of all the name brand cleansers and moisturizers available, but they all contain basically the same ingredients. So if you first find out what base of cream is most suitable for your skin, whether lanolin or glycerin or something else, and then find the least expensive one of that type that suits you. You don't have to buy the cheapest but you don't have to pay several dollars an ounce either.

Soap can be considered as a cleanser and moisturizer because it does soften your skin. There really is not that much difference between soaps. Any soap is pure and has to meet certain standards. A soap may appear to dry your skin slightly but the fat or oil contained in the soap is softening your skin at the same time.

Deodrants make all kinds of claims in advertising about how dry they will keep you, but these claims cannot be supported. Now everyone needs to use an anti-perspirant. In addition, aerosol spray deodorants can be a cause of cancer. Roll-ons and sticks are longer lasting and less expensive. Some of the roll-ons may be sticky or cause irritation, so try several until you find the one that suits you.

The advertising of toothpaste would make it seem as if the answer to cavities has been found. But basically one toothpaste is no better than the other, the brushing is the important factor. You can buy a private brand that has fluoride and still save at least 30 cents on the large size.

When you buy mouthwash check the label to see that it contains at least 25% alcohol. Some contain as little as 12%. So check this before you buy and choose the stronger. The ones with less alcohol still cost you more because you are getting mostly water. The private brands meet the same standards as the name brands and usually contain the same flavorings.

The best bath oil you can use is also the cheapest baby oil. Bath oils contain scents and coloring to look more attractive, but it is basically not any different or better than bath oils you can mix yourself.

The cheapest bath powders are the baby powders because they don't contain a lot of special scents.

Shampoos cannot possibly perform miracles as they are advertised to do. The purpose of a shampoo is to remove dirt, oil, and dandruff from your hair and leave as little soap or detergent residue as possible in your hair. Most of us have enough natural oils to replace any lost during shampooing, protein shampoos are not necessary either, because your hair is a living thing, and the protein it needs must come from you and not out of a shampoo bottle. Coating the hair temporarily may aid in styling but it will not solve any problems your hair may have. The use of egg or gelatin is the most common protein source in shampoo and this merely coats the hair temporarily. Some of the special texturizing and protein shampoos have caused the hair to split or break very badly, but unfortunately it takes several years of being on the market before these things are found out.

A cream rinse usually contains glycerin, water, perhaps alcohol, coloring, and scent. The ycerin helps to keep the hair tangle free because it penetrates and releases tangles. One brand is usually as good as another.

A setting otion or cream has a main ingredient that is some sticky gelatinous, glutinous substance. The other ingredients include water, alcohol, and scent. Denture adhesive powder can even be used to make setting lotion. The setting lotion surrounds the hair and gives it extra body as the hair dries around the curler. Then as time passes and you continue to comb and brush your hair, this proecire aser consisting of the dried lotion that holds the curl and body in place is brus ed and aears out. Your hair then begins to lose its curl and body. Any of the brands of setting lotion will serve he same purpose.

Do not buy any cosmetic or toiletry item just because it is on sale. Many of the companies na adcertise a free travel kit or free product wi a ninimum order of $5.00, eucts are always so expensive that you are probably paying for the free product as well. Don't try a new product just because it is on sale. It is better if you stick to a brand that suits you.

Be very careful about buying eye make-up. Allergies to eye make-up are more common than other allergies, so find a medium priced brand that suits you and stick with it. You can waste money by trying many different ones that you may not be able to use because of allergies.

Cosmetics are a thing of fashion just like clothes. If you don't like lipstick, powder or blusher, then don't buy them just to be in style. Don't be influenced by the different types of applicators, such as the various types of brushes that mascara comes with. Each company tries to outdo the other by coming up with new shapes of bottles, containers, and applicators, and raising the price accordingly.

Allergy to nail polish and nail polish remover is one of the most common allergies, and most people who have it don't even realize it. If you find your face is breaking out or the skin on your hands is peeling, quit using nail polish for a month and see if the condition clears up. Since a bottle of nail polish lasts a long time you'll probably tire of the color before the bottle is empty anyway. But there is not that much difference in the durability between the expensive and the moderate priced. They all wear off and begin chipping at the same rate.

If you have problem nails, don't fall for those miracle protein polishes that are supposed to cure your problem. They don't work. Oily nail polish remover is supposed to be less drying on your nails, and it is recommended that you not use it more often than once every 5-7 days.

For the purpose that hair spray is supposed to serve, the cheaper brands should be as good as the more expensive ones. Almost any hair spray will make your hair feel stiff and unnatural looking. As for as holding your hair even in the rain, imagine what ingredients must be in it that it is not water soluble. It is also believed that continued use of hair spray can cause cancer because when you spray it on your hair, a certain amount of the spray goes into the air and you breathe it into your lungs.

The best and cheapest astringent lotion may not be very popular as such, because it is known under another name, witch hazel. Astringent lotions are mostly water and alcohol. Try mixing your own using witch hazel or alcohol.

For face masks try using some of the old standbys that are made up of products from the kitchen, including eggs and lemon juice, oatmeal, fruits and vegetables. But price the ingredients you will be using to make sure that it is cheaper than the packaged facial masks since the price of foods flucuate from season to season.

Making Your Own Cosmetics

The following recipes were selected from A GUIDE TO NATURAL COSMETICS, Connie Krochmal. Quadrangle The New York Times, New York, N.Y., 1973.

HERBAL BATH BAGS

Rosemary	1 cup
Dill Herb	1 cup
Mint, dried	1 cup
Linden flowers, dried	1 cup

Combine all the ingredients. Tie in cheesecloth bags. Then tie the bag on the faucet and let it hang down so the running water will flow through it.

WITCH HAZEL SKIN FRESHENER

Alcohol	¾ cup
Glycerin	2 teaspoons
Oil of jasmine	5 drops
Witch hazel	2 teaspoons

Combine all the ingredients and shake well to mix.

MINT LOTION

Tragacanth   1 teaspoon
Water, hot   ⅓ cup
Alcohol   ½ cup
Glycerin   2 tablespoons
Menthol   ¼ teaspoon
Oil of peppermint   ¼ teaspoon

Soak the tragacanth in the water to form a mucilage. Dissolve the oil of peppermint and menthol in the alcohol and add the glycerin. Combine the mucilage with the alcohol mixture.

COCOA BUTTER SHAVING SOAP

Soap flakes   3 tablespoons
Water   ½ cup
Cocoa butter   1 tablespoon
Tincture of benzoin   1 teaspoon
Oil of bitter almond   5 drops
Glycerin   2 tablespoons

Dissolve the soap in the water. Melt the cocoa butter, and add the water mixture. Add the remaining ingredients. Blend in a blender until the mixture emulsifies.

BUYING CHRISTMAS TREES

There is nothing to match a living green Christmas tree in the home, no matter how good looking a synthetic tree may be. With everyone concerned about environment and ecology, more and more Christmas trees are appearing on the market with a ball of dirt and a burlap sack so that the trees can be planted out. Some cities have actually established collections for Christmas trees to be planted.

Christmas trees most often are a renewable resource. People grow them on plantations just like any other crop and harvest them every year in time for marketing.

To pick a fresh tree that will not lose its needles, just bang the stump on the ground. If it holds its needles, buy it. Another simple test is to feel the base of the cut trunk. Fresh trunks are usually moist.

Many Christmas tree growers sell trees right on the farm. You and your family can go in and buy the tree you like.

Once you get the tree home put it into a bucket of damp sand and keep it there, to help keep the tree fresh. Just before putting it into the bucket cut off an inch or two of the lower trunk.

When time comes to dispose of the tree, if it is not to be planted, get it out of the house as soon as you are finished with it.

A most attractive leaflet on Christmas trees, with handsome sketches and a brief history of the Christmas tree, comes from the Northeastern Forest Experiment Station, United States Department of Agriculture, Forest Service, 6816 Market Street, Upper Darby, Pa., 19082. It's called Buying Your Christmas Tree, and it's free.